ALIEN ZONE II

ALIEN ZONE II

THE SPACES OF SCIENCE-FICTION CINEMA

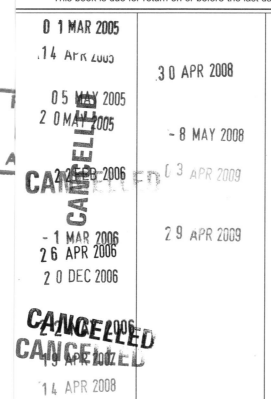

First published by Verso 1999
This collection © Annette Kuhn 1999
Individual chapters © the authors
All rights reserved

The moral rights of the authors have been asserted.

3 5 7 9 10 8 6 4 2

Verso
UK: 6 Meard Street, London W1F 0EG
USA: 180 Varick Street, New York, NY 10014–4606

Verso is the imprint of New Left Books

ISBN 1–85984–259–3

British Library Cataloguing in Publication Data
A catalogue record for this book is available from the British Library

Library of Congress Cataloging-in-Publication Data
A catalog record for this book is available from the Library of Congress

Designed and typeset by Lucy Morton & Robin Gable, Grosmont
Printed and bound in Great Britain by Bath Press Ltd, Avon

CONTENTS

INTRODUCTION

In 1997, a survey of science-fiction studies courses in North American universities and colleges revealed that *Blade Runner* was far and away the most widely assigned film. Its closest rival, *2001: A Space Odyssey*, received considerably fewer votes, while *Metropolis* came in at a close third place. The films in the *Alien* series were rated at fifth place, after *The Day the Earth Stood Still*. The absences from the list are interesting, too: the box-office successes *Star Wars* and *Close Encounters of the Third Kind*, for example, appear nowhere on it. While this survey makes no claim to representativeness, it is certainly indicative, at least as a snapshot of a science-fiction film canon in the process of formation.[1]

If this does constitute a canon, though, it is of a singular kind. A science-fiction buff's top ten films, for example, would quite probably be different from this pedagogic pantheon – which is not, of course, to say that a degree of 'fannish' investment must necessarily be absent from a university teacher's choice of films to screen on a science-fiction course. Nonetheless, given the genre's nature, history and characteristic modes of reception, a particular set of pedagogical imperatives, intertexts and cultural references comes into play whenever science-fiction cinema enters an educational context. Since most higher education courses in science-fiction studies concern themselves primarily with literary rather than with cinematic science fiction, their central theoretical and methodological agendas are rarely those of screen studies. At the same time, while the constituencies and agendas of, say, film studies, literary science-fiction studies, and science-fiction fandom may differ from one another, there are undoubtedly areas of overlap and common interest.

Within screen studies scholarship, for example, there has often been less interest in science-fiction cinema as a genre than in certain science-fiction films as self-contained objects of analysis. A rough count of publications in the field suggests that the screen studies science-fiction canon is headed more or less equally by the *Alien* films and *Blade Runner*,[2] but if these have become cultural icons, objects of fascination and fodder for commentary and analysis by film scholars, this is not necessarily, nor indeed only, because they are science-fiction films. Any scholarly or pedagogical canon of science-fiction cinema is ultimately bound up with other canons: in particular those of science-fiction studies more generally, and those of film scholarship. What then are, or ought to be, the objects and substantive concerns of a screen studies approach to science-fiction cinema? How – with what methodologies – are these objects most appropriately approached? Above all, perhaps, whom ought such studies to address?

Science-fiction cinema challenges several screen studies agendas, and the encounter between science-fiction studies and screen studies raises a number of as yet unanswered questions. A look at the literature suggests, for example, that within the broader study of film genres there is relatively little sustained reflection on science-fiction cinema, and that extensive studies of science-fiction cinema as a *genre* are few and far between. At the same time, and perhaps in consequence, discussions of individual science-fiction films are frequently uninformed by genre criticism or by awareness of science-fiction cinema's considerable history. This state of affairs clearly has implications for the manner in which criticism and analysis of science-fiction films is conducted. Such work is frequently confined to discussions of plot and character, for instance, paying relatively little attention to questions of film form and cinematic address. Where these latter are considered, it is usually in the context of readings of single films rather than treatments of the genre. In consequence, the key question as to whether there are modes of cinematic enunciation peculiar to, or particularly associated with, science-fiction cinema as against other film genres remains largely unaddressed by screen studies scholarship.

In generic terms, science-fiction cinema may be approached in four ways: in terms of its *themes*, its *iconographies*, its *modes of address*, and its *uses*. Vivian Sobchack, one of the few film scholars to have undertaken a systematic analysis of science-fiction cinema as a genre, has proposed that, thematically, science fiction offers a 'poetic mapping of social relations as they are created and changed by new technological modes of "being-in-the-world"'.[3] This suggests that science fiction's characteristic themes are basically twofold, having to do with technologies on the one hand and with modes of societal organization on the other. The preoccupation with technology gives the genre its peculiar fluidity, says Sobchack: for technologies – and, it might be added, the cultural attitudes and competences that go with them – are in constant flux. It is the emphasis on the social which gives science-fiction narratives their characteristic coolness, in that they display a tendency to eschew the motivations and psychological development of characters in favour of a detached, even Olympian, stance towards the social arrangements governing the fictional worlds they construct and the fictional characters who inhabit these worlds.

It is surely no coincidence, then, that among popular fictional genres science fiction above all appears to solicit critical commentary of a sociological kind. This is apparent in readings which in one way or another address the relationship between the social worlds of science fictions and the 'real' worlds outside them. Overviews of the genre, for example, very often adopt a historical approach in which science fiction's thematic preoccupations are tracked alongside social events and attitudes prominent at the time the work first appeared. With science-fiction cinema, the trajectory typically runs from the Cold War obsessions of American 1950s science fiction (*The Thing, Invasion of the Body-snatchers*), through the ecological disasters predicted in 1970s films like *THX-1138* and *Soylent Green*, to the post-industrial and postmodern cityscapes of more recent productions like *Blade Runner* and the *Terminator* films. In close analytic encounters with science-fiction films, critics mine thematic and iconographic subtexts for insights into their ideological workings.[4] It is in this spirit that Sobchack advances the view that contemporary science-fiction films offer 'new symbolic maps of our social relationship to others in what has become the familiarity (rather than the novelty) of a totally technologised world';[5] and that, with their rubbish-strewn ruined cityscapes, these films take for granted, even eroticize, the effects of disaster.

The social and technological thematics of science fiction often go hand in hand with certain iconographies – with dominant visual facts, motifs or symbols in a film's, or in the genre's, overall organization. Prominent in popular imaginings of science fiction are such familiar icons as spaceships, robots and aliens. These, however, are probably more prominent in science fiction in non-cinematic media, figuring particularly memorably in the science-fiction comics and pulp literature of the 1940s and 1950s. Indeed issues of narrative theme, as well as of iconography, cut across all the media forms in which science fiction finds expression: the themes and iconographies associated with science fiction, that is, are not confined to science-fiction cinema.

Is there, then, anything peculiarly distinctive about science-fiction in *cinema* as against science fiction in other media? Sobchack has suggested that the science-fiction film provides 'concrete narrative shape and visible form to our changing historical imagination of social progress and disaster':[6] in other words, the genre's fictions of progress – as well, *pace* Susan Sontag, of disaster[7] – are precisely rendered *visible* in science-fiction films. Visibility, of course, is not an attribute confined to cinematic science fiction: science fictions are told through visual media and matters of expression other than cinema, from comic books to television to computer games and the Internet. If it has this much at least in common with other media, then, how is cinematic science fiction different?

Perhaps the main site of potential distinctiveness is cinema's specific apparatus and modes of address – the manner and context in which films are consumed, and the ways in which they interpellate, or speak to, the spectator. When viewed in cinemas, science-fiction films foreground spectacle at the levels of both image and (if the term may be thus extended) sound. Big-budget science-fiction extravaganzas offer the total visual, auditory and kinetic experience of the *Gesamtkunstwerk*: the spectator is invited to succumb to complete sensory and bodily engulfment. Wherever cinema exhibits its own distinctive matters of expression – as it does with science fiction in displays of state-of-the-art special effects technologies – there is a considerable degree of self-reflexivity at work. Indeed, when such displays become a prominent attraction in their own right, they tend to eclipse narrative, plot and character. The story becomes the display; and the display becomes the story. Does it really matter, for example, that a film like *2001: A Space Odyssey* effectively lacks a plot? The enticement is not narrative involvement, nor even identification with characters, but rather the matters of expression of cinema itself, and this film's awe-inspiringly unfamiliar imagery. Spectators are invited to gape in wonder and abandon themselves to the totality of the audiovisual experience.

If this is the case, the singular address of science-fiction cinema rests on a particular gaze, a form of looking which draws in senses other than vision: hence Vivian Sobchack's suggestion that, more than any other film genre, science fiction repays analysis in terms of a phenomenonology of vision – analysis, that is, which attends to the sensuous immediacy of the viewing experience. Such vision-implicated sensuousness might well, of course, derive its power in part from its evocation of primal fantasies and pre-Oedipal pleasures.[8] These defining features of science-fiction cinema's metapsychology ground the uses and instrumentalities of science-fiction films as a body of cultural texts.

The 1990s have seen significant shifts in the central *topoi* of screen studies, shifts which have accompanied a general move away from grand theory towards more grounded and inductive approaches to the study of culture. This is evident, for example, in an increased attention to microhistories of cinema, of its institutions and intertexts, and in refinements in the ways in which interconnections between film texts and their contexts of production and reception are conceptualized. At the same time, the rise of cultural studies within the academy has energized debates around the cultural instrumentalities of a wide range of media forms; and a number of studies of science-fiction fandom and of the reception and uses of science fiction in cinema and other media have been conducted within this framework.[9] These studies raise urgent questions about the continuing cultural significance of distinctions between the various media in which science fiction finds expression.

One of the consequences of a shift of focus from the specifically cinematic to the more broadly cultural is a deflection of attention away from the cinematic apparatus, from cinema's own institutional and spectatorial mechanisms and their intersection in the conscious and unconscious psychical and affective processes evoked in the act of film spectatorship. This point is of some significance in light of the rise during the 1990s of new technologies of communication and vision, and of the revolution currently under way in systems for the delivery and reception of moving-image media. Science fiction figures prominently in this context, and not only at the level of media content: questions concerning metapsychology, textual specificity, and cultural instrumentality are in fact more centrally at issue here. Meanwhile, the very concept of science-fiction *cinema* is undergoing transformation at every level, from the metapsychological to the institutional to the economic.

Among screen theory's new *topoi* is space; and this is a development whose import for the study of science-fiction cinema goes far beyond mere wordplay. In classical film theory, cinematic space is codified primarily in terms of diegetic space and spectatorial space, each qualifier implying a particular locus. Diegetic space is the organization of space on screen, within a film's fictive world; in particular the mapping and rendering intelligible of a fictive geography. Assuming the act of viewing – as against the film text – as its locus, spectatorial space is the space between spectator and screen, the space which organizes the ensemble of screen, spectator and cinematic apparatus. If diegetic space is primarily about the film text, then, spectatorial space is primarily about the metapsychology of cinema.[10] For film theory which takes classical Hollywood cinema as its cornerstone, the spectator is not a passive recipient of messages but actively, if not necessarily consciously, involved in the relay of meanings and subjectivities produced within and by the cinematic apparatus.[11] In their construction of a fictive, or virtual, geography for the spectator, however, spectatorial space and diegetic space are conjoined and mutually dependent.

Classical film theory holds that a necessary condition of this imbrication of spectatorial and diegetic spaces is a distinctive type of viewing situation, involving a large cinema screen viewed in a darkened cinema auditorium. However, given that the cinema auditorium is now only one of a number of possible venues for viewing films, the classical configuration of diegetic and spectatorial space must be regarded as historically and culturally specific. Nonetheless, given the peculiar importance of sound and spectacle in science-fiction cinema, the classical spatial model arguably remains serviceable, in this context at least. As a set of institutions and a mode of textual organization, classical Hollywood cinema may indeed be history; and yet science-fiction films continue to demand certain engagements with diegetic, spectatorial – and perhaps also with other – spaces. Ironically perhaps, these engagements are rather different from those proposed by classical cinema and classical film theory. What, then, is distinctive about the spaces of science-fiction cinema? And how might these spaces be conceptualized in relation to science-fiction films when these are consumed outside the cinema auditorium? What, in other words, is the difference between the spaces inhabited by the spectator of science-fiction films in the cinema and those inhabited by the consumer of science fiction delivered in other moving-image media? To what extent do these spaces remain separate, and to what extent – and with what possible consequences – do they leak into one another?

NOTES

1. *Science-Fiction Studies*, vol. 24, no. 1, 1977.
2. The count is based on publications listed in the Bibliography: see Appendix. *Metropolis* takes third place, well behind the leaders, and is followed by *Star Wars*, the *Terminator* films, *2001*, *Close Encounters of the Third Kind*, and *Robocop*.
3. Vivian Sobchack, 'Science Fiction', in Wes D. Gehring, ed., *Handbook of American Film Genres*, Westport, CN: Greenwood Press, 1988, p. 229.
4. See, for example, Peter Biskind, *Seeing is Believing: How Hollywood Taught Us to Stop Worrying and Love the Fifties*, New York: Pantheon Books, 1983; H. Bruce Franklin, 'Visions of the Future in Science Fiction Films from 1970 to 1982', in Annette Kuhn, ed., *Alien Zone: Cultural Theory and Contemporary Science Fiction Cinema*, London: Verso, 1990.
5. Sobchack, 'Science Fiction', p. 237.
6. Ibid., p. 231.
7. Susan Sontag, 'The Imagination of Disaster', in *Against Interpretation*, London: Eyre & Spottiswoode, 1966.
8. Vivian Sobchack, *Screening Space: The American Science Fiction Film*, New York: Ungar, 1987, ch. 4; Sobchack, 'Cities on the Edge of Time', in this volume; Daniel Dervin, 'Primal Conditions and Conventions: The Genre of Science Fiction', in Kuhn, ed., *Alien Zone*.
9. Kuhn, ed., *Alien Zone*, p. 9; Henry Jenkins and John Tulloch, *Science Fiction Audiences: Watching Star Trek and Doctor Who*, New York: Routledge, 1995; Constance Penley, 'Brownian Motion: Women, Tactics, and Technology', in Constance Penley and Andrew Ross, eds, *Technoculture*, Minneapolis: University of Minnesota Press, 1991.
10. Stephen Heath, 'Narrative Space', *Screen*, vol. 17, no. 3, 1976; David Bordwell, *Narration in the Fiction Film*, London: Methuen, 1985, ch. 7.
11. For a discussion of spectatorial space and the mobility of spectatorial subjectivity in relation to unconscious fantasy, see Elizabeth Cowie, 'Fantasia', *m/f*, no. 9, 1984.

PART I

CULTURAL SPACES

INTRODUCTION

Teasing out the interconnections between science-fiction film texts, their spectators and the social-cultural discourses and practices in which they are embedded requires conceptualising the genre not only in its specificity as cinema but also in terms of its cultural instrumentalities. This, however, exposes a number of inconsistencies in science-fiction film criticism and theory. In particular, it becomes apparent that the critical and scholarly attention which has been devoted to science-fiction cinema does not add up to an actively evolving body of critical work on science fiction as a film genre. Built as it largely has been around a handful of classical Hollywood genres – the western, the film noir, the melodrama – film genre criticism does not find science fiction easy to deal with.[1] If science-fiction cinema possesses any distinctive generic traits, these – unlike those of other genres – have to do in large measure with cinematographic technologies and with the ways in which these figure in the construction of diegetic and spectatorial spaces: while science-fiction films may certainly tell stories, narrative content and structure *per se* are rarely their most significant features. In these respects, science-fiction films mark themselves out not only from other types of film but also from science-fiction literature.

In '"Sensuous Elaboration": Reason and the Visible in the Science-Fiction Film', Barry Keith Grant explores the relationship between science fiction as a cross-media genre and cinema as a vehicle for science fictions. Looking first at the differences between science fiction and adjacent genres, especially the horror film, he argues that the distinctiveness of science fictions, in whatever medium, lies in their *expansiveness* – their opening out of new worlds, new ways of seeing and being. This attribute clearly runs counter to the classical narrative's impetus towards closure. The distinctiveness of science-fiction *cinema*, Grant contends, lies in special effects, with their accentuation of visual surfaces and their sensuous and kinetic potential. In combination with its positive emphasis on 'the surface of things', science-fiction cinema's de-emphasis of narrative process and closure allows corresponding weight to the sense of awe and wonder evoked by many science-fiction films. This is particularly apparent in films like *Close Encounters of the Third Kind*, in which a child character, responding with amazement at some miraculous apparition, functions as a stand-in for the film's spectator: to this extent, the spectator of science-fiction film is addressed as a 'wide-eyed child'. A sense of wonder, says Grant, is a key generic feature of science-fiction cinema; and indeed this constitutes the genre's 'ontological fulfilment'.

In 'Diegetic or Digital? The Convergence of Science-Fiction Literature and Science-Fiction Film in Hypermedia', Brooks Landon explores differences between science-fiction literature and science-fiction cinema, concluding that a convergence between science fiction's various media of expression is currently taking place. In reaction against what he characterizes as an overprivileging of questions around narrative, theme and character in science-fiction film criticism, Landon draws on and extends Christian Metz's arguments concerning *trucage* in cinema,[2] arguing that in science-fiction cinema the point is not so much the story as the response invited by the film's visual surface, and the ways in which the film depicts technologies and deploys them in its production. Exactly as with the earliest 'cinema of attractions', therefore, the point at issue is the medium's fascination and the spectacle it offers of its own production technology.[3]

Landon's concern is at this level with cinema, and more precisely with the distinctive traits of science-fiction cinema: 'Could the spectacle of [film] production technology deserve and reward our attention as surely as do narratives about the impact of technology?' he asks. However, with developments in special effects technologies – Computer Generated Imagery, especially – now making such an impact on the genre, it is becoming increasingly difficult to ignore the genre's 'visual surfaces'. At the same time, these developments are also breaking down technological and expressive boundaries between cinema and other visual media. Ironically perhaps, developments in special effects technologies have particularly significant consequences for the ways in which science-fiction narratives are structured. Focusing on digital hypermedia science fiction, Landon examines the 'multiform narrative' made possible by interactive hypertexts; and concludes that science-fiction narrative is both discovered in, and shaped by, special effects technologies.

Grant and Landon are both concerned with the *address* of science-fiction films, with the modes of spectatorial subjectivity proposed in their textual organization. Digital hypertext narratives pose an intriguing challenge to conceptualizations of cinematic address. Because these narratives can only be read, they do not merely propose an active spectatorial subjectivity but positively demand activity – bodily activity, at that – on the part of a user who must collaborate simultaneously in both the telling and the reception of the story by clicking his/her own path through a range of (albeit predefined) narrative possibilities. At this point, narration and reception are telescoped: textual address – which is about the 'spectator-in-the-text', or the implied spectator – converges with actual user activity. Digital hypertext narratives thus raise immediate questions around cultural instrumentality, and demand that attention be given to the responses and activities of their consumers.[4]

Consumers of science fiction appear to be a singularly communicative and creative group. In a study of fans of the television science-fiction series *Star Trek*, for example, Henry Jenkins discovered that fans adopt a distinctive mode of reception, involving conscious selection and repeated consumption of material; and that they translate the material and their reception of it into social activities of various kinds (including talk with other fans, membership of fan clubs, attendance at conventions, and exchanges of letters). Also, says Jenkins, fandom constitutes a particular interpretive community – fan club meetings, newsletters and fanzines all offer forums for collective negotiation of the meanings of texts, as well as an alternative social community ('the fans' appropriation of media texts provides a ready body of common references that facilitates communication with others scattered across a broad geographic area'). Jenkins discovered that fandom even constitutes a particular 'Art World', wherein fans use their selected texts as bases for new cultural creation.[5]

The attributes of *Star Trek* fandom are interesting in light of Will Brooker's discussion of 'Internet Fandom and the Continuing Narratives of *Star Wars*, *Blade Runner* and *Alien*'. Brooker, like Jenkins, undertook an empirical study of fan activity; but his inquiry was focused on science-fiction cinema, and on fan interaction in Internet discussion groups. However, both the topic and the medium of the fan activity Brooker investigated clearly lent themselves to fan behaviour of the sort observed by Jenkins. These fans' highly active and in-volved responses to their favoured films are apparent in the effectively social activity of their Internet conversations. Moreover, fans of the three films form a self-contained and highly distinctive interpretive community, in which shared meanings are taken for granted by participants and the chosen film serves as a basis for new, and often cumulative and collective, 'acts of enthusiastic and dedicated creation'. At the same time, there is a degree of self-referentiality about Internet science-fiction film fan activity, in that it depends upon and makes use of the very sorts of technologies that are depicted in many science-fiction films and are deployed in the production of special effects in them.[6] Fan activity of this sort is far from homogeneous, however: Brooker observed marked differences between his three groups in their styles of selecting favoured films and their attitudes towards, and modes of celebration of, these 'canonical' texts. Aside from the insights it offers into the singular cultural instrumentalities of science-fiction cinema, Brooker's study affords fascinating insights into some of the cultural processes through which science-fiction film canons are formed and transformed.

NOTES

1. For a more detailed discussion of these issues, see Annette Kuhn, ed., *Alien Zone: Cultural Theory and Contemporary Science Fiction Cinema*, London: Verso, 1990, pp. 1–11.
2. Ibid, p.148; Christian. Metz, 'Trucage and the Film', *Critical Inquiry*, vol. 3, no. 4, 1977.
3. Landon is referring to the argument advanced by Tom Gunning in 'The Cinema of Attractions: Early Film, Its Spectator and the Avant-Garde', *Wide Angle*, vol. 8, nos 3–4, 1986.
4. On the role of the user in hypertext narratives, see Ruggero Eugeni, '*Myst*: Multimedia Hypertexts and Film Semiotics', *Iris*, no. 25, 1998.
5. Henry Jenkins, '"Strangers No More, We Sing": Filking and the Social Construction of the Science Fiction Fan Community', in Lisa A. Lewis, ed., *The Adoring Audience: Fan Culture and Popular Media*, London: Routledge, 1992.
6. On virtual reality as a plot device in science fiction, see Mark Dery, ed., *Flame Wars: The Discourse of Cyberculture*, Durham, NC: Duke University Press, 1994; see also Claudia Springer, 'Psycho-cybernetics in Films of the 1990s', in this volume.

I

'SENSUOUS ELABORATION': REASON AND THE VISIBLE IN THE SCIENCE-FICTION FILM

BARRY KEITH GRANT

In this chapter I want to explore the relation of science fiction to the cinema – that is to say, the relation between the genre of science fiction and the medium of film. [1] As I shall argue, the inherent nature of cinema as a visual medium has tended to work against the distinctive dynamics of science fiction as a genre. My intention is not to claim, as indeed some critics have, that 'Science fiction film … is an intellectual impossibility.'[2] Clearly such a sweeping claim would be absurd, yet fans of science-fiction literature have lodged this complaint against science-fiction film frequently.

For my purpose here, we might begin to hack our way through what Darko Suvin calls the 'genealogical jungle' of science fiction by distinguishing it from horror.[3] Although the two genres share some of the same generic elements (iconography, character types, conventions), their treatment is notably different. So while the genres of science fiction and horror often overlap, even more so in film than in literature, the contrasts between them are rooted in the particular nature of science-fiction *film*.

Both science fiction and horror, along with fantasy, are types of narrative that have been called speculative fiction or structural fabulation.[4] Horror and science fiction are both rooted in the real world: the former works by positing something as horrifying in contrast to the normal, quotidian world; the latter by acknowledging to some extent contemporary scientific knowledge and the scientific method. Hence the close relationship between the two genres. Such works as Mary Shelley's novel *Frankenstein* (1817), Ridley Scott's *Alien* (1979), and the two versions of *The Thing* (1951, 1982) have been categorized as both science fiction and horror, for all employ iconography and conventions found in both genres. By contrast, fantasy narratives are based neither in the natural world nor in the supernatural, but the *supra*natural. As Robert Heinlein notes,

> Science fiction and fantasy are as different as Karl Marx and Groucho Marx. Fantasy is constructed either by denying the real world *in toto* or at least by making a prime basis of the story one or more admittedly false premise – fairies, talking mules, trips through a looking glass, vampires, seacoast Bohemia, Mickey Mouse.[5]

The distinctive aim of fantasy, then, according to Lester del Rey, is to present 'alternative *impossibilities*'.[6]

Despite the narrative relation between horror and science fiction, the two genres offer experiences and pleasures strikingly different, in fact almost opposite, in nature. As such critics as Robert Scholes and Bruce Kawin have argued, the appeal of science fiction is primarily cognitive, while horror, as the genre's very name suggests, is essentially emotional.[7] Linda Williams has discussed the horror film as a 'body genre' – that is, one of those genres (like pornography and melodrama) that works by eliciting pronounced emotional and physiological excitation. Science-fiction, by contrast, is often defined more cerebrally as a philosophical openness described as a 'sense of wonder'. Science-fiction critic Sam Moskowitz, quoting Rollo May, for example, invokes the phrase as the essential quality of science fiction and defines this sense of wonder as a heightened awareness and open attitude to new ideas.[8] Science fiction, quite unlike fantasy and horror, works to entertain alternative *possibilities*.

Perhaps, then, the fundamental distinction between the two genres is one of attitude: a closed response in horror, an open one in science fiction. Horror seeks to elicit terror and fear of something unknown or unacknowledged. According to Robin Wood's highly influential Freudian/Marxist analysis of the horror film, the genre's monsters represent a 'return of the repressed', forbidden desire disowned and projected outward by the protagonist.[9] Accordingly, in horror stories narrative consciousness is often trapped or contained, set in claustrophobic, enclosed places, as in the countless castles, vaults, tombs and chambers that typify the genre's dramatic spaces. And vision is often obscured, from Poe's 'The Pit and the Pendulum' (1843) to John Carpenter's *The Fog* (1979). Because the sleep of reason breeds monsters, horror tales emphasize darkness and night (Stephen King's *The Dark Half* [1990], the numerous movies entitled *Night of…*) and superstition (*Halloween* [1978], *Friday the 13th* [1980] and the various *Curse(s) of…*).

Tellingly, the narrator's struggle in Poe's story 'Descent into the Maelstrom' (1841) to employ empirical reasoning so as to prevent being sucked below the surface is paradigmatic of the horror tale. By contrast, the rapt upward gaze of faces bathed in beatific light in Steven Spielberg's *Close Encounters of the Third Kind* (1977) is emblematic of the expansive thrust of science fiction. Vision in horror tales tends to focus down and inward, as in Poe's 'The Premature Burial' (1844) or David Cronenberg's *Parasite Murders* (a.k.a. *Shivers/They Came From Within*, 1975), while science fiction gazes up and out – from man's one small step in Jules Verne's *From the Earth to the Moon* (1865) to the giant step for mankind through the stargate in Stanley Kubrick's *2001: A Space Odyssey* (1968). Kawin sums up the difference by comparing the last lines of *The Thing* – the dire warning 'Keep watching the skies!' – and *Brainstorm* (1983) – the hopeful and expansive invitation to 'Look at the stars!'[10] It is no coincidence that one of the first science-fiction movies of the sound era was entitled *Just Imagine* (1930).

For Damon Knight, 'Some widening of the mind's horizons, no matter in what direction' is what science fiction is all about.[11] In this sense science-fiction narratives are, to use Méliès's own phrase, *voyages extraordinaires* which, befitting their frequent setting in the future and/or on parallel worlds, emphasize the vastness of space and the fluidity of time. Thus in science fiction, narrative point of view expands to entertain rather than contain new possibilities. As in, say, Olaf Stapledon's novel *Last and First Men* (1930) or H.G. Wells's *The Shape of Things to Come* (1933) and the film version *Things to Come* (1936), which Wells scripted, the dramatic conflict in science fiction is quite often exactly this: the difficulty of accepting rather than combating forces larger than the individual will. According to Suvin, the genre works by providing us with an experience of 'cognitive estrangement': as in Russian Formalism, our attention is returned to reality by the premises of science-fiction tales, which make us question the givens of our world.[12]

In both Richard Matheson's *The Shrinking Man* (1956) and the film adaptation *The Incredible Shrinking Man* (1957), the mental perspective of the protagonist expands even as his body dwindles. At first Scott Carey is terrified by the new, challenging world in which he finds himself, but ultimately he achieves spiritual transcendence. His epiphanic perception, on the novel's final page, is that he has moved from the 'universe without' to the 'universe within': 'Why had he never thought of it; of the microscopic and the submicroscopic worlds? … He'd always thought in terms of man's concept, not nature's…. But to nature there was no zero. Existence went on in endless cycles' (or, as the film concludes: 'To God there is no zero').[13]

The horrible dangers of an enlarged world are embodied in both novel and film in the spectacular form of a spider that comes to seem monstrously large. Both horror and science fiction make generic claims to monster movies – 'the Creature film sits (awkwardly, for some) between horror and SF', observes Vivian Sobchack[14] – but they are represented quite differently in the two genres. This difference follows from their respective orientations of vision. In horror, creatures are monstrous violations of ideological norms, while in science fiction monsters are often simply a different life form. Because of this difference in the treatment of the Other, as Sobchack observes, horror monsters threaten the disruption of moral and natural order, while those of science fiction address the disruption of the social order.[15]

So the monsters of horror are typically abject, occasionally even unnameable, as in Stephen King's *It* (1986); but in science fiction they may be subjects of rational scrutiny, as in John W. Campbell, Jr's novella 'Who Goes There?' (1938), the source of both versions of *The Thing*. Because the monsters of horror commonly represent 'the return of the repressed', they tend to be anthropomorphic (the vampire, the zombie, the mummy) and animalistic (the wolf man, cat people), to spring from our physical nature, albeit in unnatural or 'interstitial' form.[16] The Other of science fiction, however, frequently takes nonhumanoid forms, whether animal (*War of the Worlds*, 1953), vegetable (*The Andromeda Strain*, 1970), or mineral (*The Monolith Monsters*, 1957).

The fundamental difference between science fiction and horror is conventionally represented within the two genres themselves as a differing emphasis on the mind (science fiction) and the body (horror). Science fiction focuses on heady issues, as in such movies as *The Brain from Planet Arous* (1958) and *The Mind of Mr Soames* (1969). The premiss in Poul Anderson's novel *Brain Wave* (1954) is that the human race is suddenly confronted with a quantum leap in intelligence. By contrast, horror commonly evokes our anxiety about the body, so vividly invoked in such horror films as *I Dismember Mama* (1972) and *The Texas Chain Saw Massacre* (1974). Indeed, contemporary horror movies focus on the graphic spectacle of the violated body to such an extent that they have been referred to as 'meat movies'. For Philip Brophy, they tend 'to play not so much on the broad fear of Death, but more precisely on the fear of one's own body, of how one controls and relates to it'.[17] In many of these movies, such as the *Hellraiser* series, evisceration and flaying – that is, exposing the body as a visible site – are treated as the privileged moments of horror, the generic 'money shots'. (Indeed, it might even be argued that the history of the horror film traces a trajectory of gradual, inexorable surrender to the allure of the visible, and that this genre's current aesthetic impasse and moribund status is precisely the result of its wholesale capitulation to the representation of horror as that which is corporeal, physical – that is, *seen*.)

For Christian Metz, the chronological development from Lumière to Méliès marks an evolution of 'cinematography to cinema' – that is, from a conception of film as a recording tool to an artistic medium.[18] But it is perhaps more accurate to say that cinema is simultaneously Lumière and Méliès, science *and* fiction, for the film image is at once a concrete, scientific record of things in the real world (*'actualités'*) and a selected account of that world (*'artificially arranged scenes'*). Dziga Vertov's Kino Eye, that unblinking machine capable of perceiving the world with a greater objective fidelity than the human eye, always open to that which is placed before it, would suggest that the cinema would be an ideal medium for conveying science fiction's sense of wonder. Indeed, cinema as a medium displays three central aspects central to the genre of science fiction: space, time, and the machine – or the apparatus, in the terms of materialist film theory. (We might note in passing that these themes appear much less often in the horror genre.)

In cinema, narration proceeds by manipulating time and space, elongating and condensing both for dramatic and affective purposes. The techniques for achieving such spatial and temporal distortions constitute the foundation of classic narrative film, but such manipulations are central to documentary and experimental cinema as well. Across the range of different film practices the camera, the recording apparatus itself, seems capable of moving through both dimensions at once. Terry Ramsaye has noted how much the cinema resembles a time machine in his discussion of H.G. Wells's description of travelling through time in *The Time Machine* (1895).[19] (Later in the year Wells's book was published, inventor William Paul, whom Wells knew, applied for a patent for a machine that would provide simulated voyages through time.)

The cinematic machine, like the Constructors in Stanislaw Lem's novel *The Cyberiad* (1967), is a device capable of imagining and 'building' (through special effects) other machines infinitely more sophisticated than itself. Science-fiction film has relied heavily on special effects, and these effects in turn constitute one of the particular pleasures of the genre. The genre's reliance on special effects is itself an enactment of science fiction's thematic concern with technology. It is therefore understandable that for many viewers the value of (that is to say, the pleasure derived from) science-fiction movies is determined by the quality (synonymous with believability) of the special effects. For these viewers, nothing destroys the pleasure of a science-fiction movie more than seeing the 'seams' in a matte shot or glimpsing the zipper on an alien's bodysuit. Even Richard Hodgens, an apparent purist who bemoans the lack of scientific knowledge in science-fiction movies, at several points seems to confuse the failure of some films' special effects to be 'convincing' with the plausibility and consistency of their narrative premises.[20]

Special effects are 'filmic moments of a *radically* filmic character',[21] for they seek to achieve unreality as realistically as possible – to engage 'our belief, not our suspension of disbelief', as Sobchack puts it. We marvel at special effects images at once for their fantastic content and for the power of their realization. They announce the powers of cinema while, paradoxically, taming the imagination through the very fact of visual representation. This visualization for the camera pulls the images from speculation to spectacle – in Sobchack's terms, it transforms the poetry of the possible into the prosaic realm of the visible.[22]

Because of the science-fiction film's emphasis on special effects, the genre's primary appeal has been the kinetic excitement of action – that 'sensuous elaboration' which Susan Sontag describes as 'the aesthetics of destruction … the peculiar beauties to be found in wreaking havoc, making a mess'.[23] (This pleasure is itself visualized in the 'bird's-eye view' shot in Alfred Hitchcock's 1963 (science-fiction?) thriller *The Birds*, as the viewer is placed with the hovering birds looking down in seeming satisfied contemplation of the picturesque destruction they have wrought in the town below.) At least one subgenre of the science-fiction film, the apocalyptic film, is founded on the promise of scenes of mass destruction. In these films, from *When Worlds Collide* (1951) to the recent *Armageddon* and *Deep Impact* (both 1998), we eagerly await the climactic tidal wave that will sweep over New York and its landmarks of western civilization.

The paradigmatic example of this difference between science fiction in the two media is, perhaps, *Frankenstein*. Shelley's novel is a central early text in the history of science-fiction literature – the 'first great myth of the Industrial age', in the words of Brian Aldiss[24] – while James Whale's 1931 movie is a classic horror film. In the film, philosophy is replaced by *frisson*, and the white magic of science becomes black.[25] Dr Frankenstein's laboratory, with its battery of crackling generators and steaming German Expressionist beakers – clearly influenced by Rotwang's laboratory in *Metropolis* (1926) – evokes not enlightened scientific inquiry but the dark supernatural world of the Gothic. The creature is transformed from a nimble and articulate being, an effective metaphor for Romantic *hubris* and encroaching industrialization, into a lumbering, grunting monster. The movie is less interested in the moral implications of human artifice than in the frightening spectacle of Boris Karloff's stiff-legged strut, and so shifts the focus from, as it were, the doctor's dilemma to the revenge of the creature. The doctor's famous cackle, 'It's alive, it's alive', as uttered by actor Colin Clive, unmistakably marks him as an unhinged man – the familiar mad scientist of horror who has committed the hubristic sin of investigating phenomena 'Man was not meant to know'.

Monsters, phaser-gun gadgetry and large-scale destruction are staple motifs of science-fiction literature, but they have been more prominent in science-fiction cinema. If the cinema's BBBs (big bosomed babes, in the jargon of the genre), as represented by *Fire Maidens From Outer Space* (1956) and Jane Fonda as *Barbarella* (1967), cannot hope to match the depictions in the science-fiction pulps in the 'Golden Age' (approximately 1938 to 1950), it is only that actresses of flesh and blood could never equal the damsels in the fantastically stylized illustrations of the pulp covers – although Russ Meyer's amply endowed women in *Dr Breedlove* (1964) come close.

Because film is primarily a visual medium, it tends to concentrate on the depiction of visual surfaces at the expense of contemplative depth. Science fiction's characteristic sense of wonder thus works differently in film than in literature. According to Cyril Kornbluth, 'The science fiction writer churns out symbols every time he writes of the future or an alternate present; he rolls out symbols of people, places, things, relationships, as fast as he can work his typewriter or his pen.'[26] Indeed, writing in the interrogative mode of science fiction rather than the declarative mode of realism is necessarily to write symbolically, for it is the extrapolative kind of writing that contemplates the potential of things, how things *might* be regarded (Suvin's 'cognitive estrangement'). Unlike words, which are rendered either as sounds or marks on paper, representational images are first and always objects in the material world, the things themselves before being symbolic of something else.[27]

In other genres, inherent symbolism is provided by visual icons which carry 'intrinsic charges of meaning independently of whatever is brought to them by particular directors'.[28] But, as Sobchack notes, the common objects in science-fiction films, like spaceships, lack the iconographic consistency of other genres and are relatively 'unfixed'.[29] But science-fiction films are are shaped by the ideological constraints of the genre system, which typically features comfortable narrative closure. So even though science-fiction movies allow us the anarchic pleasure of witnessing civilization's destruction, the genre also offers us, at least in its classic form (similar to the gangster film, to which monster movies are closely related), the satisfaction of the restoration of social order. So in the monster movies that typified science-fiction film during the 1950s (the period John Baxter refers to as 'Springtime for Caliban'[30]), the creatures, which almost always appear as the result of nuclear testing, are often finally destroyed with an 'ultimate weapon' that uses similar technology. In other words, the unfortunate results of sophisticated and potentially lethal technology are defeated by the creation of even more sophisticated and lethal technology.

In *The Beast from 20,000 Fathoms* (1953), one of the movies that initiated the 1950s monster cycle, the elegiac atmosphere that informs Ray Bradbury's 1951 source story 'The Fog Horn' is emphatically sacrificed for visual spectacle. The story is a mood piece about a lonely prehistoric creature drawn from the sea to a lighthouse by the melancholy sound of its horn. Bradbury's prose is more suggestive than concrete in its description, but the movie features a radioactive, mutated Rhedosaurus that wreaks havoc in New York City, with the requisite shots of physical destruction and stampeding pedestrians. In the film's climax, the army pursues the creature to Coney Island, for no particular reason other than the visual interest in showing the creature in proportion to the famous Cyclone roller coaster, where it is killed with a new nuclear warhead. Thus our fears about the possibility of nuclear holocaust are at once aroused and assuaged in a narrative trajectory that in short order became a soothing ritual in the myriad movies featuring genetically altered insects, reptiles, and other asserted BEMs ('bug-eyed monsters') that soon followed. Of course, the ideological assurance of such narrative closure works across numerous genres, but in the specific case of science fiction it compromises the radical potential of the genre's extrapolative, speculative dynamic.

In recent years, the science-fiction film has placed great emphasis upon the child, and this is no accident. Robin Wood has argued convincingly that recent American cinema generally has tended to construct the viewer as childlike,[31] in thrall to the illusion. In science fiction specifically, the generic sense of wonder, and by extension the position of the spectator, has been located in the image of a wide-eyed child. This development, of course, is largely the result of the huge commercial success of George Lucas's *Star Wars* trilogy and Steven Spielberg's *Close Encounters* and *ET: The Extra-terrestrial* (1982), all of which rank among the top box-office winners in film history. (The *Star Wars* cosmology became even more firmly entrenched in American cultural consciousness when former President Ronald Reagan named his national defence programme after Lucas's film and referred to the Soviet Union as the 'Evil Empire'.) Subsequent science-fiction movies such as *Starman* (1984), *The Explorers* (1985), *Short Circuit* (1986), *Tron* (1982) and *The Last Starfighter* (1984) exhibited a new adolescent orientation, clearly showing the influence of the Lucas and Spielberg films. *Cocoon* (1985), with its premiss of alien lifeforms that change a swimming pool into a fountain of youth, even manages to make children of senior citizens.

Before Spielberg and Lucas, children were as sparse in science-fiction films as in the stylized towns of the classic Western. Aside from such rare exceptions as *Invaders From Mars* (1953) and *Village of the Damned* (1960, based on John Wyndham's *The Midwich Cuckoos*, 1957), until recently children tended to be

DBS Arts Library

neither heard nor seen in science fiction. In horror, however, children have been presented frequently as figures of evil rather than innocence. From *The Bad Seed* (1956) to Stephen King's *Pet Sematary* (1983), horror tales have depicted children as figures of demonic possession. Many of these movies, following upon the popularity of *Rosemary's Baby* (1968) and *The Exorcist* (1973), may be read as embodying adult fears of being 'possessed' by children – that is, of being obligated to them, an expression of cultural backlash against the centrality of the nuclear family in a period of dissolving marriages and more open sexual mores.

Discussing the infantilization that informed much of Hollywood cinema in the 1980s, Wood refers to special effects as the exhibition of technological 'magic'. Tellingly, Lucas's special effects company is called Industrial Light and Magic – the name itself suggesting the kind of totemic power the popular audience ascribes to the sophisticated technology required to produce such visual illusions. As Carl Freedman notes, special effects tend to 'overwhelm the viewer, to bathe the perceptual apparatus of the filmgoer in the very "filmicness" of film'.[32] This position is literalized by the placement of the camera (and hence the position of the spectator) in the genre's now-conventional special effects image described by Martin Rubin as 'a shot … of an enormous spacecraft rumbling over the camera position, so that the entire underside passes overhead, massive, ominous, bristling with special effects paraphernalia'.[33] (The convention is nicely parodied in the opening shot of Mel Brooks's 1987 science-fiction parody *Spaceballs*, with its enormous ship that rumbles past – and past, and past.)

The scopophilic pleasure of cinema is mobilized most intensely in special effects images, as viewers are swathed in their power. This wondrous dependence on special effects imagery is itself the subject of Paul Verhoeven's *Total Recall* (1990), based on Philip K. Dick's short story 'We Can Remember It For You Wholesale' (1966). Like Dick's story, the movie is a reflexive science-fiction film about the extent to which we look to the image to provide our reality. The protagonist, Douglas Quaid, because of his memory implant, becomes incapable of distinguishing reality from fantasy: he does not know whether his adventure is the program he requested at Rekall, Inc, or if his actual identity has been accidentally uncovered. Viewers share Quaid's lack of epistemological certainty since they are incapable of detecting – indeed, are virtually challenged to detect – a flaw in the state-of-the-art special effects, that is, of distinguishing between what is 'real' and what is 'imagination'. Inevitably, the viewer regresses to that earliest phase of childhood Jacques Lacan calls the pre-Oedipal Imaginary, unable to distinguish the nature of the visual field. The world of the film, with its domestic wall projections of make-believe environments, mechanical taxi drivers and holographic projections, is a postmodern simulacrum, just as the visual media are for us in the real world. The landscape of recent popular cinema offers ample evidence that, like Quaid, we enjoy imagining ourselves as Arnold Schwarzenegger in non-stop action movies – just like *Total Recall*.

Verhoeven follows the same approach in his more recent *Starship Troopers* (1997), based on Heinlein's 1959 novel. The book is a rather straightforward account of the military mindset and values in the future when the human race is threatened by an extraterrestrial army of giant intelligent insects. Without a trace of irony, Heinlein uses the story to offer extended passages about the benefits of a social order organized by militaristic principles. The film, however, completely subverts the book's conservative ideology by deconstructing military guts and glory even as it provides it so completely. Again with state-of-the-art effects, Verhoeven shows us graphic battles between bugs and humans as soldiers are impaled, eviscerated and dismembered. The protagonists are all played by beautiful young actors, with whom the audience can easily identify. But these scenes alternate with images of official government propaganda films (obviously inspired by the nationalistic fervour of Frank Capra's *Why We Fight* documentaries from World War II) that clearly contradict the bloody truths of the war. In the film, the young people still march off to war full of optimistic faith, just as audiences flocked to the film to see the much-touted violence of its battle scenes.

Apart from Verhoeven's postmodern critiques, much of contemporary science-fiction cinema has replaced the sense of wonder with the awe of mystification. Popular science-fiction movies like *The Terminator* (1984) and *Predator* (1987), offering almost continuous spectacular action, seem to have succumbed almost entirely to the siren call of the sensuous spectacle. Other science-fiction films like *Alien, Blade Runner* (1982, based on Dick's 1968 *Do Androids Dream of Electric Sheep?*) and John Carpenter's 1982 version of *The Thing*, which propound ostensible humanist messages, are devoid of rounded characters and overwhelmed by production design and special effects, thus contradicting their own themes.

The starchild of *2001* looking down at Earth, returning our gaze to us for self-scrutiny, has become the regressive child/man of *Close Encounters* who, wanting to escape his adult responsibilities and enter the womb of the 'Mother' ship, gazes upwards, as if in religious devotion. If the reverential awe we accord science-fiction images is a debasement of science fiction's distinctive philosophical attitude, it is because the film medium, and the generic system which organizes so much of popular cinema, work to discourage the kind of speculative narrative that has challenged us to embrace what Arthur C. Clarke calls *Childhood's End*. Embodied in science-fiction films most fully in special effects, the genre's characteristic sense of wonder is perhaps the ontological fulfilment of the nature of science-fiction *cinema*.

NOTES

1. This is a substantially revised version of an essay originally published in *Literature/Film Quarterly*, vol. 14, no. 3, 1986.
2. John Baxter, *Science Fiction in the Cinema*, New York: Paperback Library, 1970, p. 8.
3. Darko Suvin, *Metamorphoses of Science Fiction*, New Haven, CT: Yale University Press, 1979, pp. 16–36.
4. Science-fiction author Robert A. Heinlein uses the term 'speculative fiction' in his essay 'Science Fiction: Its Nature, Faults, and Virtues', in Basil Davenport, ed., *The Science Fiction Novel: Imagination and Social Criticism*, Chicago: Advent, 1969, pp. 14–48. 'Structural fabulation' is Robert Scholes's term in *Structural Fabulation: An Essay on Fiction of the*

Future, Notre Dame, IN: University of Notre Dame Press, 1975.

5. Robert Heinlein, 'Preface' to *Tomorrow, the Stars*, New York: Doubleday, 1967, p. 8. See also Heinlein, 'Science Fiction'.

6. Lester del Rey, *The World of Science Fiction, 1926–1976: The History of a Subculture*, New York: Ballantine, 1979, pp. 6–9.

7. Scholes, *Structural Fabulation*; Bruce Kawin, 'Children of the Light', in Barry Keith Grant, ed., *Film Genre Reader II*, Austin: University of Texas Press, 1995, pp. 308–29.

8. Linda Williams, 'Film Bodies: Gender, Genre, and Excess', in Grant, ed., *Film Genre Reader II*, pp. 140–58; Sam Moskowitz, *Seekers of Tomorrow*, Westport, CT: Hyperion Press, 1974, p. 211.

9. Robin Wood, 'An Introduction to the American Horror Film', in Barry Keith Grant, ed., *Planks of Reason: Essays on the Horror Film*, Metuchen, NJ: Scarecrow Press, 1984, pp. 164–200.

10. Kawin, 'Children of the Light', p. 256.

11. Damon Knight, *In Search of Wonder*, 2nd edn, Chicago: Advent, 1967, p. 13.

12. Suvin, *Metamorphoses of Science Fiction*.

13. Richard Matheson, *The Shrinking Man*, New York: Bantam, 1969, p. 188.

14. Vivian C. Sobchack, *The Limits of Infinity: The American Science Fiction Film*, New York: A.S. Barnes, 1980, p. 47.

15. Ibid., p. 30.

16. For a discussion of Julia Kristeva's concept of abjection as applied to the horror film, see Barbara Creed, *The Monstrous-Feminine: Film, Feminism, Psychoanalysis*, London and New York: Routledge, 1993. On monsters as interstitial beings, see Noel Carroll, *The Philosophy of Horror, or Paradoxes of the Heart*, New York and London: Routledge, 1990, pp. 31–5.

17. Philip Brophy, 'Horrality – The Textuality of Contemporary Horror Films', *Screen*, vol. 27, no. 1, 1986, p. 8.

18. Christian Metz, *Film Language: A Semiotics of the Cinema*, trans. Michael Taylor, New York: Oxford University Press, 1974, p. 44.

19. Terry Ramsaye, *A Million and One Nights: A History of the Motion Picture through 1925*, New York: Touchstone, 1986, pp. 153–4.

20. Richard Hodgens, 'A Brief and Tragical History of the Science Fiction Film', *Film Quarterly*, vol. 13, no. 2, 1959, p. 31.

21. Carl Freedman, 'Kubrick's *2001* and the Possibility of a Science Fiction Cinema', *Science Fiction Studies*, no. 75, 1998, p. 305.

22. Sobchack, *The Limits of Infinity*, p. 88.

23. Susan Sontag, 'The Aesthetics of Destruction', in *Against Interpretation*, New York: Delta, 1966, p. 212.

24. Brian Aldiss, *Billion Year Spree: The True History of Science Fiction*, New York: Schocken Books, 1974, p. 23.

25. Hodgens, 'A Brief and Tragical History'.

26. C.M. Kornbluth, 'The Failure of the Science Fiction Novel as Social Criticism', in Davenport, ed., *The Science Fiction Novel*, p. 54.

27. Of course, the recent use of Computer Generated Imagery in science-fiction special effects complicates such claims about cinema's indexical fidelity to the real world.

28. Colin McArthur, *Underworld USA*, New York: Viking Press, 1972, p. 19.

29. Sobchack, *The Limits of Infinity*, pp. 64–87.

30. Baxter, *Science Fiction in the Cinema*, p. 100.

31. Robin Wood, *Hollywood from Vietnam to Reagan*, New York: Columbia University Press, 1986, p. 163.

32. Freedman, 'Kubrick's *2001*', p. 306.

33. Martin Rubin, 'Genre and Technology: Variant Attitudes in Science Fiction Literature and Film', *Persistence of Vision,* nos 3/4, 1986, p. 107.

2

DIEGETIC OR DIGITAL? THE CONVERGENCE OF SCIENCE-FICTION LITERATURE AND SCIENCE-FICTION FILM IN HYPERMEDIA

BROOKS LANDON

Although almost all histories of film in general, and of science-fiction film in particular, credit Georges Méliès as the genre's first significant practitioner, with his *Le Voyage dans la lune* (1902) being its first significant work, I would contend that alternate or revisionist histories of science-fiction film might argue for the Lumières' *Charcuterie mécanique* (1895) as equally deserving of that distinction. Furthermore, I would suggest that such a revisionist history might well see *all* films made before 1906 as science fiction. My proposed revisionist history starts from the assumption that science-fiction film does not necessarily have to present a science-fiction story, that the look of the film and its use and depiction of technology might be enough to evoke a response quite similar to that evoked by science-fiction stories.[1]

This assumption, in turn, builds on the recognition that 'primitive' cinema, the period beginning with the first commercial uses of moving picture technology in 1894 and lasting until around 1906, was primarily a non-narrative phenomenon. 'During most of the primitive period', Kristin Thompson reminds us, 'films appealed to audiences primarily through simple comedy or melodrama, topical subjects, exotic scenery, trick effects, and the sheer novelty of photographed movement'.[2] Tom Gunning calls this period – in which actuality films depicting motion as spectacle or new locations outnumbered fictional films, and in which 'trick' films employed only the most nominal narrative touches – the time of the 'cinema of attractions'. Gunning argues that this period of exhibitionist cinema

> sees cinema less as a way of telling stories than as a way of presenting a series of views to an audience, fascinating because of their illusory power (whether the realistic illusion of motion offered to the first audiences by Lumiere, or the magical illusion concocted by Méliès), and exoticism.[3]

It is Gunning's contention that many of the films made before 1906, including those by Lumière and Méliès, created a very different primary relation to the spectator than that created by the narrative film after 1906. This argument has fascinating implications for the history of science-fiction film, since it suggests the possibility that the genre has its roots in spectacle rather than in narrative, an essential originary difference from the history of science-fiction writing. 'Cinema *is*, of course, a special effect', Scott Bukatman insistently reminds us, 'and that's how it was regarded by its initial audiences':

> The illusion of motion, with its consequent sensations of temporal flow and spatial volume provided enough innovation for spectators *already familiar* with a range of spectacular visual novelties. If cinema's blend of spatiotemporal solidity and metamorphic fluidity was largely assigned to the representation of narrative, these effect(s) of the medium nevertheless remained central to the experience. Special effects redirect the spectator to the visual (and auditory and even kinesthetic) conditions of the cinema, and thus bring the principles of perception to the foreground of consciousness. 'Cinematic images are not representations', Shaviro writes, 'but *events*'.[4]

Accordingly, judged by the standard of attractions – by the nature of its events – rather than by the prevailing conventions of written science-fiction narrative, it can be argued that since primitive cinema used the spectacle of its production technology to elicit the same sense of wonder and discovery elicited by science-fiction writing, all cinema-of-attractions films can be thought of as science fiction.

What has been a pointed privileging of narrative and consequent denunciation of special effects in discussions of science-fiction film is part of a larger privileging of narrative in film criticism in general. Gunning has attempted to redress this distortion in film history by pointing out that the history of film is not necessarily the history of film's narrative accomplishment. He reminds us that the classical style codified by Bordwell, Staiger and Thompson in *The Classical Hollywood Cinema* was not just the development of primitive cinema, a refinement of its crude attempts at narrative, but the development of *one kind* of primitive cinema, while the non-narrative focus of what Gunning calls the 'cinema of attractions' represents another kind of primitive cinema, whose traditions continued even after the codification of the classical style. Significantly, most of what we loosely claim to be pioneering science-fiction films better fit the paradigms of Gunning's 'cinema of attractions', and a historical view of science-fiction film that recognizes the primacy of spectacle in those early films will also suggest a very different view of more recent science-fiction film, in which special effects – increasingly digital attractions – have overshadowed or usurped narrative elements. Indeed, Gunning's work to explain the cinema of attractions helps us to understand the non-narrative value of some of science-fiction film's great spectacles, films such as *Metropolis* (1926), *Things to Come* (1936), *2001: A Space Odyssey* (1968), and *Blade Runner* (1982).

Most early films which have been retrospectively labelled science fiction were initially classified as 'trick films' on the basis of their special effects, offering viewers a series of magical tricks more than a story. Singling out the work usually identified as the first science-fiction film, Gunning explains:

> Many trick films are, in effect, plotless, a series of transformations strung together with little connection and certainly no characterization. But to approach even the plotted trick films, such as *Voyage dans la lune* (1902), simply as precursors of later narrative structures is to miss the point. The story simply provides a frame upon which to string a demonstration of the magical possibilities of the cinema.[5]

Primitive films such as *Le Voyage dans la lune* based their appeal more on the attractions of fairground exhibits and rides than on that of the theatre, as can be most easily seen in the hyperreal *Hale's Tours*, with its films of train rides supplemented by other physical simulations of the sensation of riding on a train.[6] Even more relevant to my approach to contemporary science-fiction media is Gunning's reminder that cinema technology itself was a featured early attraction:

> Early audiences went to exhibitions to see machines demonstrated (the newest technological wonder, following in the wake of such widely exhibited machines and marvels as X-rays or, earlier, the phonograph) rather than to view films. It was the Cinematographe, the Biograph or the Vitascope that were advertised on the variety bills in which they premiered, not *The Baby's Breakfast* or *The Black Diamond Express*.[7]

While the revisionist history of science-fiction film I have derived from Gunning and Bukatman may not be accepted by many in the science-fiction community, the received history the science-fiction community does generally accept also supports – even if it does not recognize – the idea that spectacle may have been more important than narrative. True, *Le Voyage dans la lune* was loosely built around events described in works by both Jules Verne and H.G. Wells, thus establishing links to narratives by two of science fiction's first significant practitioners; but anyone who has seen this film should agree that it is more a caricature than an adaptation of written science fiction. Even if – *particularly if* – the history of science-fiction film starts from Méliès, it starts from a magician who called his trick films 'little abracadabras', and whose interest clearly lay with technological *trucage* rather than with speculation, with tricks rather than with discovery. Indeed, Méliès himself specified that narrative considerations had little importance in his filmmaking and declared that he used story 'merely as a pretext' for his stage effects or tricks.[8] Yet, despite the fact that most historians of science-fiction film point more to the 'attractions' or special effects of the Méliès films than towards their ties to written science-fiction narratives, the clear, and clearly unexamined, tradition in science-fiction film criticism has been to identify science-fiction films primarily in terms of their narrative aspects.

Against this very understandable, but very limiting, privileging of narrative in discussions of science-fiction film, I have proposed a revisionist discussion that would start by attempting to rethink science-fiction film in film-specific terms, opting variously for epistemologically based or image-based criteria instead of the source-based or narrative-based assumptions that have so far shaped most discussions of science-fiction film. Central to any such reconsideration would be the question of whether cinematographic aspects of film production could themselves mark film as science-fictional or provide in themselves phenomena worthy of consideration. Could the spectacle of production technology, increasingly a kind of digital narrative, deserve and reward our attention just as surely as do narratives about the impact of technology? While not limiting his concern to science-fiction film, Scott Bukatman has provocatively explored this line of thought, taking it in new directions by focusing on the 'hallucinatory excess' of special effects sequences in which 'narrative yields to kinetic spectatorial experience', and suggesting:

> A consideration of special effects might help to restore a balance between the ideological critiques of representation (and narrative) which have long dominated cinema studies, and a phenomenological approach that acknowledges that, as Steven Shaviro puts it, 'Cinema is at once a form of perception and a material perceived, a new way of encountering reality and a part of the reality thereby discovered'.[9]

It is crucial to note that while science-fiction writing has always been a narrative medium, science-fiction film actually began as a non-narrative one, its influences and traditions being quite different from those of science-fiction writing. The two media have developed along widely divergent trajectories, only occasionally intersecting in a film that earns the respect of both film critics and science-fiction critics. (Another important difference between these two trajectories stems from the fact that science-fiction literature has also pursued several teleological agendas hidden within its ostensible goal of interrogating and/or advocating change and the impact of science and technology on humanity; science-fiction film does not seem to have shared these 'hidden' agendas.[10]) I believe that we, the audience for the seemingly disparate twins of science-fiction film and science-fiction literature – twins separated at birth –

stand to benefit from their being reunited, even if only in critical discourse and not in production practice. Furthermore, I believe that advances in representation and simulation technology are making such a reunification inevitable, the challenge which faces us being only to recognize the process. Computer animation, Computer Generated Imagery (CGI), virtual reality, virtual reality modelling language (VRML), virtual actors, and the new possibilities offered by hypermedia creations on the World Wide Web may lead to an exciting blending of state-of-the-art art with state-of-the-art science in a new hyper-technologized production matrix for science-fiction media that itself invokes or enacts the science-fiction ethos as much as or more than the narratives it presents. Indeed, there is every reason to predict that digital production technology will determine the future trajectory of science-fiction 'film' and will reshape our understanding of its functionality.

There is a striking irony implicit in the effort of so much critical discourse within the science-fiction community to decry science-fiction stories in film as bad science fiction while we ignore the fact that the history of science-fiction film is itself a science-fiction story turning on technological axes of wonder and featuring filmmakers – and now increasingly computer artists – who almost perfectly exemplify the written genre's longstanding fascination with Edisonades (the celebration of the myth of the lone wizard/inventor) and its cyberpunk-led interrogation of the technosphere. And by overlooking the conceptual implications of science-fiction film or science-fiction media technology, I believe we miss an important opportunity for rethinking what science fiction is in an increasingly science-fiction world – and for rethinking what it might be. Just as Gunning's understanding of the cinema of attractions helps us rethink primitive cinema, the notion of a 'digital cinema of attractions' can help us rethink and 'resee' the history and the future of science-fiction film.

I have elsewhere signalled a number of aspects of such a digital cinema of attractions, and considered some of the different ways in which special effects 'mean' in science-fiction film and some of the ways in which they transcend the science-fiction story depicted in the science-fiction film to constitute a new science-fiction story that *is* science-fiction film. [11] The appearance during the past several years of films such as *Jurassic Park* (1997), *Toy Story* (1995), *Species* (1995), *Twelve Monkeys* (1995), *Contact* (1997), *Alien Resurrection* (1997), *Small Soldiers* (1998), *Independence Day* (1996), *The Fifth Element* (1997), *Men in Black* (1997), *Starship Troopers* (1997), *Godzilla* (1998) – not to mention the non-science fiction but special-effects-heavy *Titanic* (1997) – has almost certainly shifted the focus of popular and critical discussion from special effects 'in' science-fiction film to the fact that science-fiction film, and indeed much – if not most – contemporary film, *has become a technology on the way to somewhere else*, whether that goal turns out to be immersive, interactive, or some holodeck-style fusion of the two. Special effects, including the whole range of 'invisible' effects having to do with costuming and makeup are more and more disappearing into science-fiction effects, an increasingly riveting electronic phenomenon and a process characterized by Vivian Sobchack as the transformation of the 'wonderfully functional' into the 'functionally wonderful'.[12] The special effects technology that has been the science-fiction genre's determining characteristic is now shading into computer animation and electronic simulation of virtual environments in such a way that we may be on the verge of a new stage in science-fiction thinking, where media offers the realization rather than just the representation of science-fiction narratives.

There are topics worth thinking about in the specific case of science-fiction film as well as in its semblances: the digital aspect of these films may prove to be inherently as much or more the stuff of science fiction than the diegetic. Rethinking science-fiction film from a perspective that centres on its special effects suggests that they function in a number of ways not necessarily subordinated to advancing narrative. 'Indeed', concludes Sobchack, 'now the primary sign-function of science-fiction special effects seems to be precisely to connote "joyful intensities," "euphoria," and the "sublime".'[13] And, in the tradition of Sobchack and of Annette Michelson's stunning meditation on *2001*,

'Bodies in Space: Film as Carnal Knowledge', Scott Bukatman has recently offered an intriguing study of *Blade Runner*, a study concerned as much with its euphoric or utopic special effects and kinetic aspects as with its discursive narrative.[14]

At the very least, spectacular special effects function as a spectacle that interrupts or even disrupts the narrative: the special effect may simply be so striking as to constitute a kind of show-stopper. Both fans and detractors of John Carpenter's remake of *The Thing* (1982) will acknowledge that this is the case with many special effect scenes in that film, as it is surely the case in many scenes in *Forbidden Planet* (1956), *2001*, *Blade Runner*, *Dune* (1984), *Terminator 2: Judgment Day* (1991), and in more recent films such as *Jurassic Park*, *Species* (1995), *Contact*, *Alien Resurrection*, *Independence Day*, and *Men in Black*. Detailing how this interruptive phenomenon works in *Alien* (1979), Annette Kuhn reminds us that this film's special effects sequences are rarely the focus of critical readings: 'And yet the narrative of this film is periodically, and significantly, halted by episodes whose only function must be to invite the spectator's awed gaze: these include lengthy special effects sequences early in the film devoted to the business of getting characters out of the mother space ship and onto the alien planet.'[15] If we think of the riveting attraction of similar process scenes in *Close Encounters of the Third Kind* (1977), the *Star Wars* films, the *Star Trek* films, *Independence Day*, *Contact*, *The Fifth Element*, *The Nutty Professor* (1996), and many other science-fiction films, we realize that many of the special effects sequences that have become so important to these films actually halt rather than advance the narrative. (Indeed, one oblique recognition of the power of special effects has been the 'making of' phenomenon, in which part of the promotion of science-fiction film rests on 'documentaries' that celebrate the special effects technology that produces these show-stopping scenes.) That these scenes are striking enough to interrupt the flow of the narrative is, in fact, the persistent complaint of detractors of science-fiction film, who see in them the tail of special effects wagging the dog of narrative. My concern, however, is not whether special effects scenes are interruptive or whether such interruptions are 'good' or 'bad', but with several important independent functions of these scenes. And here I would suggest that special effects events in science-fiction film can be profitably considered as self-reflexive celebrations of film technology itself, as a kind of counter-narrative that often conflicts with the ostensible discursive narrative, and even as a kind of liberatory or utopic moment quite independent from the utopian representations of science-fiction narrative.

Against the charge that special effects in science-fiction film do not adequately subordinate themselves to the narrative, we can specify some of the non-diegetic roles that special effects do seem to play. Garrett Stewart assigns one such important function to science-fiction film special effects when he details their self-referential celebration of the technologies of the cinema itself – that special effects serve to reveal and emblematize not the idea of future technology, but the state of the art of current film technology. Stewart details the ways in which science-fiction film characteristically 'shifts the cutting edge of technological ingenuity … from machines in outer space to the logistics of their replication in inner or screen space, from aeronautics to cinematics'; or, as he sums up: 'Movies about the future tend to be about the future of movies.'[16] Returning to this thesis in a more recent essay, Stewart both updates it, considering what he sees as 'a postcinematographic iconophobia' resulting from pervasive digital effects, and explores the implications (particularly for our understanding of the human body) of mixing electronic effects in a film with their photographic ancestors.[17]

One clear implication of Stewart's earlier thesis is that science-fiction film has become the showcase genre for cinema technology, and that science-fiction special effects are increasingly *representations* of what is technologically possible rather than *simulations* of what is technologically impossible. On the other hand, his more recent meditation on the place of digital special effects in science-fiction film seems to lament that current electronic simulations are a kind of deadly digital virus, threatening the life of cinema as a photochemical technology:

As the most durable of screen genres in the second half of this century, science fiction has continued, more and more vividly, to imagine the technologies that would outdo it, do it in. In the digital era, however, futurist cinema has for the first time mobilized rather than merely evoked its own self-anachronizing upgrades. Engineered by computer enhancements, the superannuation of a suddenly hybrid medium has become a manifestly planned obsolescence, performed from within rather than simply foreseen. The technological overkill has spilled back into plot as an ontological dead end.[18]

While I do not share his nostalgia for film unpolluted by electronic simulation, I offer Stewart's challenging reading of the story of special effects as a model for what science-fiction film criticism might discover if it can draw back from its preoccupation with narratives in science-fiction films and consider the science-fictional story that science-fiction film production has itself become. For instance, if science-fiction film has become 'the cinema's own genre', then the time-travel films may be seen as offering the most intensely self-reflexive formula within an already self-reflexive genre. Considered broadly, the special effects on which the cinematic apparatus relies for its most basic illusion of motion makes all science-fiction film time-travel film, makes the time-travel formula particularly powerful in film, and may even be said to make our experience of any film, science fiction or otherwise, a kind of time-travel experience.

While Stewart suggests a sense in which one ubiquitous kind of special effect – screens and other imaging devices shown in science-fiction film – can be thought of as telling the story of science-fiction film production technology, other critics note ways in which special effects may actually exist in competition, or conflict, with the film's science-fiction narrative. J.P. Telotte discusses this phenomenon as a conflict between the film's *production technology* and its *reproductions of technology*.[19] For instance, a series of special effect interruptions may also be seen as a kind of counter-narrative or competing techno-narrative in its own right. Raymond Durgnat has famously written of *This Island Earth* (1955) as a sequence of special effects sequences marking a crescendo of voyages and a progression of breached barriers.[20] And Albert LaValley has described *Forbidden Planet* as 'three distinct plots on its narrative level' which are 'superseded by the feeling of another kind of discursive voyaging, a trip into technology's wonders and its future', a feeling structured by 'four levels of wonder' provided by the film's special effects.[21] Both Durgnat and LaValley cite films in which the image track offers a kind of techno-narrative that exists in parallel relationship to the film's plot- or story-based narrative.

Indeed, genre theorist Stephen Neale goes so far as to suggest that in science-fiction film 'narrative functions largely to motivate the production of special effects, climaxing either with the "best" of those effects (*Close Encounters of the Third Kind*), or with the point at which they are multiplied with greatest intensity (*Star Wars*).'[22] In this sense, science-fiction film's special effects can be thought of as existing not to support the narrative or the plot, but to provide their own formal rhythm and logic – the special effects story that the film is 'really' built around. Offering a more specific reading of one important consequence of 'the formal rhythm and logic' of special effects, Bukatman has recently suggested that we attend to the kaleidoscopic 'displacement and defamiliarization' accomplished by such scenes – in a sense their illogic, their 'flights from the strictures of instrumental reason'.[23] Referring to a recurrent twist of camera angle in *Forbidden Planet* and *The Incredible Shrinking Man* (1957), and relating this to similar phenomena in *2001*, *Close Encounters*, *Altered States* (1980), *Brainstorm* (1983), *Johnny Mnemonic* (1995), and *Contact*, Bukatman likens it to the play of the kaleidoscope:

> But there is also something liberatory about these movements, especially in the context of the mundane camera that precedes them both. If they destabilize us, then it should be acknowledged that we welcome the effect. We are moved away from the mundane, away from the ordinary – in some sense, we are moved away from the narrative and into the pleasures of the spectacle.[24]

Suggesting that the *movement* inherent in special effects sequences in science-fiction film actually 'performs an idea of utopia', Bukatman clarifies:

> The special effects sequences of science fiction cinema are not literally utopian – neither are they, in fact, non-narrative, anti-rational, or transgressive. Instead, they articulate, as

an embodied knowledge, a utopian discourse of possibility – they present the possibility of utopia, not its realization. They show us what utopia might feel like.[25]

Bukatman's meditation on the meaning of special effects thus effectively moves the consideration of these effects from ways in which they might offer a counter-narrative within a particular science-fiction film to the notion that they may advance an essentially oppositional epistemology. 'Science fiction is a notoriously rationalist genre', he concludes, 'but in the kinetic delirium of many effects sequences, the genre detaches from disembodied, de-sensationalized knowledges', serving to 'exemplify the *function of unreality* in representations of technology', thus offering 'an escape from technocracy through the window of technological immersion'.[26]

There is another significant difference between science-fiction literature and science-fiction film, one almost too obvious to cite, but hugely important: most science-fiction literature is created by individuals, while almost all science-fiction film is manufactured by production 'teams', each responsible for one part or aspect of the overall film. Developments in digital cinema, however, may actually be in the process of erasing this distinction, as digital technology can more and more be controlled by a single artist. In a recent interview, George Lucas invoked the comparison between writing and filmmaking, but concluded that new technologies were allowing him to bridge the gap:

> Instead of making film into a sequential assembly-line process where one person does one thing, takes it, and turns it over to the next person, I'm turning it more into the process of a painter or sculptor. You work on it for a bit, then you stand back and look at it and add some more onto it, then stand back and look at it and add some more. You basically end up layering the whole thing. Filmmaking by layering means you write, and direct, and edit all at once. It's much more like what you do when you write a story.[27]

What is so striking about Lucas's view of the future of filmmaking from the very top of the 'New Hollywood' production hierarchy is that it is almost exactly mirrored by the view of independent moviemakers at the bottom or on the margins of that hierarchy. For example, Scott Billups, a self-styled outlaw digital effects artist, has called attention to the phenomenon cited by Lucas, concluding: 'It's getting back to the single person, the author, who has an idea and can go with it.'[28] In this respect it grows ever more possible for science-fiction film to be made not only through a process much more like that which produces science-fiction literature, but for the two endeavours to be guided by much more similar teleologies. And, just as digital technology gives the kind of creative control to the science-fiction filmmaker previously enjoyed by science-fiction writers, that same digital technology increasingly offers the science-fiction writer the kinds of multiform and multimedia options previously reserved for science-fiction filmmakers.

Indeed, one possible future for science-fiction film would collide the parallel worlds of science-fiction writing and science-fiction film in the 'holonovel' of virtual reality considered by Janet H. Murray. Invoking the idea of the 'holo-deck' made familiar on *Star Trek: The Next Generation* and its spinoffs, *Deep Space Nine* and *Voyager*, Murray calls attention to an episode of *Voyager* in which captain Janeway uses a holosuite to insert herself in a three-dimensional computer-driven sensorium that instantiates the semblance of a Victorian world reminiscent of Charlotte Brontë's *Jane Eyre*. Captain Janeway 'assumes' the role of governess 'Lucy Davenport' in this semblance, and Murray simply dubs the resulting 'holonovel' *Lucy Davenport*.[29] This holodeck, Murray concludes, is a 'universal fantasy machine, open to individual programming: a vision of the computer as a kind of storytelling genie in the lamp'. Starting from this imaginary 'virtual literature of the twenty-fourth century', Murray quickly turns to a discussion of existing virtual literatures of the end of the twentieth century – computer-driven games and hypertexts, which she characterizes as 'multi-form narratives'. Citing numerous recent examples ranging from novels such as *The Dictionary of the Khazars*, to films such as *Groundhog Day*, to CD-ROMs such as *Myst*, to hyperfictions such as Michael Joyce's *Afternoon* and Stuart Moulthrop's *Victory Garden*, Murray suggests a kind of cultural inevitability to multiform narrative:

> As this wide variety of multiform stories makes clear, print and motion picture stories are pushing past linear formats not out of mere playfulness but in an effort to give expression to the characteristically twentieth-century perception of life as composed of parallel possibilities. Multiform narrative attempts to give a simultaneous form to these possibilities, to allow us to hold in our minds at the same time multiple contradictory alternatives. Whether multiform narrative is a reflection of post-Einsteinian physics or of a secular society haunted by the chanciness of life or of a new sophistication in narrative thinking, its alternative versions of reality are now part of the way we think, part of the way we experience the world. To be alive in the twentieth century is to be aware of the alternative possible selves, of alternative possible worlds, and of the limitless intersecting stories of the actual world.[30]

Murray's use of the term 'multiform narrative' conveniently lets us sidestep the question of whether a 'holonovel' such as *Lucy Davenport* would actually be an example of science-fiction writing or of science-fiction film, combining as it would salient characteristics from both traditions.

Of course, what we have available at the end of the twentieth century is not quite the sensorium of the holodeck, but rather the new space of hypermedia, where hypertexted narratives can be advanced by multimedia. Perhaps closest to the ideal of the holodeck is VRML (Virtual Reality Modelling Language) on the World Wide Web, a technology that permits immersive 3-D modelling even if it can only be experienced through the 2-D interface of a computer screen.[31] One pioneering VRML project in particular deserves attention for what it has already achieved: David Blair's *WAXWEB*,[32] whose title references its science-fiction film precursor: *WAX, or the Discovery of Television Among the Bees*.

Premiered at a private screening in the Museum of Modern Art, New York, in September 1991, and seen in art houses throughout the USA and Canada as part of a seven-film theatrical package entitled 'The Festival of Grand Illusions', *WAX* almost perfectly represents the idea of a cinema of digital attractions. *WAX* is like no other science-fiction film, if not like no film of any sort. It has been called postmodern, postcyberpunk, postfuturist, postavant-garde, or postcinema; but attempts to label *WAX* 'post' anything are probably a mistake: this highly technologized experimental work is more appropriately considered 'pre' something – pre-virtual reality theatre, pre-virtual surreality, pre-image processing cinema.... Indeed, *WAX*'s 85-minute celebration of the possibilities of 'electronic cinema' may well indicate one future direction for science-fiction film, if not for 'film' itself.

WAX tells one story to do with beekeeping and war that is very hard to describe, while its making illustrates another, actually more important, story having to do with the emergence of what might be called 'techno-narrative'.[33] Like David Lynch's early films or David Cronenberg's most recent, *WAX* does not derive its power from any rational sequence of events. While its narrative is more or less linear, it is also more or less a collage or cutup, with events proceeding in the smooth but impossible logic of a very realistic dream – the result being that *WAX* derives its impact from its look and feel and experiential logic rather than from its discursive story. What it does is combine seemingly incongruous found footage, impressively sophisticated computer animation, and eerily banal location shots of its protagonist Jacob Maker, always dressed in his white beekeeping suit and hood, always reminding us more of Dave Bowman in *2001* or of men in radiation or toxic cleanup suits than of bee-keepers. These images are processed with state-of-the-art electronic post-production non-linear editing, allowing a degree of control over each shot, sequence and scene never before seen in a low-budget feature. The resulting hallucinatory ride of heavily processed images has the formal coherence and slickness of a big budget music video – one that lasts for eighty-five minutes.

Taking a trend in commercial science-fiction film to its ultimate conclusion, *WAX* discovers its narrative in special effects technology, finding new images in the electronic processing of older ones, its story turning in new directions supplied by image processing technology. In this sense, production technology drives its narrative, yielding the strangely disconnected but somehow inevitably 'right' effect that William Burroughs achieves in writing through his cut-ups and fold-ins. Rather than trying to come up with some traditional story that would allow him to make use of new special effects, *WAXWEB*'s 'writer' David Blair has tried to discover the story *inherent in* the technology he employs, so that his production has to do with the technological and ontological concerns of postmodern simulation and with a metacritical response to the affective impact of earlier science-fiction film. Blair wanted to capture in *WAX* the odd effect of watching the strangely disconnected narratives, 'understandable and complicated at the same time', that he saw in bad science-fiction films like *It Conquered the World* (1956) and *Zontar: the Thing from Venus* (1966). Accordingly, one of his goals in *WAX* was to 'fuse narrative, sound, and image to concretely describe a virtual world, and at the same time hypnogenetically induce a strong sense of hallucination'.

Although Blair says he did not necessarily plan for *WAX* to be science fiction, that genre seemed to him to offer a singularly technologically focused medium for his technological subject. He thinks of the finished product as science fiction, with an emphasis on the grotesque; and the reviews suggest that Blair succeeded in catching the interest of the science-fiction world. Moreover, in deconstructing and reconstructing *WAX* into the hypermedia *WAXWEB*, Blair has demonstrated how the narratives of science-fiction literature and the technologies of hypertext and multimedia can fuse into a new interactive experience on CD-ROM or on the World Wide Web.

WAXWEB combines the nonsequential or multisequential links of hypertext with still images, sound, video clips, and (provisionally) 3-D VRML environments. Having intuited structural affinities between his original film and hypertext, Blair decided to try to remove the time base from the film by turning it into a spatial structure of some six hundred nodes, each roughly corresponding to one line in the film's voice-over monologue. This base-layer was then indexed in a number of different ways, including a linear/chronological path through the film, a hierarchical act/scene structure, shot overview maps indexed to similar pictures, textual thematic paths, and a random index. Or, put somewhat differently, the site can be navigated by following a shot-by-shot breakdown of the film, by following its story, superstory, or contract overviews of the plot.[34] What this means is that *WAXWEB* is a multimedia environment that can be explored or toured or navigated in a vast number of radically different ways. If *WAXWEB* offers a unique way to experience narrative and special effects in a totally defamiliarizing new context, it is not the holonovel envisioned by Janet Murray. But it is the most intriguing and most promising example to date of the ways in which film and text may recombine in cyberspace, suggesting an immersive and interactive future for science-fiction film.

NOTES

1. See also Brooks Landon, *The Aesthetics of Ambivalence: Rethinking Science Fiction Film in the Age of Electronic Reproduction*, Westport, CT: Greenwood, 1992.
2. In David Bordwell, Janet Staiger and Kristin Thompson, *The Classical Hollywood Cinema: Film Style and Mode of Production to 1960*, New York: Columbia University Press, 1985, p. 157.
3. Tom Gunning, 'The Cinema of Attractions: Early Film, Its Spectator and the Avant-Garde', *Wide Angle*, vol. 8, nos 3–4, 1986, p. 64. This essay has been reprinted in Thomas Elsaesser, ed., *Early Cinema: Space – Frame – Narrative*, London: British Film Institute, 1990, pp. 56–62.
4. Scott Bukatman, 'The Ultimate Trip: Special Effects and Kaleidoscopic Perception', *Iris*, no. 25, 1998, p. 79. Bukatman's reference to Shaviro is to Steven Shaviro, *The Cinematic Body*, Minneapolis, MN: University of Minnesota Press, 1993, p. 24.
5. Gunning, 'The Cinema of Attractions', p. 65.
6. For a reconsideration of *Hale's Tours* that ties that pioneering ridefilm to contemporary immersive technologies such as Disney's *Star Tours* and Trumbull's *Secrets of the Luxor Pyramid*, see Lauren Rabinovitz, 'From *Hale's Tours* to *Star Tours*: Virtual Voyages and the Delirium of the Hyper-Real', *Iris*, no. 25, 1998, pp. 133–52.
7. Gunning, 'The Cinema of Attractions', p. 66.
8. Ibid., p. 64.
9. Scott Bukatman, 'The Ultimate Trip', p. 77.
10. See Brooks Landon, *Science Fiction After 1900: From the Steam Man to the Stars*, New York: Twayne, 1997.
11. Landon, *The Aesthetics of Ambivalence*, particularly chs 4 and 7. See also Scott Bukatman, *Terminal Identity: The Virtual Subject in Postmodern Science Fiction*, Durham, NC: Duke University Press, 1993.
12. Vivian Sobchack, *Screening Space: The American Science Fiction Film*, New Brunswick, NJ: Rutgers University Press, 1987, p. 283.
13. Ibid.
14. Scott Bukatman, *Blade Runner*, London: British Film Institute, 1997; Michelson's 'Bodies in Space' originally appeared in *Artforum* vol. 7, no. 6, 1969, pp. 54–63.
15. Annette Kuhn, 'Spectators: Introduction', *Alien Zone: Cultural Theory and Contemporary*

Science Fiction Cinema, London: Verso, 1990, p. 148.

16. Garrett Stewart, 'The "Videology" of Science Fiction', in George Slusser and Eric S. Rabkin, eds, *Shadows of the Magic Lamp: Fantasy and Science Fiction in Film*, Carbondale: Southern Illinois University Press, 1985, pp. 159–60.

17. Garrett Stewart, 'The Photographic Ontology of Science Fiction Film', *Iris*, no. 25, 1998, pp. 99–132; and 'Body Snatching: Science Fiction's Photographic Trace', in this volume.

18. Stewart, 'The Photographic Ontology', p. 129.

19. J.P. Telotte, 'Film and/as Technology: An Introduction', *Post Script: Essays in Film and the Humanities*, vol. 10, no. 1, 1990, p. 4.

20. Raymond Durgnat, *Films and Feelings*, Cambridge, MA: MIT Press, 1967.

21. Albert J. LaValley, 'Traditions of Trickery: The Role of Special Effects in the Science Fiction Film', in Slusser and Rabkin, eds, *Shadows of the Magic Lamp*, p. 154.

22. Stephen Neale, *Genre*, London: British Film Institute, 1980, p. 31. Neale has explored this thesis more specifically, discussing John Carpenter's 1982 remake of *The Thing*, in "You've Got To Be Fucking Kidding!' Knowledge, Belief and Judgement in Science Fiction', in Kuhn, ed., *Alien Zone*, pp. 160–68.

23. Bukatman, 'The Ultimate Trip', pp. 80–81.

24. Ibid., p. 80.

25. Ibid., p. 92.

26. Ibid.

27. Kevin Kelly and Paula Parisi, 'Beyond Star Wars', *Wired*, vol. 5, no. 2, 1997, p. 2 of 11 online at http://www.hotwired.com/collections/film_special_effects/5.02_lucas1.html

28. Paula Parisi, 'Shot By An Outlaw', *Wired* vol. 4, no. 9, 1996, p. 2 of 6 online at http://www.hotwired.com/collections/film_special_effects/4.09_billups1.html.

29. Janet Murray, *Hamlet on the Holodeck: The Future of Narrative in Cyberspace*, New York: Free Press, 1997, pp. 13–17.

30. Ibid., pp. 37–8.

31. One of many FAQ (Frequently Asked Questions) pages for VRML can be found at http://www.h2o.hiroshima-cu.ac.jp/h2o-misc/vrml-related-docs/VRML_FAQ.html.

32. This hypermedia feature, produced with support from the Brown University Graphics Lab and now made available by the Institute for Advanced Technology in the Humanities at the University of Virginia, exists in a CD-ROM version (with the 3-D version still to come) and was once available in the immersive space of a MOO on the World Wide Web, but is most easily available as a 2-D website at http://jefferson.village.virginia.edu/wax/index.html. For a description of its VRML version, see Blair's narrative at http://www.village.virginia.edu/wax/wax.html and an interview/article at http://shrine.cyber.ad.jp/~etienne/nikkei/waxweb.html; and the initial news release for the now taken down VRML site can be found at http://vag.vrml.org/www-vrml/arch/1162.html. For a description of the MOO version, see http://cair.kaist.ac.kr/Archive/

Announce/01/0065.html, and Blair's brief overview at http://www.mca.com.au/burning/statements/blair.html.

33. *WAX*'s plot has been summarized by Blair in publicity releases as follows: 'Jacob Maker makes weapons guidance systems and keeps bees. While tending his bees, he falls into a reverie and visits roughly rendered spaces where linear thought struggles with warped axes of time and space. Agents of dead souls, the bees insert a crystal television in his head. The television guides him to the planet of the dead where planar, skeletal animations take him through the creation of the world and into the eye of God. (God's eye, it turns out, is roughly equivalent to a cathode ray tube.) When, in the form of a smart-bomb's gun site, he murders Iraqi tank commandos in the desert near Basra, all is right with his past, and he has secured his future.'

34. Instructions for using each navigation strategy are available online. For example, instructions for using the Shot By Shot index can be found at http://jefferson.village.virginia.edu/wax/html/1014.html.

3

INTERNET FANDOM AND THE CONTINUING NARRATIVES OF STAR WARS, BLADE RUNNER AND ALIEN

WILL BROOKER

Star Wars: A New Hope, Alien and *Blade Runner* were all released between 1977 and 1982; yet, almost two full decades later, the narratives of Luke Skywalker, Ellen Ripley and Rick Deckard maintain their grip on popular culture. While texts of the same period like *Jaws, Close Encounters of the Third Kind* and *Saturday Night Fever* are now regarded as nostalgic exhibits in film 'history', these three science-fiction sagas endure vividly in the 'present' of the late 1990s. This endurance is due partly to an extension of the 'official' narratives, most obviously through sequels, directors' cuts and prequels, but also through secondary texts such as CD-ROMs, comics and novels, which often bear only a quasi-canonical status due to their sanctioning by a production company but lack the director's 'personal' authorial stamp. Finally, a wealth of fan-based material, rich in detail and imagination, is left to fill in the gaps of these official plots, to suggest new directions, flesh out secondary characters and build on or knock down the framework imposed from 'above'.

The crucial role of secondary texts in maintaining these film series as ongoing concerns rather than as historical relics can be demonstrated if we examine more closely the parallels with other 1970s cinema such as the films cited above – none of which, after all, was simply an individual text. *Jaws* spawned three sequels, *Saturday Night Fever* was followed up with *Staying Alive*, and *Close Encounters* was extended into a Special Edition which earned the film theatrical redistribution. In every case, then, the 'official' primary text was extended beyond a single instalment.

The merchandising for these films, however, constituted a single wave of spinoffs rather than the constant ripple of ongoing comics, novels and computer products which make up the secondary textual level of *Alien*, *Blade Runner* and *Star Wars*. There were albums released on the back of all three films, of course, with the Bee Gees providing the soundtrack for *Saturday Night Fever*, but these were self-contained spinoffs rather than the first in an ongoing series. *Jaws* and *Close Encounters* were marketed as novels and between them inspired rub-down transfers, a Marvel comic, a board game and a satire in *Whizzer and Chips* called 'Gums'. As I suggested in an earlier essay,[1] *Star Wars* also went through a phase where its merchandise was limited to cheap, ephemeral items such as penny chews and tinned sausages, but products related to the saga have grown up with the audience. While not forbiddingly sophisticated or expensive, the *Star Wars* paperbacks and PC games currently on the market are clearly aimed at an audience of older teens and upwards, and constitute a thriving industry despite the lack of any sequels, or prequels, between 1983 and 1999. There is to the best of my knowledge no series of *Jaws* CD-ROM adventures currently available, nor a recent bestseller exploring the further adventures of Roy Neary from *Close Encounters*.

It could be argued that *Jaws*, *Saturday Night Fever* and *Close Encounters* still inspire admiration and respect in the late 1990s as classics of 1970s cinema, and that prestige boxed editions of the films continue to find a market. And yet by contrast *Star Wars*, *Blade Runner* and *Alien* have retained an immediacy to the point that we would barely think to cite them as examples of a 'late seventies' or 'early eighties' mode.[2] Their secondary texts are not nostalgic archive collections but supplementary narratives which push back the boundaries of the existing stories. That said, merchandise alone would never be enough to keep a film series 'alive' some twenty years after its first instalment. As

Henry Jenkins has argued, texts, like stuffed toys, become 'real' through being loved.[3] Fandom is built around love. It is this emotional investment in the continuing lives of the protagonists and intense dedication to the faintest detail of the story world that continually revives and rejuvenates *Alien*, *Blade Runner* and *Star Wars*, that makes them not 'seventies cinema' nor even 'nineties cinema'. They are more than cinema: they are phenomena.

This chapter will explore the various levels of 'official' narrative around each of the chosen film texts, from the canonical originals through the much-debated special editions to the ambiguous status of novels and comics. It will investigate the ways in which contemporary Internet fandom works with, around or against these official texts in what I see as a unique moment of cultural limbo. Unlike the *Doctor Who* fans of John Tulloch's study,[4] or the *Twin Peaks* audience discussed by Henry Jenkins,[5] these viewers are constrained by an ongoing official narrative rather than knowing that their chosen text constitutes a vast but never-changing archive which they are free endlessly to revisit and rework.

On the other hand, their position is equally removed from that of the Internet X-Philes described by Susan J. Clerc,[6] the Batman fans of Roberta Pearson and William Uricchio's anthology[7] and the Trekkers investigated by Henry Jenkins,[8] in that the ongoing narrative with which they engage is constructed mainly of secondary texts, widely regarded as open to debate and negotiation: the spaces for fandom to enter, to create, argue and suggest, are therefore much wider. We might choose to set aside the feature films, which some fans view with ambivalence; but even so, the textual archives of *Star Trek* and *The X-Files* are augmented almost every week with a new and instantly canonical television episode, while Batman's canon of primary texts builds at the rate of six comics per month, from *Detective* through *Gotham Adventures* and *Legends of the Dark Knight* to *Shadow of the Bat*. All of these new episodes in the lives of the protagonists are officially sanctioned, bear a stamp of authenticity through authorship (created by Chris Carter, by Bob Kane, by Gene Rodden-berry) and come from the same production stable (Fox, DC, Paramount) that gave birth to the beloved 'original'.

By contrast, the *Alien* saga was passed from helm to helm and to date constitutes four films by four different directors, each with his own distinctive visual style and thematic concerns. Ripley is therefore flung not just across massive gulfs in time and space but from one aesthetic and generic universe to another, with only her alien nemesis providing continuity. The *Star Wars* universe has been kept alive on an 'official' level largely through a series of novels and comics, ranging from Timothy Zahn's bestselling trilogy set immediately after *Return of the Jedi* to the Dark Horse monthly comic books which explore minor characters and loose ends from both the films and the novels. This extended universe has travelled so far under its own steam that Han Solo and Leia Organa, barely reconciled at the end of *Jedi*, have now not just married but brought up three children; and yet all the intricacies of this secondary world would be made redundant in the eyes of most fans if their detail were to be contradicted in the slightest by the forthcoming prequels from Lucasfilm. Although fans rate the novels and comics in a hierarchy of quality and fidelity to the 'original', this remains very much a second-order ranking which the gospel of George Lucas would collapse in an instant: even the 'best' novels are widely regarded as a collection of fables about Solo, Skywalker and Organa which will pass the time pleasantly enough until the prequels are released but which ultimately have no canonical status.

The world of *Blade Runner*, finally, was jolted back to life ten years after its inception by the director's cut, which for most fans managed the unprecedented coup of replacing the 'original' as the preferred version, despite its significant reworking of both the ending and the protagonist's human status. This contrasts with the Special Edition of *Aliens*, which – as a limited video release intended for collectors only – attracted none of the critical attention afforded *Blade Runner*'s new cut, and in turn with the widespread fan rejection of the *Star Wars* Special Editions as unnecessary and gimmicky. Since the early 1990s, the *Blade Runner* world and cast have been taken up by two novels, which currently hold much the same ambivalent status as the *Star Wars* secondary texts, and by a CD-ROM, which while officially sanctioned by the 'Blade Runner Partnership' must inevitably occupy some intermediary position as neither unauthorised spinoff nor yet authored text. A sequel to the film has been rumoured many times and to date also exists only in limbo, raptly desired by some fans and feared by others for its potential threat to the thus far self-contained and precisely balanced world of the 'original'.

These secondary texts and the rationale behind the hierarchies which fandom has built around them will be discussed more fully below, in sections on the individual sagas. It should be clear already, though, that afficionados of *Alien*, *Star Wars* and *Blade Runner* celebrate and negotiate their chosen objects in a cultural phantom zone which both unites them all and distinguishes them from other fans. It seems fitting, then, to focus on the fan activity around these three science-fiction narratives which finds its platform in the inherently paradoxical global no-place of the Internet.

I am choosing to focus on Internet fan activity rather than other forms such as print fanzines, conventions and 'real life' discussion groups for various reasons, the first of which is the fact that Internet fandom combines elements of these other forms within a global medium while retaining elements unique to itself. It might also be noted that print fanzines and discussion groups around science-fiction series have already been thoroughly discussed in the work of John Tulloch and Henry Jenkins, detailed above, while Internet science-fiction fandom – a hybrid of ephemeral text, 'printed' only on a screen, and textualized 'speech' which appears as dialogue transcriptions – strikes me as offering an intermediate territory which has yet to be exhaustively mapped out and charted by academic research.

Nevertheless, the relation between Internet fandom and other, more traditional forms of debate and celebration is worth examining for its areas of overlap and difference. Consider first the questions of production and audience with relation to print and online fan culture. Even the most modestly produced fanzines, such as the *Star Wars*-related *Force Sensitive* and *Jedi Holocron*, involve costs for copying and distribution which have to be covered by subscription, and therefore depend upon a dedicated core readership willing to commit to several issues. The Internet equivalent, on the other hand, allows a potentially infinite audience from around the world to drop in and read articles or features at whim, with no such commitment. Its readership is therefore very different – far larger, more anonymous, more casual – than that of a print 'zine.

These potentially vast fan groups, linked by 'webrings' which connect one *Blade Runner* or *Alien* site to the next through a simple mouseclick, have significant ramifications for organized fan protest against producers' decisions. While dedicated viewers who despaired at losing *Star Trek* or *Twin Peaks* from network television turned to letter-writing campaigns, radio appeals and conventions, late-1990s Internet fandom can sound an alarm from site to site, the message spreading like signal fires along a webring, and theoretically draw on a worldwide body of fans to launch emails of protest at Fox, Paramount or Lucasfilm within the space of mere hours.

Due to the minimal cost of 'publishing' on the Web, an online fanzine can incorporate full-colour images and scanned photos. In this respect the Internet serves as a democratic arena within which distinctions between 'professional' and 'amateur' productions are eroded, and the 'official' site for a film will not automatically be afforded more status than a good fan site – if, indeed, either can be recognized as such. Even more importantly, Internet sites almost invariably include bulletin boards where visitors can post up their own comments and reply to others. A fanzine editor may select and type out a couple of readers' letters per issue; a discussion panel at a convention permits debate within a formal structure, under a chairperson and with deference to any 'celebrity' guests. Internet boards, by contrast, allow any reader instantly to become a participating writer on an equal footing with fellow contributors, including the site's creator or even the published authors who occasionally visit to post their own responses to discussion.

While debates do of course rage across the letters pages of print fanzines, the month, or more usually the three-month, gap between issues results in a pace which seems archaic compared to the immediate return provided by the

Internet. On the other hand, while many fans relish the informal debates in the bar at conventions and even arrange their own social pub meets – I have myself travelled to Lincoln, London and Birmingham for such reunions – these face-to-face discussions are often months apart, while Internet boards can be accessed during a lunch break, after homework, even in the middle of the night.

Clearly, print fanzines, conventions and social groups still offer unique pleasures; otherwise they would surely have died out in the last two or three years, as Internet access has spread through the workplace and the academy and into the domestic sphere. For the purpose of examining the nature of fan response to three film series at this specific cultural moment – which is, as I have argued, a particularly interesting one – the Internet offers unparalleled immediacy. However, I strongly suspect that the fan activity detailed below would be echoed, though with a different expression, in the less ephemeral discourse of the fanzine and in the more occasional debate of the face-to-face discussion forum. From the frequent reference on Internet boards both to print magazines – invaluable as sources for interviews, rumours and photographs – and to panel groups at conventions it is clear that, to an extent at least, the same people are participating in all three forms of fandom, with the platform offered by the Net – in its combination of immediacy and interactivity with a relative permanence and textual 'status' – falling somewhere between the two poles of printed word and face-to-face contact.

While this is a study of audiences, it does not aspire to sociology. I would maintain that audiences always become texts in the process of analysis, whether we study them through letters and statistics or through our own transcriptions of their interviews; and the Internet makes this point particularly evident by transmuting all communication, whether question, response, insult or endearment, into the same currency of words on a screen. Any study of Internet audiences is therefore textual analysis.

For my research on Internet fan activity, I trawled the Internet for sites related to the three film series, narrowing my list to the ten listed at the end of this chapter. On the five of those sites which offered bulletin boards I posted a list of questions, a version of which is appended to this chapter. It will be noted that I felt it more honest to declare my academic interest and the purpose of my questions rather than pretend to be simply an interested fan.

Since I gave an email address with my post, some of the responses came as letters, while others appeared as part of the discussion 'thread' I had begun on the board. I visited the five sites at least once a day during the last week of April 1998 and printed hard copy both of the responses to my post and of the other ongoing discussions during that period. It is these printed versions that I later studied, sifted through and quote in the study that follows, which is divided into three parts and identifies a slightly different mode of fan activity around each of the sagas under discussion. The *Blade Runner* fans, for example, appear to practise a form of 'forensic detection' involving constant return to the primary, original, text for 'truth'. *Alien* fans, faced with a range of apparently canonical films which nevertheless contradict each other in aesthetic, tone and characterization, are concerned with 'debating the canon', arguing the merits of one version over another and imposing their own frameworks of inclusion and exclusion even on primary film texts. At the time of my investigation, the *Star Wars* fans were at a point of intense speculation as to when the first of a new trilogy, longed for by many for over fifteen years, was to be released. Fan discussion on *Star Wars* sites was therefore buzzing with an ecstasy of rumour, fuelled by snatches of information of various degrees of authority. As the sketchy outlines of Lucas's proposals for *Star Wars 1* took gradual shape, fans attempted to fill in the gaps with an enthusiasm and anticipation verging on mania, backing up their proposals with an incredible knowledge of the existing trilogy's every detail. I have called this process 'speculative fiction'.

These subtitles and divisions are merely a device. Of course, *Star Wars* fans debate the canon; of course, their piecing together of the 'prequels' jigsaw is a form of forensic detection. The different headings suggest my own shift in approach, rather than the fan groups' exclusive content, and as such imply a clarity of focus which is in fact rarely evident on Internet message boards.

However, it will be appreciated that the fluidity of Web discussion cannot easily be transposed to the more traditional form of academic scholarship without imposing a degree of structure and a certain loss in the translation.

Blade Runner has, of course, a prehistory in Philip K. Dick's *Do Androids Dream of Electric Sheep?*, which Internet fandom shortens to the evocative 'Dadoes'. If *Blade Runner* adapts selectively from the novel, its borrowing from William S. Burroughs's *Bladerunner (A Movie)*, itself a reworking of a short story by Alan E. Nourse, can only be described as minimal. Ridley Scott, the film's director, was interested not in Burroughs's plot but in the potential of the title, and bought the rights to the words only. In Nourse's story the term referred to a smuggler of illegal medical implements. In William K. Jeter's novel, billed as a sequel to the film, it is explained as a corruption of *bleibruhiger*, someone who makes replicants 'stay quiet'.

An album called *Blade Runner* was released in 1982. It consisted not of the actual movie score but of a version of the tracks performed by the New American Orchestra. Shortly afterwards, a *Blade Runner* game was produced for the ZX Spectrum and Commodore 64 computers. The makers, CRL Software, had been unable to secure the rights to the film, and so marketed the game as 'an adaptation of the Vangelis soundtrack', whose grandiose swoops and fanfares were reduced, on the Spectrum version at least, to a tinny one-channel burble.

The 1992 director's cut, supposedly discovered by accident at a film festival, omits completely the Chandleresque narration of the 1982 version and cuts short the optimistic finale which suggested Deckard and Rachael's escape from the city. Its one addition, in which Deckard dreams of a unicorn, seemed in context to suggest that the central character was himself a replicant and thus overturned all prior audience assumptions about stable human identity and the dividing lines between self and other. Even the director's cut retains 'mistakes', some considered deliberate and others – like the numerous internal contradictions over the exact number of escaped replicants – further expressions of the obscurity which has given the film its aura of myth. These ambiguities are highlighted rather than resolved by the critical texts clustered around the film: Judith B. Kerman's anthology of essays and Scott Bukatman's BFI monograph celebrate and annotate the layers of complexity, but make little attempt to provide definitive answers.[9] To confuse matters further, the Marvel Comics' adaptation of the film, though published a decade before the release of the director's cut, contains narration which strongly suggests Deckard's replicant status.

William K. Jeter's two novels, *Blade Runner 2: The Edge of Human* and its sequel *Replicant Night*, pick up Deckard's story from the end of the existing narrative, assuming his escape with Rachael but complicating his subsequent existence by revealing Pris to have been a human and Roy Batty one of just many identical clones, and confusing the reader further by attempting to reconcile the significant inconsistencies between Dick's novel and Scott's film.[10] *Replicant Night* brings Batty back as a talking briefcase and pairs Deckard with Eldon Tyrell's daughter Sarah, the 'original' woman from whom his beloved Rachael was replicated. In the subplot of *Replicant Night* a film is being made of Deckard's most famous case: its title is *Blade Runner*.

Finally, Westwood Studios released a *Blade Runner* game in 1997. Computer technology having progressed at a fair lick in the previous fifteen years, this version shares only its name with the CRL effort. The plot is open-ended and follows multiple storylines to numerous possible endings, involving animated video clips of characters who talk back to the player. Although set in the same near-future Los Angeles, the protagonist is not Rick Deckard but a lookalike called Ray McCoy, and the supporting cast features both familiar characters – Rachael, Tyrell – and new faces like the blade runner Crystal and Nexus-6 replicant Clovis. Any hierarchy of authenticity between 'original' and 'invented' cast members is flattened by the glossily hyperreal aesthetic of the CGI animation, just as the soundtrack seamlessly blends elements of Vangelis with near-identical pastiche. As such, this game occupies an intriguing middle ground between prose fiction, interactive simulation and cinematic text – for if Ridley

Scott ever does make the rumoured follow-up, *Metropolis*, this will itself surely draw heavily on computer animation. It is perhaps unsurprising, then, that the project of *Blade Runner* Internet fandom involves a search for answers, an obsessive return to the 'original' text(s) in this wealth of false leads, in order to pick over the clues and build threads of logic which explain some of the film's unsolved mysteries. Westwood was shrewd in modelling its recent game on a 'rep-detect' mission in which the player's task is one of interrogation and deduction.

Like the game, the Internet sites I visited attempt to re-create the world of *Blade Runner* – one of them even has that name – simulating, or perhaps replicating, the atmosphere of Los Angeles 2019 through elaborate graphics and sound. These sites invite a total immersion in the film's story space, a nostalgic return to the future: 'we can remember it for you wholesale', as Philip K. Dick once put it.[11] Visitors to *Los Angeles 2019* are greeted with a midi version of the Vangelis 'Love Theme', while *The World of Blade Runner* opens with 'Memories of Green'. Both sites are elaborate constructions of neon text and Chinese characters against a dark background. Beyond these gateways the visitor is invited to take on the role of detective, opening up new avenues by selecting images and clicking on text; and although the process is mouse-activated rather than voice-controlled, the extent to which it parallels Rick Deckard's examination of photographic evidence in *Blade Runner* itself is star-tling. The hypertext of 1998 has, it becomes clear, very nearly caught up with the ESPERs and Voight–Kampff machines of 2019, and these sites make full use of that similarity to transform reading and viewing into writing and par-ticipating. You are no longer simply a fan of *Blade Runner*: you are part of the world of *Blade Runner* or even a blade runner yourself. If this is only simula-tion, it is nevertheless a 'consensual hallucination', in William Gibson's phrase,[12] and one shared by creators and participants. *The Off-World Connection* has the following preface:

> I have created this web site not just to be a collection of images, but an adventure, a place to explore. I have used the resources of the Internet, images, sound clips, text

research, and put them all together to tell a story. You become the main character in this story. It will be you who makes the decisions.[13]

As indicated, there are two core texts behind this simulation: the original *Blade Runner* and its director's cut, which together are assumed to hold 'answers' to the inconsistencies, ambiguities and 'frequently asked questions', or FAQs. These 'truths' will become clear through immersion in the text and close analysis of the kind Deckard performs on his photographic evidence. As an example, consider the *Blade Runner FAQ* written by Murray Chapman. A few clicks take the visitor to a page where queries and answers are laid out with the authority of a transcribed interrogation:

> Q: How can Deckard be a replicant, when he's physically outmatched by Roy, Leon, Zhora, and Pris?
>
> A: The videos that Bryant shows Deckard include a mental and physical rating for each of the replicants. (See here, here, here, and here.) In all cases, they are rated 'A' physically. If Deckard was a replicant designed to think it was human, it would probably be made a 'B' physical, which would correspond to average human strength.
>
> Q: How can Tyrell tell Roy that 'We made you to the best of our abilities', when he deliberately gave him a four year lifespan?
>
> A: Tyrell probably means they couldn't risk making him any better because they can only control them for so long. This assumes Bryant is correct in saying the 4-year lifespan is intentionally built-in. Tyrell also says 'the light that burns twice as bright' suggesting improved performance may be a trade-off with lifespan. Since Tyrell's goal is commerce, he may have turned a biological problem into a benefit by taking advantage of the 4-year lifespan – planned obsolescence. When Sebastian says, 'There's some of me in you,' he might be referring to the intentional use of the genes responsible for Methuselah Syndrome.[14]

These answers are backed with intensely close reference to the cinematic text, with links to images for 'proof'. However, some intertextual material is accepted as helpful and valid; other answers are supported by interviews with Scott or Harrison Ford, draft scripts and pre-production sketches, elements of 'Dadoes' and, significantly, academic studies such as those by Kerman and Bukatman.[15] Further proposals seek ingenious backing from the Internet's treasure house of miscellany: for Deckard's ability to hold onto a ledge with two fingers, for example, we are referred to a rock-climbing newsgroup. The canon of valid 'evidence', however, does not extend to the Jeter novels, nor to the Westwood game. *The Edge of Human* earns a scathing review from several sites ('I'm sad to say that this book is one of the worst things I've ever read, I love the *Blade Runner* universe and all the characters, but this was just too much. The story isn't good enough and it's not a worthy follow up to the movie'[16]), while the game is regarded as a suitable homage to the film but of no relevance to its internal questions: 'I think the game is fine as it deals with a separate narrative and the world of *BR* was so well researched. The story of *Blade Runner* was told in the film.'[17]

For *Blade Runner* fans to go forward, then, they have continually to return to the past – or perhaps look sideways. In April 1998 the latest buzz on the *Blade Runner* pages was for a film scripted by *Blade Runner*'s David Peoples, originally scheduled for October 1998. *Soldier*, starring Kurt Russell, is billed as a 'sidequel, set in the *Blade Runner* universe'. As *Los Angeles 2019* has it, 'it should be enough to satisfy us until the real sequel comes out. If ever'.

The overall 'text' of *Alien* is characterized, like the alien xenomorph and Ellen Ripley themselves, by a mode of hybridity. As noted above, each of the four existing films – *Alien* (1979), *Aliens* (1986), *Alien3* (1992) and *Alien Resurrection* (1997) – was under the command not just of a different director but of a different *auteur*, each with a highly distinctive personal style. The four films are united by two central characters, Ripley and the xenomorph in all its forms, and by a science-fiction setting and mise-en-scene; beyond this, however, each is a mutant crossbreed between genres. To simplify, Ridley Scott's *Alien* is a horror film in space while James Cameron's *Aliens* draws on all the conventions of the 1980s Vietnam film and transports them to a far-future mining colony. David Fincher's *Alien3*, meanwhile, is born from *Porridge* out of Carl Dreyer's *La Passion de Jeanne d'Arc*, and Jean-Pierre Jeunet's *Alien Resurrection* is something of a European science-fiction art-horror with an injection of black comedy. This distinction between directorial styles is entirely recognized by fans, one of whom sums up:

> Each of them have their own 'trademark'. Scott has his dark and gloomy big space. Cameron has his big budget spending. Fincher is quite similar to Scott in some ways, with his gloomy corridors. Jeunet has his dark sense of humor mixed with excellent effects and a more pristine view on the aliens.[18]

The film series is supplemented by an extensive range of toys, models and computer games, and by a long-running series of Dark Horse comics which, like the *Star Wars* titles, expand on characters and settings established in the films, taking them off at tangents and suggesting new possibilities: the story in which the aliens battle Superman remains perhaps the most extreme example.

The first difference between *Alien* and *Blade Runner* fandom is that the canon itself is far less rigid. The *Alien* feature films are not regarded as sacred texts simply by merit of their cinematic status, and their respective qualities are entirely open to debate, as the following posts – responses to my questions about the canon on two message boards[19] – aptly demonstrate:

> The first two films are canon; they just form one long film, really. *Alien3* exists in a parallel, overlapping universe.... *Alien Resurrection* would have made an interesting comic book. The first two comic series are as 'real' as the third and fourth films ... from there it's hit and miss. [20]

> As far as I'm concerned, STORY wise, the movies all count. I'm also willing to let the novels (based on the comics) count.[21]

> I would say that the first two (three, pushing it) constitute the original story. The comic books are great, they expand the story rather than trash it like *Alien 4* did.[22]

> I believe that all four movies ARE the *Alien* story. The comics are fun reads, but mostly seem like spoofs of the movies. The novels are a great insight into the movies but basically are just opinions, not facts, of the author who tries to fill the space between the lines.[23]

Second, perhaps because of the ongoing nature of the film series over the last twenty years and the strong possibility of its continuation into the new millennium, fan attention is not really concerned with looking back to favourite texts in a search for underlying themes of, say, human versus alien and android identity, nor with exploring each director's use or otherwise of Freudian vaginal imagery. While Scott Bukatman's essays are treated as key references by *Blade Runner* fans, who subscribe to much the same project of enquiry as Bukatman himself, I have seen no mention of Barbara Creed's equivalent work on *Alien*[24] on Internet fan sites. The *Alien* fan agenda is concerned, by contrast, with predicting the future: second-guessing the production companies' plans for *Alien 5* and arguing over the best choice of cast and directors. Third, as a probable consequence of the *Alien* series's fluidity and openness to diverse authorial styles, Internet fans have no qualms about posting their own full-length scripts for *Alien 5* or even *Alien 6* online, frequently in the understandable belief that their knowledge of and investment in the previous texts makes them better qualified than most Hollywood scriptwriters to create the next instalment.

In place of *Blade Runner*'s widely accepted canon, then, there is diversity and debate. In place of reverence for the screen texts, there is scepticism. And in place of the obsessive project of detection and enquiry after truth in which the *Blade Runner* fans mimic Rick Deckard, there is more the sense of a marine barracks or mess hall, full of challenge, boast and putdown. Sigourney Weaver is referred to as 'Siggy', *Aliens* is described as 'pure crap', and fans who 'rip on' (insult and disrespect) *Alien Resurrection* are decried as 'louzy [*sic*] hypocrites'.[25] Here, assertions are backed not so much through the academic rationality we would see on *Blade Runner* sites or the faith and humanism surrounding *Star Wars*, but by an in-depth knowledge of technical production detail and appeals to the craft of screenwriting, informed by a cut-the-crap approach and a military intolerance of sloppy workmanship:

> *Alien 4* started well but then halfway through it fell apart. Where'd the aliens go? They're running amok, but then they're nowhere to be found, which is too bad because if they'd been attacking the party left and right we may have avoided the Ripley/Call whine whine I'm not human stuff. And the hybrid? Bad bad bad. You don't introduce something new

then blow it out the window in the same breath. Complete waste of time and story. Also, apart from Call and Ripley the characters weren't fleshed-out.[26]

In point form, I censure *Alien Resurrection* for:
* failing to adequately explore the character Call (Winona Ryder)
* failing to develop the adjunctive 'Newborn' sub-plot
* not giving enough screen-time to Vriess (Dominic Pinon)
* obtrusive computer-generated animation
* too much light! Hollywood seems to think audiences are too dim-witted to understand any action that doesn't take place amid four-point lighting.[27]

This display of expertise extends beyond plot and character to production design and effects, where the discussion also takes on a certain posturing and machismo:

> Stan Winston is the best FX guy out there. He only had 16 million to work with on *Aliens*, and look what he came up with. Think if he had a 70 million budget!! It hurts me on the inside thinking how the Newborn could have looked, and was messed up sooo bad! Give the Alien jointed legs, give him a lean physique, but muscular one. Whatever, Stan the Man would come up with something.[28]

Unlike *Blade Runner*, where the pleasure comes from picking over a single text's rich detail, and *Star Wars,* with its guessing games and anticipation, *Alien* fandom posesses a large and diverse canon and thrives on argument over its merits. This is a largely masculine sphere, and the almost universal use of science-fiction/military nicknames rather than real identities suggests that much of the banter may have its roots in role-playing games, where the insults and competition are part of a forum of teenage male friendship. There is, after all, an underlying commonality behind the argument. 'The Alex', having proposed his outline for *Alien 5* and challenged 'anyone got a better suggestion?', can only conclude, perhaps reflecting on how much he enjoys this participatory online society, '*Alien* is a great movie, man!!'

As already suggested, *Star Wars* Internet fandom overlaps in many ways with the activity around *Alien* and *Blade Runner*. In other respects, it operates somewhere between them. The main focus at the time of writing was on the forthcoming prequels and discussion looked ahead, like *Alien* fandom, to movies with a guaranteed release within the next year. Fan predictions and rumours about the next trilogy were drawn, however, not just from a knowledge of the production process but from an intimacy with the original texts which required a constant return to the existing material of the *New Hope – Empire – Jedi* trilogy.

Based on leaks, official press releases, stolen photographs from the Tunisia set and deductions based on textual evidence, the game of anticipation around *Star Wars 1* resembled nothing so much in fandom as the 'Who Killed Laura Palmer' mystery of *Twin Peaks* Net discussion.[29] As in the groups Henry Jenkins studied, expertise and kudos in this discourse stem from piecing together visual clues which are presumed to have been included deliberately by the omniscient author, in this case George Lucas rather than David Lynch:

> George has stated that the prequels are going to dramatically change the way we perceive the current trilogy. Would George add a droid torture sequence to *Return of the Jedi* for no good reason? Not likely. Notice C3PO's reaction to this scene. There is more going on there than we can understand right now.[30]

> Recently I noticed something interesting in the opening 'roll-up' of *A New Hope*. It reads, 'Rebel spaceships, striking from a hidden base, have won their first victory agains the evil Galactic Empire'. If that is their FIRST victory, doesn't that imply that there'd either be no rebellion in Episode Three … or that perhaps Episode Three doesn't end with the birth of Leia and Luke after all, but instead has an ending more 'recent' to the time frame of the trilogy?[31]

> It is pretty much accepted that we will see two planets in Episode One – Coruscant and Tatooine. But classically, if you look to Episodes 4–6, each movie features THREE different planets – Tatooine/Death Star/Yavin, Hoth/Dagobah/Bespin and Tatooine/Dagobah/Endor. So it's a pretty safe bet that at least three planets will be seen in Episode One.[32]

To the outsider, and even to many fans, this kind of obsession with minute detail will seem arcane, even pedantic – the kind of activity that prompted one of Henry Jenkins's group to protest 'do you enjoy making the rest of us feel stupid?' Indeed, one contributor to the *Star War Prequels Rumors* site takes a similar tone:

I have found all the speculations amusing, but it reminds me a little too much of funda-
mentalists picking over what a specific verse in the Bible means, without ever understanding what the whole thing is really about.[33]

Note that, despite the huge range of novels, comics, soundtracks, computer
games, radio scripts, toys, television cartoons, fan writing and role-playing
games around the saga,[34] the only texts considered to hold any real validity in
terms of predicting the future *Star Wars* narratives are three films released
between 1977 and 1983 – literally 'a long time ago', particularly when we
remember that a sizable proportion of *Star Wars* fans were born in the mid to
late 1980s or even the early 1990s.

There is, however, a subtle differentiation around the various secondary
texts in terms of their canonical status. As with *Alien*, the position of specific
texts in the hierarchy is considered to be open to discussion; but there has
clearly emerged a certain consensus, based around what can only be called a
fetish for authorship – George Lucas's involvement is absolutely paramount
for a text to be considered genuinely canonical. The original trilogy is therefore the gold standard against which other texts are to be compared, though
there is a significant preference for the first and second films in the saga
against the more sentimental *Jedi*, and a concomitant preference for *Empire*
director Irvin Kershner over Richard Marquand.

Along with fan fiction and role-playing scenarios, comic books and computer games occupy the opposite position: these are by definition far removed
from Lucas's authorship and can only be regarded as tributes to his original
creation. As regards novels, there is again an internal hierarchy which favours
the work of Timothy Zahn – *Heir to the Empire, Dark Force Rising, The Last
Command* – and Steve Perry's *Shadows of the Empire*. What Zahn's and Perry's
novels have in common is a proximity to the events of Lucas's films – Perry's
fits between *Empire* and *Jedi*, Zahn's come on the trilogy's heels – which elevates
them in the minds of many fans above those novels which attempt to detail
the more distant further adventures of Leia Organa-Solo, her husband and her
three children. *Shadows of the Empire*, furthermore, attained the unique status of

earning an accompanying soundtrack, computer game and range of action figures, and became almost problematically close to 'canon' when a spacecraft invented by Perry was retroactively added to the Mos Eisley scenes of *A New Hope*'s Special Edition.

The overview of my correspondent Gini McDonagh, from the *Echo Station* message boards,[35] sums up this hierarchy neatly, while conveying the compexity of distinction between various authored texts:

> I accept as total, unquestionable canon ONLY the original trilogy. The Special Editions don't get that treatment. Second tier are the radio dramas, since they are based so closely on the original movies and Lucas' notes. The books, I'm very pick and choose about. Zahn happened, at least his original trilogy. Certain events chronicled by Anderson may have happened. Hambly, K-Mac and McBride Allen's contributions do little to the history of the Star Wars galaxy. McIntyre did NOT happen!!! [36]

Even the best-liked novels are considered by the message board contributor 'BetsyK' as

> legends about our favorite characters, something to give us some insight into what might have happened, but to be taken with a grain of salt regarding their 'factuality'.... I consider them original stories, using only names and props from the original trilogy. Among other things are the fact that the books have lost the spiritual message that GL wove into the movies.[37]

'Jody' responds to this post that, 'while I enjoy reading the novels, I tend to think of those as a parallel or alternative universe. GL didn't write them … and only GL should be able to tweak the characters' personalities, because only what he writes directly counts for me.'[38] Finally, 'Admiral Motti' echoes both opinions: 'I lean towards saying that George's works are the only ones that count. If the characters from the Bantam continuum appear in the prequels it will only mean than George endorses the "glorified fan fiction" and thinks that the stories merit being in his canon.'[39]

A number of points can be drawn from this *Star Wars* discussion forum. First, every single post deifies George Lucas as the guarantor of 'authenticity', as if the director had acquired a quasi-mystical Force about himself and taken

on the role of a shamanic Jedi Master to his respectful and obedient fandom. Second, the discussion is measured and entirely friendly – unlike some of the infighting on the *Alien* boards – with much use of 'smiley' emoticons, interjections of '*laugh*' or '*grin*' and mentions of the trilogy's inherent humanity or spiritual content. If *Alien* sites resemble Colonial Marine barracks, this is perhaps the democratic arena of the *Star Wars*' 'New Republic'. Third, all the participants here are women, with the possible exception of 'Admiral Motti' – who, perhaps significantly, takes on an Imperial nickname. 'Jody' explains that 'I do believe *SW* has more appeal to women than, say, *Blade Runner*. *SW* doesn't bog down in technospeak, touches on familiar themes and has all the classic elements of a good epic story.'[40] It may not be coincidence that of all the sites surveyed, this board comes closest to constructing an online 'community', with long-running dialogues, affectionate in-jokes, digressions into 'personal' information and plans to meet 'irl' – that is, in real life.[41]

In conclusion, then, we can see various inflections of fandom across these boards, each with distinctive qualities in terms of its selection of 'valid' – canonical – texts, its attitude towards that canon and its mode of celebrating the favoured objects. Crudely speaking, *Alien* fandom might seem to resemble most the 'buddies shooting the bull' mode identified by Susan J. Clerc around the *X-Files*-based Gillian Anderson Testosterone Brigade; or alternatively, as I have suggested, an online equivalent of the role-playing groups whose popularity peaked in the mid to late 1980s. *Star Wars* fandom, at least within *Echo Station*, comes closer to the female net groups of Clerc's study, or perhaps even to the romance readers of Janice Radway's research:[42] recall that 'Jody' loves the saga for its 'classic elements of a good epic story', a preference which would hardly be out of place at one of the midwestern coffee mornings Radway describes. *Blade Runner*, finally, as what my correspondent John Zaozirny calls 'very much an introspective film',[43] attracts a project based not so much around community but solitary dedication, and is as such something quite unique among the Internet fan groups described in academic study to date. These three fan groups, though, clearly have more links and shared agendas than they have differences. All are engaged in acts of enthusiastic and dedicated creation; and all are engaged in a constant process of negotiation as they work within, around and against an existing and ongoing framework, lovingly crafting their own culture in the chinks of the producers' world-machines.

Sample post to discussion boards, April 1998

I am researching an article on *Star Wars, Alien* and *Blade Runner* fandom for a book to be published in 1999. I would very much appreciate responses to some questions.

1. Which of the films, if any, do you feel are the weakest, and why?
2. Are there characters which you or other fans feel are particularly weak?
3. Do you feel any actors in the series are particularly weak?
4. Do you feel any preference for specific directors within the series over others?
5. What do you feel constitutes the [film title] 'canon', that is, the 'official' story? Is it just the original film[s]? Do the Special Editions count?
6. What about spinoff novels and comics? Do they have 'official' status in your view?
7. What is the status of computer games within the canon?

NOTES

1. Will Brooker, 'New Hope: The Postmodern Project of *Star Wars*', in Peter Brooker and Will Brooker, *Postmodern After-Images*, London: Arnold, 1997.
2. Partly, of course, because the science-fiction and fantasy genres usually manage to avoid the mise-en-scene of 'seventies' wardrobes and hairstyles which inevitably dates some of their contemporaries.
3. Henry Jenkins, *Textual Poachers*, New York: Routledge, 1992.
4. John Tulloch and Henry Jenkins, *Science Fiction Audiences: Watching Doctor Who and Star Trek*, London: Routledge, 1995.
5. 'Do You Enjoy Making the Rest of Us Feel Stupid?', in David Lavery, ed., *Full of Secrets: Critical Approaches to Twin Peaks*, Detroit: Wayne State University Press, 1995.
6. 'DDEB, GATB, MPPB, and Ratboy: The *X-Files*' Media Fandom, Online and Off', in Lavery, Hague and Cartwright, eds, *Deny All Knowledge: Reading the X-Files*, London: Faber & Faber 1996.
7. Roberta Pearson and William Uricchio, *The Many Lives of the Batman: Critical Approaches to a Superhero and his Media*, London: BFI, 1991.
8. Jenkins, *Textual Poachers*.

9. Judith B. Kerman, ed., *Retrofitting Blade Runner*, Ohio: Bowling Green State University Press, 1991; Scott Bukatman, *BFI Modern Classics: Blade Runner*, London: BFI, 1997.

10. Scott renamed Dick's character 'Isidore' as 'J.F. Sebastian'; Jeter includes both as different characters, and returns to Dick's original spelling of 'Rachael'.

11. Philip K. Dick's 'We Can Remember It For You Wholesale', a short story first published in 1966 and reprinted in *The Preserving Machine* (1969), was adapted into Paul Verhoeven's film *Total Recall* (1990).

12. This was Gibson's term for 'cyberspace': see *Neuromancer*, New York: Ace Books, 1984.

13. Lee Stevenson, *The Off-World Connection*, http://www.geocities.com/Area51/Nebula/7445/index.htm.

14. Murray Chapman, http://www.bit.net.au/~muzzle/bladerunner/.

15. *2019 Off-World* runs a special feature on Bukatman's study, with a scanned cover and enthusiastic review; and most sites refer to *Retrofitting Blade Runner* as a key purchase for fans.

16. Nicklas Ingels, *Los Angeles 2019*, http://home4.swipnet.se/~w-47416/blade/.

17. John Zaozirny, email reply to enquiry, 29 April 1998.

18. Christian Fowler, Webmaster of *The Unofficial Alien 5 Site*, message-board response to enquiry, 29 April 1998.

19. *The Alien V Discussion Forum,* http://apps.vantagenet.com/aforums/thread.asp?id=199818114639 and *Alien Central*, http://207.244.122.48/discussion.cgi?id=15798.

20. 'KC', message-board response to enquiry, 25 April 1998.

21. 'Mazvec', message-board response to enquiry, 26 April 1998.

22. 'Corporal Hicks', message-board response to enquiry, 25 April 1998.

23. 'St Just', message-board response to enquiry, 26 April 1998.

24. Barbara Creed, 'From Here To Modernity: Feminism and Postmodernism', *Screen*, vol. 28, no. 2, 1987, pp. 47–67.

25. This irreverence reaches an extreme in the *Unofficial Newt Hate Page* of the *Alien 5 Discussion Forum,* dedicated to abusing Carrie Henn's character in *Aliens*. It opens with the boast 'In *Alien3*, I cheered when I realized she had drowned. If only she had died in the previous film, we would all have been happier.'

26. 'Mazvec', post on *The Alien 5 Discussion Forum*, 26 April 1998.

27. 'KC', post to *The Alien 5 Discussion Forum,* 26 April 1998.

28. 'The Alex', post to *Alien Central*, 18 April 1998.

29. See Jenkins, 'Do You Enjoy Making the Rest of Us Feel Stupid?'

30. 'NYC', post to *DarkSide Prequel Rumors*, http://members.tripod.com/~prequelrumors/soguco.html, February 1998.

31. 'DB', post to *DarkSide Prequel Rumors*, February 1998.

32. Matt Hecht, post to *DarkSide Prequel Rumors*, February 1998.

33. Thomas J. Mosbo, post to *DarkSide Prequel Rumors*, February 1998.

34. These secondary texts are too numerous and diverse for me to expand upon here: but

my essay 'New Hope' attempts to convey the scope of the surrounding *Star Wars* culture in the late 1990s.

35. *Echo Station*, http://www.echostation.com.

36. Gini McDonagh, message-board response to enquiry, 29 April 1998.

37. 'BetsyK', message-board response to enquiry, 30 April 1998.

38. 'Jody', message-board response to enquiry, 30 April 1998.

39. 'Admiral Motti', message-board response to enquiry, 30 April 1998.

40. 'Jody', message-board response to enquiry, 30 April 1998.

41. Compare with the 'David Duchovny Estrogen Brigade' of Susan J. Clerc's study, and with other research into Internet 'communities': Heather Bromberg 'Are MUDs Communities?' in Rob Shields, ed., *Cultures of Internet*, London: Sage, 1996; Katie Argyle, 'Life After Death', in ibid.; Shawn P. Wilbur, 'An Archaeology of Cyberspaces: Virtuality, Community, Identity', in David Porter, ed., *Internet Culture*, London: Routledge, 1997; Derek Foster, 'Community and Identity in the Electronic Village', in ibid.; Howard Rheingold, *The Virtual Community: Homesteading on the Electronic Frontier*, Reading: Addison-Wesley, 1993.

42. Janice Radway, *Reading the Romance*, London: Verso, 1987.

43. John Zaozirny, email response to enquiry, 29 April 1998.

PART II

CITY SPACES

INTRODUCTION

In science-fiction cinema, place often assumes a special significance. Some types of literary science fiction trace their roots to utopian literature – writings about non-existent places (utopia means 'nowhere') whose politics, laws and living conditions are ideally perfect. Science fiction's attitudes towards such places fluctuates between idealism and cynicism, but a common plot element in utopian science fiction involves an intrusion from outside into, and an ensuing disruption of, a utopia: the narrative then explores the consequences of the changes brought about by the intrusion. The utopian tradition also embraces dystopias, places which are the very opposite of perfect. In constructing and exploring these extreme forms of social organization, utopian narratives are doubly fictional: they set up a utopian or dystopian place as a setting for a story, while at the same time the place itself becomes the story.

In cinema, and in science-fiction cinema especially, place carries an additional expressive burden: in its function as the setting for a story, a place becomes visible as mise-en-scene. At the same time, place frequently functions as pure spectacle, a site for the display of *tours de force* of art direction and special effects. At the level of spectacle, the degree to which – and indeed the manner in which – stories and settings are interwoven varies from film to film.

In the 1926 science-fiction feature *Metropolis*, for example, the two elements are highly imbricated. The film's architectural and design references and its organization of diegetic space combine to produce a visible expression of the societal organization underpinning the film's fictional world. In turn, the visibly apparent social structure of Metropolis is what motivates the film's narrative. At one level, *Metropolis* inaugurates a continuing strand of cinematic science fiction in which imagined places – future cities in particular – constitute settings for narrative action. But even where a cityscape figures as little more than a backdrop (as is arguably the case in a film like, say, *RoboCop*), the backdrop is never entirely neutral: at the very least, its visibility adds a layer of cultural meaning and intertextual reference to events in the story.

Science-fiction cinema's visions of urban utopias and dystopias tend to invite reflection on social and political questions. Even if social and political issues are not explicitly addressed in the film itself, science-fiction cityscapes invariably invoke cultural meanings around, for example, scientific progress, urban decay, nuclear holocaust, and other preocccupations. Science-fiction film criticism has not been slow in taking up the invitation to see in these imaginary cityscapes commentaries on contemporary modes of social organization.[1] David Desser's essay, 'Race, Space and Class: The Politics of Cityscapes in Science-Fiction Films', extends this line of genre criticism by setting out a historical overview of cities in science-fiction cinema, beginning with an analysis of the spatial representation of a social class division represented in the upper city/lower city geography set out in the founding text *Metropolis*. Desser's account of science-fiction cinema's cityscapes culminates with *Blade Runner*, a film whose spatial articulation of power relations, he suggests, intertextually reworks *Metropolis* in significant respects, whilst bringing into focus questions of race as well as of social class. These two films – *Metropolis* and *Blade Runner* – are repeatedly referenced in writings on science-fiction cinema and the city; the one arguably belonging to, and the other commenting upon, a tradition in modernist art of portraying the city as 'a place of delirious chaos, alienation, resistance and even improbable liberation'.[2]

In 'Future Noir: Contemporary Representations of Visionary Cities', Janet Staiger takes a somewhat different approach towards questions of intertextuality and the cityscapes of science-fiction cinema. She searches for meanings of science-fiction cinema's virtual cities not in the history of science-fiction cinema itself nor in contemporary society, but in instances of real-world urban social reform, utopian architecture and progressive town planning such as Ebenezer Howard's 'Garden City' and Le Corbusier's 'Radiant City'. In the 'future noir' science-fiction films she discusses, Staiger identifies a series of iconographic motifs which are culturally associated with these utopian visions and are quoted in the films – but with irony. As such, in characteristically postmodern vein, 'future noir' films draw upon and quote from a reserve of shared cultural images of 'progress' in the built environment, whilst at the same time expressing loss of faith in the idealism from which these images first sprang.

The cities of science-fiction cinema provide settings and often subject material for stories. They invoke – and in recent science fiction more often than not pour scorn upon – yearnings for better ways of organizing society. Or they voice fears about decay, degeneration and danger in the public sphere. They may even reference or recycle city images from earlier science-fiction films. At the same time, these places are also constructed as spaces for the film's spectator to enter, map and explore: that is, they interpellate the spectator. How do they do this? What information is contained in the organization, within and between shots, of these filmic spaces? How is this information given, and what does it ask of the spectator? Classical Hollywood cinema, of course, has its own ways of constructing diegetic spaces and of drawing the spectator into and through its virtual worlds. But is there anything special about the ways in which diegetic and spectatorial spaces are organized in the cityscapes of science-fiction cinema?

While these questions are about cinematic address, from the spectator's standpoint they are also phenomenological: that is to say, they have to do with what presents itself as an immediate object of perception, what 'makes itself sensuously and sensibly manifest'.[3] A phenomenological approach to film spectatorship brings vision to the fore, and acknowledges the embodied potential of vision and the kinetic quality of the experience of film space. So, for example, in phenomenological terms navigating the virtual space of a film's diegetic world may involve experiencing the body 'as if' drawn into and moving through that space. While such sensuousness might characterize the experience of classical cinema's narrative space, science-fiction films are singular in that at the levels of image and spectacle they 'real-ize' the genre's *topoi* of the imaginary and the speculative, proposing a necessary connection between the visible worlds created in films and the stories for which these worlds constitute the settings. In consequence, the kinetic experiences they offer are of a very particular kind.[4]

In 'Cities on the Edge of Time: The Urban Science-Fiction Film', Vivian Sobchack considers cityscapes in science-fiction cinema as poetic images with an affective power which conjoins a phenomenology of actual urban experience. In her historical and phenomenological description of science-fiction film cityscapes, Sobchack revisits a long tradition of visualizations and visions of cities in science-fiction films, tracing a shift from the utopian yearnings of the 1920s and 1930s to the dizzyingly bottomless 'grunge-pits' of the 1990s. She notes the instrumentality of special effects in these cinematic experiences, arguing that effects such as digital morphing and warping, with their capacity to destabilize the groundings of space, are implicated in the vertiginous experience offered by a number of recent science-fiction films. This history of 'cities on the edge of time' emphasizes emotion as well as movement: the sensuous and affective qualities of the spaces of science-fiction cinema, and the instrumentality of special effects in these spatial experiences, are further explored in Part IV.

NOTES

1. See, for example, H. Bruce Franklin, 'Visions of the Future in Science Fiction Films', in Annette Kuhn, ed., *Alien Zone: Cultural Theory and Contemporary Science Fiction Cinema*, London: Verso, 1990.

2. Scott Bukatman, *Blade Runner*, London: British Film Institute, 1997, p. 61. See also Eric Alliez and Michel Feher, 'Notes on the Sophisticated City', *Zone*, vol. 1, no. 2, 1986; Giuliana Bruno, 'Ramble City: Postmodernism and *Blade Runner*', in Kuhn, ed., *Alien Zone*; Steve Carper, 'Subverting the Disaffected City: Cityscape in *Blade Runner*', in Judith B. Kerman, ed., *Retrofitting Blade Runner: Issues in Ridley Scott's Blade Runner and Philip K. Dick's Do Androids Dream of Electric Sheep*, Bowling Green, OH: Bowling Green State University Popular Press, 1991; Anton Kaes, '*Metropolis*: City, Cinema, Modernity', in Timothy O. Benson, ed., *Expressionist Utopias: Paradise, Metropolis, Architectural Fantasy*, Los Angeles: Los Angeles County Museum of Art, 1993.

3. Vivian Sobchack, *The Address of the Eye: A Phenomenology of Film Experience*, Princeton, NJ: Princeton University Press, 1992, p. 3.

4. On kinesis and cinema spectatorship, see Lauren Rabinowitz, "From *Hale's Tours* to *Star Tours*: Virtual Voyages and the Delirium of the Hyper-Real', *Iris*, no. 25, 1998; and in relation to science-fiction cinema, see Annette Michelson, 'Bodies in Space: Film as "Carnal Knowledge"', *Artforum*, vol. 7, no. 6, 1969.

4

RACE, SPACE AND CLASS:
THE POLITICS OF CITYSCAPES
IN SCIENCE-FICTION FILMS

DAVID DESSER

The imaginative films of Georges Méliès notwithstanding, the first flowering of cinematic science fiction appears in Weimar Germany, that era of films so memorably, if controversially, discussed in Siegfried Kracauer's *From Caligari to Hitler*.[1] However reductive his analysis may appear to contemporary critics more used to seeing contradiction and ambiguity in filmic texts, there is surely something to be said about the appearance of so many films of fantasy, horror and science fiction during an era of societal confusion and uncertainty. Many of the films reveal the covert play of ideology and cultural tensions amidst the overt big-budget gloss of commercial filmmaking in the international arena. Nowhere is this more apparent than in Fritz Lang's famed *Metropolis*.

The influence of *Metropolis* on the history of screen science fiction is almost incalculable. Douglas Menville and R. Reginald have called it 'The first great achievement of the science-fiction cinema [whose] atmosphere and visual style … were to influence the concept of virtually every filmic portrayal of the future for many years to come.'[2] As one of the towering achievements of the Golden Age of German cinema, *Metropolis* lent intellectual respectability to screen science fiction and started a series of cycles of big-budget science-fiction films. And although today critics and historians concentrate on the

fabulous architectonics of the film and decry its naive, seemingly simplistic, politics, it is the very attempt to politicize the genre that accounts for the film's historical significance.

The film's politics owe much to its historical moment in Weimar Germany's precarious economic and cultural situation. *Metropolis* reveals strong fears of economic collapse and Communist revolution overlaid with anxieties about modernization and urbanization and barely repressed fears of racialized Others. Alternately, it revels in the modern, with its magnificent vistas of towering cities and wondrous technology. It is contradictory, conflicted and ambiguous, precisely the qualities which make it endlessly fascinating.

Kracauer's reductionism notwithstanding, however, within these tensions and contradictions can be detected the ideological motifs central to Nazism:

anti-urbanism, anti-modernism, anti-communism and anti-Semitism. These fears and attractions are structured into the text through an intertwining of visual and thematic elements revolving around race, space, and social class. Repeated shots of the magnificent, towering skyscrapers creating canyons through which aeroplanes travel may be the most memorable of the film's visual motifs (Figure 1), and have proved the most influential in films to follow, but no less memorable and influential are the linked associations between high and low, inside and outside, self and Other.

The cityscape in *Metropolis* is divided between high and low: the city dwellers who live above the ground are contrasted to, and in conflict with, those who dwell beneath the streets. This dialectic above/below corresponds to a difference in class. The workers labour below; the upper classes who benefit from their labour frolic above. Scenes of upper-class life revolve around pleasure, even debauchery; scenes of the workers reveal mechanized, depressed figures who seem barely human (Figure 2). Lang envisions the high vs low, upper class vs working class dichotomy as inevitable, but not necessarily inevitably in conflict. He thus imagines a mediator: the labour/capital conflict is allegorized as a necessary union between hand and mind mediated by the heart. The Lord of Metropolis is the mind, the foreman of the workers is the hand, and the mediator is the son of the master of Metropolis. To this mixture of class conflict Lang, however, adds the element of race through the figures of Rotwang, the mad scientist – a combination of technocrat and alchemist – and Maria, the working-class girl who is also the model for the robot.

In the ultra-modern city of Metropolis, Rotwang is an anachronism, a figure out of an earlier time and age. He lives in a house of mediaeval design and dresses and acts like a figure out of earlier Expressionist films. His associations with mediaeval images of the Jew, which would be reinstitutionalized in Nazi propaganda – the scientist, the magician, the alchemist – bring forth associations of racialized conflict, further impacted both by the use of the robot Maria and the Orientalism of the setting in which she first appears. Maria is Other by virtue of her social class and, of course, by virtue of her gender. The

2

Robot Maria, Rotwang's most fearsome creation, is introduced to an intra-diegetic audience in a nightclub of 'Oriental splendour', the Yoshiwara (the name of the traditional pleasure quarter of Japan's Edo, now Tokyo). This association between an overtly sexualized female and the decadance associated with the Orient also feature in anti-Semitic images of the Jew as 'Oriental'.

These may all very well be unconscious traces of contemporary fears of modernization, urbanization and racial and sexual 'mongrelization'. Lang's attempt to mediate all of this, to turn these fears into a happy ending, are largely unsuccessful, but perhaps well intentioned. The Robot is destroyed, Rotwang is killed, Maria is lifted out of her lower depths, and the workers and the capitalists seem to live happily ever after. But whatever the success (or failure) of Lang's political vision, he introduced into the cinema what we might call a *politicized production design*, a way of imagining through physical space the contemporary conflicts surrounding issues of race, class, and gender. In highlighting social concerns and societal tensions, science-fiction films for decades to follow would utilize the binary oppositions high/low, inside/outside, order/ disorder, technology/nature to translate into thematic issues of male/female, middle class/working class, self/Other, and human/non-human. This chapter will trace the development of a strand of science-fiction cinema which utilizes the contemporary or futuristic cityscape for the purposes of sociopolitical commentary.

While much science-fiction or fantasy literature of the precinematic age was concerned with the creation of utopias, cinema would carry forward the dystopic tradition inaugurated by *Metropolis*. This tradition is on view, for example, in *Just Imagine* (1930), one of the few overtly science-fiction films of Hollywood's classical era. A combination of the newly popular genre of the musical and the still-palpable influence of German Expressionism on Hollywood cinema, *Just Imagine* uneasily swings between dystopic fiction and standard 'boy gets girl' comedy. Thematically, the film looks forward to George Lucas's early chase thriller, *THX-1138* (1970), with its use of letters and numbers in place of names and the overall dystopic dehumanization of its urban citizenry. John Brosnan notes the source of the film's 'lavish and very expensive' production design:

> The huge model set of New York is really the film's most interesting aspect. Obviously inspired by *Metropolis* but much more elaborate than the city in the German film, it cost a quarter of a million dollars to build and contained miniature skyscrapers supposedly 250 storeys high.[3]

Like *Metropolis*, too, with its coded images of Jews, *Just Imagine* links the city of the future with America's newly emergent middle class. Comedian El Brendel stars as a man newly awakened into a marvellous, but also dehumanized, city of the future: New York in 1980. The romance between J21 and LN18 is like many a romance in early musicals: forgettable. So, too, proved *Just Imagine*.

The politics of race and space also commingle in *King Kong* (1932). This story of a giant ape on the rampage in New York may be a mythic reworking of the struggle between nature and culture, but it is also, among other things, a thinly veiled allegory on race relations. Although the Freudian imagery is obvious, there is nevertheless something to be said concerning middle-class fears of sexuality manifest in the film. A fear of blacks, of the African, has had a long and unhappy association with fears of sexuality, a motif in cinema history which stretches as far back as D.W. Griffith's *The Birth of a Nation* (1915). In *Metropolis*, sexual licentiousness, at once fearful and attractive, underlies much of the fear of the working class as well as providing motivation for the Orientalist imagery and giving expression to the ever-present fear of the feminine and of feminized sexuality. In *King Kong*, the fear of racialized sexuality is translated into the figure of a fearsome ape whose attraction to, and pursuit of, the white heroine is an unmistakable projection of middle-class white male fears of black sexuality. Thus the dialectic human/animal is visually reinforced by the opposition light/dark. Representing blacks by a giant ape renders black sexuality as animal-like and in so doing renders blacks as animals: that is, it dehumanizes them, makes them other than human.[4]

Fear of the Other typically manifests itself in terms of sexuality. Maria is doubly frightening in *Metropolis* for her gender as well as for her class status: the Robot Maria embodies the further, perhaps deeper, association between sexuality and racialized Others. The figure of King Kong is an overvaluation of the African, the native, the beast with uncontrollable urges, capable of wreaking havoc not only on the body of the white woman but on the body politic as well. He is let loose in New York, the fearsome city, a place where familial ties are weak, and where the races mingle in the pleasure districts. King Kong is both object of fear, the projection of the freedoms the city has to offer, and object of this city's destruction. Unlike the monsters who would in later years destroy the most modern of urban enclaves (Tokyo, London, New York, by Godzilla, Rodan, Mothra and the Giant Behemoth), King Kong is not so alien as to be unalterably Other. And the New York he invades is both dystopia and utopia. King Kong's destruction provides a foretaste of the genocidal fervour that would pervade both future science-fiction films and future world events.

Things to Come (1936), based on and given intellectual kudos by H.G. Wells's novel, attempted a rare utopic vision. This utopia, oddly enough, has much in common with the conclusion of *Metropolis*. In Wells's future, the human race will be saved by benevolent despots, technocrats all, who have rationally determined humankind's appropriate course of action. The film *Things to Come* is divided into three parts. The first presciently dramatizes the next world war's unleashing of the destructive powers of aerial warfare and the devastation such a war would bring. The second concerns the rebuilding of civilization amidst the reversion of world culture to warring tribes. The tribal leaders (exemplified in the character of Boss) are forced by the newly emergent technocrats to bring an end to the warfare.

The underlying worldview of *Things to Come* is a valorization of the idea that the capitalist system is the true, natural order. The technocrats are the natural leaders by dint of their superior technology, and in the society they create, non-productive (i.e. technologically inferior) citizens are denigrated and de-valued. In the mythic struggle between technology and art enacted in it, the film aligns itself with the technocrats. Art represents the emotional, non-rational, side of humanity all but abolished in the film's technocratic utopia. Rationality, the film asserts, would 'overcome the grubby, emotional and aggressive beast that dwells within'.[5] Unlike so many recent films which decry the failure of science and technology to solve human problems, *Things to Come* looks forward optimistically to future scientific triumphs.

In positing humankind's tendencies towards irrationalism and emotionalism as the cause of war, *Things to Come* gives expression to the novelist's Victorian roots. Emotionalism – associated with the lower classes, with women, with racialized others – is to be feared, repressed, or literally conquered. Great Britain, its imperial power imperilled by the forces of anti-colonialism and the stirrings of another world war in Europe, thus produces a film which has much in common with *Metropolis* in its highlighting of underlying discontent with the shape of the modern world and of fears of things to come. More than in *Metropolis*, and more than in most science-fiction films, technology is imaged as humanity's positive side, a motif taken up in another adaptation of an H.G. Wells story, *The Time Machine*.

The Time Machine (1960), from producer-director George Pal, puts state-of-the-art science-fiction special effects to dramatic use in highlighting the politicized spatial structuring begun in *Metropolis*. This time, however, it is the underground dwellers who control the technology, the means of production, while the surface dwellers are the victims consumed, quite literally, by these futuristic capitalists. Victorian values are again present as the time traveller hero begins his journey from late-Victorian London into the future. After passing through wars and other cataclysms, man-made and natural, he comes upon a seemingly bucolic setting. But he soon discovers that he has entered a world rigidly structured by differences – non-human/human, below/above – and that it is the non-humans who are in command. The fierce Morlocks live below the Earth's surface, while the gentle, placid Eloi cavort above in childlike fashion. The question of difference is highlighted in the visible distinction between the blonde, slender Eloi and the dark, bestial Morlocks. In this respect, human vs non-human is drawn exactly as in *King Kong*'s deployment of the light/dark opposition. As in *Metropolis*, too, though here its meaning is reversed: the surface-dwelling Eloi are the labourers consumed by subterranean masters. The Morlocks betray no feelings, no sign of any sort of humanity; the Eloi, by contrast, are all emotion. Again as in *Metropolis*, a mediator, someone who combines rationality and technological skill with an emotional life and commitment, must enter the picture. Here, however, no compromise is possible. The Morlocks must be destroyed and the more human-like Eloi set on a proper course. The apelike Morlocks, with their exaggerated facial features, preying on the Aryan Eloi, offer a powerful image of racial difference and of the horrors of war between races.

The film, however, can also be viewed as an allegory of the rapacity of capitalism. The Morlocks, owners and controllers of the means of production below the surface, enslave and devour the Eloi, providing them with just enough sustenance to maintain them in a fit state to work the machines. The film retreats from the above/below allegory, however, and moves closer to a colonialist ideology. Under the leadership of the scientist/narrator, a Great White Leader and technocrat, the Eloi defeat the Morlocks and, it is implied, will establish a new society.

Images of urban dystopias and concerns about the future of humanity arise, too, in French cinema of the 1960s. In Jean-Luc Godard's *Alphaville* (1965), Lemmy Caution participates in a science-fiction/film noir adventure in which he is pitted against a supercomputer which, like the Lord of Metropolis, runs a future Paris. The computer suppresses political opposition through mind control and, when that fails, through murder. It is emotion which brings down the computer, and Lemmy Caution's romantic interlude is very much in keeping with the film's positing of rationalism vs irrationalism, and with its siding with the latter against the repressive force of the former.

Godard's contemporary François Truffaut turned to urban dystopic fiction for source material in his 1966 adaptation of Ray Bradbury's *Fahrenheit 451*. Here the future city is a technological marvel: monorails transport its citizens quietly and efficiently to work; while wall-size big-screen interactive televisions dominate domestic space. The city is lifeless, alienating, stultifying. Conformity, forced inclusiveness, and elimination of difference are the codes by which citizens are forced to live. As in *Alphaville*, the plot is structured around the struggle between emotionalism and rationalism, life vs lifelessness. Montag, the quiet hero, is at first linked with the forces of totalitarianism, an enforcer of immoral laws, a fireman who burns books. He is redeemed by love, a new-found love of the imagination, of emotionalism, a world of difference brought to him by a woman. Truffaut's film ends differently from Bradbury's novel, with Montag retreating from the dystopic city into a 'green world' where books provide the means of genuine human connection. The woman, associated with transgression and with fertility, has freed him from the masculinist ideals of technological sameness and sterility.

During the 1960s, US science fiction was boosted by the launch of the television series *Star Trek* (1966–69), many of whose episodes (such as 'Let that Be Your Last Battlefield' [10 January 1969], in which half-white/half-black humanoids are locked in genocidal conflict) addressed current issues around race and racism, by displacing contemporary concerns onto future locales, while claiming that racism is a thing of the past.[6]

Another episode, 'The Cloud Minders' (28 February 1969), reworks *Metropolis*'s oppositions of high vs low, intellect vs labour, light vs dark. Here, the *Enterprise* crew must obtain a rare mineral from the planet Ardana, which is currently engaged in a fierce struggle between the cloud minders, the ruling class who live in a magnificent city high above the ground, and the Troglodytes who mine the mineral deep within the bowels of the planet. As in *Metropolis*, enmity between rulers and workers is extreme, the rulers insistent that the workers are mentally inferior, incapable of ruling themselves let alone of sharing power with the cloud-dwelling elite. Again, as in *Metropolis*, a mediator must be found to resolve the divisions. This is a typical move for the *Star Trek* series, in which mediation, accommodation, synthesis are always preferred solutions. Dystopic urban cinematic science fiction and attendant issues of self/Other, human/non-human, surface in films of the 1970s which deal with issues of overpopulation and ecological awareness. Two films in particular are worth noting: *ZPG* (1971) and *Soylent Green* (1973). Interestingly, both films situate themselves in a desperately overcrowded world, and yet side with a liberal-humanist ideology of freedom of choice, which here includes freedom to reproduce; and both mandate escape from the city, from bureaucracy, from technology, as a means of holding on to one's humanity.

ZPG (the letters stand for Zero Population Growth) is set in a world in which overpopulation has caused severe air pollution. A yellow smog covers the city; people wear face masks to filter out the dirt. In this dystopic future, all births have been banned. One couple disobey this law and both are sentenced to death. They manage to trick the authorities, however, and the film ends with the newly formed family journeying 'by rubber raft down a huge sewer to freedom'.[7] Again, as in *Fahrenheit 451*, escape from the dystopic city into a green world brings with it a promise of freedom and more human and humanistic values.

A similar liberal, anti-totalitarian ideology pervades *Soylent Green*. Set in the New York City of 2022, the film details the hopeless overcrowding of the city and desperate shortage of food and other vital resources, like housing. In this dystopic future, a policeman discovers, with the aid of an old friend, that the primary foodstuff of the culture (soylent green) is made by processing the bodies of the many people encouraged to commit suicide. The film's moral centre rests upon a character named Sol Roth, described by Patricia Erens thus:

> Amid all the changes of the new era Sol is an old-fashioned man, a Jewish survivor, although no mention of religion is actually made. It is Sol who discovers that the soylent green distributed by the government is really dead bodies and thus the Jew becomes the bearer of the truth.[8]

More than that, the Jew is living testimony to the destructive power of totalitarianism, the authentic man, the truly human, for having survived the greatest attempt at dehumanization in the Nazi genocide. The figure of the Jew as the real man, the authentic human, emerges more recently in *Independence Day* (1996), with its imaging of the Jew as the humanistic survivor, the Ur-human whom the aliens would destroy along with the rest of humanity.

If *ZPG* and *Soylent Green* are relatively minor works in urban dystopic cinema, *A Clockwork Orange* (1971) is a major statement on the problem of human free will and the question of genuine humanness. Situated in the very near future, in a recognizably contemporary urban nightmare, the film poses the problem of the essence of humanity thus: Is it better to be a vicious thug or a mind-controlled, pacific nerd? With a vision of fears of violence leading to totalitarian solutions, *A Clockwork Orange* challenges the viewer to choose between authentic humanity and technologized automatons. The cityscapes here are deteriorating to a shocking degree, the streets overrun by armed groups of young rapists in outlandish costumes. Grownups, the average citizenry, cower behind fenced-in compounds or secure themelves in heavily alarmed highrises. As in many dystopic films, the police are vicious psychopaths or uncaring bureaucrats. The film's anti-hero, Alex, roams the lawless streets, at home in the filth, the grime, and in the grip of uncontrollable rage and lust. Humanity is indeed messy, difficult, sometimes violent: but is there a better alternative?

THX-1138 (1970) presents a future society every bit as sterile and as controlled as *A Clockwork Orange*'s is messy and anarchic. The colourful costumes and wild energy of the young protagonists of Kubrick's film are replaced by a predominantly black-and-white production design which extends to the appearance of the characters. The environment in Lucas's film is completely lifeless and antiseptic. If Kubrick's city requires a little law and order to ensure a greater level of comfort, Lucas's dystopia needs a little disorder to restore some humanity.

The spatial patterning of above/below is here transformed into inside/outside. The totalitarian computers which seem to run this colourless future culture have decreed that its citizens must live inside a protective shell, outside which there is nothing but desolate waste. This concept of a shell, literalized on the spatial level with its stark white, empty interiors and a total absence of exterior space, is symbolized on the social level. The citizens are completely cut off from genuine emotions and real connections, isolated by drugs and constant computer monitoring. Names have been replaced by letters and numbers; conformity is ensured by physical resemblance – all the inhabitants have shaven heads and wear stark white uniforms. All differences – of class, race and gender have thus been eliminated. To assert difference is to take the first step towards rebellion.

The dehumanized quality of this dystopia is further highlighted by the presence of robots, who seem at times more lively than the people. Nancy Schwartz notes indeed that

These law enforcers are in many ways more animate than the shaven-headed, white clad body of citizens whose stern but benevolent guides and safeguards they are. The identifiable qualities which are supposed to mark the point where metal diverges from mind and flesh are distorted and invalidated. Man replaced by machine is less frightening than Man dehumanized to a level at which machines seem more lively.[9]

Again, as in much earlier science-fiction cinema, a return to emotions and a rejection of technology are necessary for the re-emergence of humanity. Escape from the sterile environment, by breaking free into the outside, is also, yet again, to return to the green world, free of the dystopic city's controls.

The contemporary city, that melting pot of races, classes and genders, represents a vision of difference gone wild, a fearsome image of loss of certainty and control, where the privilege of the dominant group is ever at risk of being undermined by a host of fearsome Others. But the city may also be a place of extreme conformity, a place where differences are erased. This image is taken up in Philip Kaufman's 1978 remake of *Invasion of the Body Snatchers* (the original, directed by Don Siegel, was made in 1956), in which the conformity of the small town is translated to a vision of urban yuppie trendiness gone wild. The corporate boardrooms, the latest 'in' restaurants and health clubs, the streets of America's premier tourist city, San Francisco, provide the settings for this updated version of the invasion of the pod people. This time, however, the vision is bleaker. Where in the 1956 version, the Kevin McCarthy character seems to escape the conformity of suburban pod-dom, Donald Sutherland in Kaufman's eerie modern classic has no such luck. The city is the victor.

This history of cinematic urban dystopias culminates with *Blade Runner* (1982), the finest achievement in the political science-fiction film, and a veritable compendium of the motifs discussed in this chapter. *Blade Runner* takes something from the ecological disasters featured in *ZPG* and *Soylent Green*; costuming motifs are inspired by *A Clockwork Orange*; policemen who enforce immoral laws are borrowed from *Fahrenheit 451*. But above all, *Blade Runner* reworks *Metropolis* in significant and deliberate ways, especially by highlighting

3

the linked issues of race, space, and class and by utilizing its production design for symbolic as well as for spectacular purposes (Figure 3).

Race is structured into the film in both the traditional and the science-fictional senses. *Blade Runner*'s futuristic Los Angeles is a densely populated melange of swarming humanity, including many Asians, Latinos and Middle Easterns. To these masses are added midgets, punks, decadent revellers, and other oddly costumed denizens of an anarchic city. The sight of an 'ordinary' white person is rare enough for one of the characters to question why Sebastian, seemingly a normal white male, has not emigrated offworld. To this urban melting pot is added another layer of race and racism in the form of replicants, artificial life forms bred for slavery in the offworld.[10] Their presence on Earth is illegal and they are held in contempt and fear by the police force, the blade runners, whose job it is to hunt them down and 'retire' (kill) them. It is never explained, either in the film or in its source novel, Philip K. Dick's *Do Androids Dream of Electric Sheep?*, just why their presence on Earth is forbidden. It might be surmised that it is a fear of difference – notably, perhaps, the replicants' alleged lack of emotions – which underlies the terror they inspire.[11]

The figuration of racism in *Blade Runner* translates into the high/low spatial metaphor present in *Metropolis* and other films. The replicants and the people of colour inhabit the teeming, rain-soaked streets, as police craft hover above (Figure 4); giant television screens similarly occupy the upper levels, beaming down their audiovisual messages to a population which cannot take advantage of the advertisements' promises of a better life offworld. Deckard, the blade runner assigned to kill a group of replicants, similarly lives high above the crowded streets, protected by ultra-modern security devices and other high-tech equipment. Highest of all, though, resides Eldon Tyrell, technocrat *extraordinaire* and Master of LA's Metropolis, in a pyramid some seven hundred storeys high.

Social class also figures in this racialized dichotomy. The replicants feel safest among the denizens of the streets, adopting working-class lifestyles. Leon takes a room on the second floor of a run-down hotel while working as nuclear fission loader, a job of marginal, blue-collar skills.[12] Zhora works in a strip joint in Chinatown. Pris becomes a street person, while Roy Batty moves freely about the city streets seeking out employees of the Tyrell Corporation.

Blade Runner also borrows from *Metropolis* the idea of the robot as doppelganger, dark double. If the replicants lack emotion, so too does Deckard the blade runner. If the replicants are at home in the streets, so too the blade runner must know his way around the lower levels. And if Leon and Rachael rely on photographic images to connect them with a past and thus with an identity, so too Deckard surrounds himself with images of a personal past, a past we are not certain is real.

Again, as in so many science-fiction films, the struggle to define real humanity revolves around emotions. In some sense, the alleged lack of emotions on the replicants' part is a projection of the emotional isolation of Eldon Tyrell himself. If *Metropolis* splits its figures of technocrat and alchemist into the Master of Metropolis and Rotwang, in *Blade Runner* these figures are combined in Tyrell. Technocrat *extraordinaire*, Tyrell surrounds himself with mere objects, creating what he regards as lifeless reproductions. While Sebastian

4

says he 'makes friends' (offbeat toys with far less genetic complexity than the replicants), Tyrell claims only to be in business to make money. It is the film's clearest irony that the replicants have far more emotion, feel more genuine connections, than their creator, Tyrell: that it is the replicants Rachael and Roy who show Deckard the way to his true humanity. If it is human to feel emotions, then to feel emotions is to be human. In a cityscape of dark complexity, Deckard retrieves something of his humanity.

Blade Runner exists, of course, in many versions. In the original US theatrical release version, Deckard and Rachael escape to the green world à la *Fahrenheit 451* or *THX-1138* – an unlikely conclusion given the ecological disaster that underlies the film's basic premiss that much animal life has been extinguished and that Earth is nearly uninhabitable, so that offworld emigration is encouraged for those who qualify racially. The director's cut (1992) ends more ambiguously, with Deckard and Rachael heading towards an unknown future. Still, as in *Metropolis*, there is a mediation figure: here Deckard is the link between the genetic engineer and the genetically engineered; with Rachael he will negotiate the landscape of this futuristic polyglot, polyracial city.

NOTES

1. Siegfried Kracauer, *From Caligari to Hitler*, Princeton: Princeton University Press, 1947. This chapter is a substantially revised version of an essay which appeared in Judith Kerman, ed., *Retrofitting Blade Runner: Issues in Ridley Scott's Blade Runner and Philip K. Dick's Do Androids Dream of Electric Sheep*, Bowling Green, OH: Bowling Green State University Popular Press, 1991, under the title 'Race, Space and Class: The Politics of SF Film from *Metropolis* to *Blade Runner*'.

2. Douglas R. Menville and R. Reginald, *Things to Come: An Illustrated History of the Science Fiction Film*, New York: Times Books, 1977, pp. 32–3.

3. John Brosnan, *Future Tense: The Cinema of Science Fiction*, New York: St. Martin's Press, 1978, p. 40.

4. Associations between blacks and apes have been common in racist imagery. Similar racialized dehumanization was reinstantiated in US World War II propaganda which frequently relied on the image of the Japanese as 'monkey men', sometimes as giant apes, sometimes as monkeys swinging through trees. See John W. Dower, *War Without Mercy: Race and Power in the Pacific War*, New York: Pantheon, 1987.

5. Brosnan, *Future Tense*, p. 57.

6. See Daniel Bernardi, *Star Trek and History: Race-ing Toward a White Future*, New Brunswick, NJ: Rutgers University Press, 1998, pp. 26–8.

7. Brosnan, *Future Tense*, p. 201.

8. Patricia Erens, *The Jew in American Cinema*, Bloomington: Indiana University Press, 1984, p. 364.

9. Quoted in Ralph J. Amelio, *Hal in the Classroom: Science Fiction Films*, Dayton, OH: Pflaum Publishing, 1974, p. 66.

10. Robert Baringer perceptively notes the almost total absence of black people in Ridley Scott's futuristic Los Angeles. In one sense, the replicants, bred to be slaves and discriminated against on Earth, are the new underclass. His subtle analysis exposes many contradictions within a film which otherwise marks a valiant effort to counter the racism it so clearly describes. See 'Skinjobs, Humans and Racial Coding', *Jump Cut*, no. 41, 1997.

11. In Philip K. Dick's original novel, Eldon Tyrell is named Eldon Rosen, Rachael is Rachael Rosen, and J.R. Sebastian J.R. Isidore. The change from book to film removes any hint of Jewishness implied in the names Rosen and Isidore.

12. Baringer, 'Skinjobs, Humans and Racial Coding', p. 14.

5

FUTURE NOIR:
CONTEMPORARY REPRESENTATIONS
OF VISIONARY CITIES

JANET STAIGER

One of the most immediate signifiers of the genre of science fiction is the representation of a known city in which readily distinguishable sections of today's cityscape are present while other parts are rewritten. Hence an advertising supplement in the *New York Times* locates its commodity, the United Nations Plaza building, within a redesigned – '100 years from Today' – New York City.[1] The proposed endurance and consequent value of the property and its address are reinforced through the supplement's second-page photo of the Dakota apartment building in 1881, which 'remains a bastion of luxury living'. Thus value exists in location and style. Good investments require a sense of the place of the building in its relation to a present and a future urban environment, including access to transportation lines and contingent developments. Furthermore, the architectural style will not only evince the present good taste of its occupants but anticipate directions of design. Consequently, within the commodity's value is incorporated its ability to forecast signifiers of 'luxury living'.

But that is not all. According to Anthony Giddens, in modern cities and within capitalist economies not only are lands and buildings situated within an exchange system but '*space itself becomes commodified*'.[2] As urbanization spreads, all environments are transformed, becoming non-natural. City parks, pedestrian precincts, a tree in a planter along the sidewalk, all represent city-dwellers' attempt to influence the milieux in which they live; as New York City residents know, even sightlines from buildings can be zoned and sold. It is not merely a rhetorical gesture of the ad to claim that one distinguishing characteristic of 'the special world of 100 United Nations Plaza' is

> views that go on and on, day after day, year after year.... In all directions dramatic and glamour-filled Manhattan vistas delight the eye. The panorama of the East River, the Rose Garden and the elegant greenery of the United Nations, the vitality of the mid-town cityscapes. They all serve to give a special aura and a special value to 100 United Nations Plaza.[3]

This utopian vision of monopoly capitalism surely invites the desire of those capable of sharing its dream ('residences from $330,000 to $5,000,000'). 100 United Nations Plaza, one hundred years from today, will be clean, sleek, accessible by land or air, and – in both meanings of the word – visionary. It is, and will be, modern.

However, as modernism continues to respond only to the aesthetics of a select few and capitalism's benefits fail to spread evenly, the signifiers for high modernism and monopoly capitalism are potential sites for a dialogical rewriting that implies the alienating decay and deadening of that vision. If corporations assume that the designs of their buildings 'communicate the company's identity to its various constituencies'[4] and TransAmerica and Citicorp (echoing the ambulatory Prudential Rock) devise commercials highlighting the pyramid towers of their corporate headquarters as signifying their mobile or personal presence in numerous cities and landscapes, then it is scarcely much of a leap to argue that in today's popular imagination modernist architecture is associated with dominant, powerful multinationals. Additionally, it is not surprising that writings and films sceptical or critical of the effects derived from the institutions housed in a specific type of architecture will 'talk back' to that institution via the appropriation, transformation and corruption of its signifiers – here the style and design of the building.

This discursive procedure is not new, being a long-standing practice in the arena of science fiction; and theorists of the genre have already noted that it is as much about the present as the future, since any envisioned tomorrow derives from premisses about today. As Samuel Delany notes about literary science fiction:

> with each sentence we have to ask what in the world of the tale would have to be different from our world in order for such a sentence to be uttered – and thus, as the sentences build up, we build up a world in specific dialogue with our present conception of the real.[5]

Such a comment applies equally well to filmic representations of future cities. Consequently, the mise-en-scene of cities in science-fiction films might be understood as utopian commentaries about the hopes and failures of today or, inversely, dystopian propositions, implicit criticisms of modern urban life and the economic system that produces it.

In this chapter, I want to look at three instances of such a criticism. While I shall draw in other examples of utopian or dystopian visions of cities for purposes of contrast, I find stimulating the similarities between *Blade Runner*, *Brazil* and the television programme *Max Headroom*. Although these three texts hardly represent the only trend in picturing the future, their appeal suggests that they tap certain strands of discontent with our society. Furthermore, even if other versions of tomorrow might not include all the aspects of 'future noir'[6] cities I shall discuss, they often produce permutations of this nexus of attributes. These permutations are significant in that they may generate political expressions very different from the future noir texts that I am treating. In fact, I will not claim any unified 'political unconscious' for these three. What the three texts do share is the strategy of quoting motifs of high modernist architecture, which then become ironic within the context of plot developments and related mise-en-scene. Additionally, interpretations of these texts indicate that they all highlight flaws of various types in the social formation, express abhorrence of the process of products signifying 'lifestyles' (late capitalist commodity fetishism) and fear the pervasiveness of information systems that overwhelm human senses. Yet they differ from each other. While *Blade Runner* and *Max Headroom* criticize elitism and class distinctions in international and monopoly capitalism, *Brazil* condemns the hierarchies and bureaucracies of the welfare state, also associated with monopoly capitalism.

Nonetheless, the mise-en-scene of their visions of another world are alike in four respects. First, present and future are conjoined via the device of a postmodern cityscape in which traces of modernist high-rises and pyramid-and-glass towers intermingle with debris from revival architecture and urban sprawl. Second, in addition these cities are dark, lit only indirectly and arguably from completely artificial light sources: while part of the dimness might be attributable to advantages for cinematic special effects technology, the meta-phoric implication of an end to civilization or alienation from natural light pervades the atmosphere. Third, darkness and urban-design chaos as bricolage also permit labyrinthine cities where only overhead schematics provide a sense of orientation. And fourth, they are entropic, characterized by debris, decay, and abandonment. Thus these dystopias' city architectures comment on a potential post-industrial, age-of-communication society. The forecast is not favourable. For the future noir city is more nightmare than vision, more anxiety than wish-fulfilment.

To understand these films' pessimistic visions of the future, it is valuable to trace their historical sources in earlier architecture and utopian social planning. Moreover, earlier and contemporaneous utopian and dystopian fictional litera-ture may have provided imagery for modern designers. Certainly from the perspective of a Foucauldian archaeology of knowledge, certain figures re-appear with eerie frequency in both fiction and reality. Having provided a cultural, symbolic and historical context for particular features of these films' representations of cities, I shall explore the four features, arguing that a cultural historian should ground interpretations of iconic representations within both the historical logic of their appearance and the specificity of their function within individual texts.

Technically, 'utopia' means 'no-place', although as originally used by Thomas More in his 1516 monograph the word suggests a spatial distance from the status quo.[7] Rather, 'euchronia' is the appropriate word for anticipations of the future while 'dystopia' derives from a prefix implying impairment or abnormality. Indeed, dystopias seem to be fabricated as corrupted versions of some utopian (or euchronian) scheme rather than initiated outright. Robert H. Walker provides another valuable distinction: that between 'communes', which usually 'offered agricultural or village models', and utopias, which 'tended to accept cities and technology and to redeploy them in ideal terms'.[8]

As historians of utopian projects report, finding the first attempts to envision some perfect social and political order probably requires turning back at least to Plato's *Republic*. After Thomas More, visions become numerous. Early founders of the United States hoped to settle the uncorrupted American wilderness as new Edens. James Oglethorpe planned for Georgia to be an orderly asylum for debtors; William Penn wanted 'a green, symmetrical, Quaker town in the woods along the Delaware'; and Cotton Mather drafted 'an HOLY CITY ... the STREET whereof will be Pure GOLD'.[9]

I find it significant that these new Edens require a specific physical structure, with plans emphasizing symmetry and order in addition to valuable building materials (green nature or golden lanes). Ease in personal transportation and interpersonal communication is important, too. Thus, from at least the 1700s in the United States, the 'new age' or the 'golden era' has an implicit isomorphic relation to spatial configurations, types of architecture, and paths of communication between people. The social and political map for the utopia is doubled in the schematics for cities and managed environments (Washington DC is a good case in point). In fact, the schematics may be part of the therapeutic process of the utopia. As Walker points out, for some 'planners of ideal communities' such as Frederick Law Olmsted, Frank Lloyd Wright, the New Dealers and Buckminster Fuller, 'whatever their scope, the design of the manmade and natural setting was a crucial factor in elevating society'.[10]

It will be certain features of some utopian designs (symmetry, order, clarity, value) off which future noir dystopias play for signification, as a sort of oppositional strategy for constructing a dialogical criticism of the social or political order the ideal community represents. Thus in film science fiction, a denunciation of the utopian vision can be elaborated and interpreted not only through narrative propositions about the society but also via mise-en-scene — as impaired physical constructions, antivisions of the makers' hopes. Consequently, understanding the specific utopias which might underpin particular architectural designs can be useful in reading science-fiction films. I would caution, however, that as meanings shift through social and historical utterance (or reader reception), it is not so much an original visionary's 'intent' that is at stake as a society's distinctive field of meanings for a style. Sketching out several varieties of utopias in relation to their specific mise-en-scene can be pertinent in setting up some parameters for the subtexts for science fiction in general, and for future noir texts in particular.

As a literary genre in the United States, utopian fiction seems to have hit a cycle in the period between 1889 and 1912, when more than a hundred works appeared following the publication of Edward Bellamy's *Looking Backward* in 1888. It is also generally considered that 1880 to 1920 marks a transitional stage in American capitalism and society: the ending of entrepreneurial capitalism and the unveiling of monopoly capitalism. On a more local scale, mass production needs to stimulate assembly-line routines and the scientific management of labour through, for example, time-and-motion studies. A predominantly rural society yields to the overwhelming hegemony of urbanism as product sources shift from farm and small town to centrally located corporations and national distribution of factory-made goods. Temporal and spatial perspectives begin to change as the telegraph, the telephone, and soon the cinema shrink distances and expand vistas. Information loads and communication channels metamorphose. Cultural historians describe this period as including a major shift in individuals' self-conception. As advertising promotes conspicuous consumption, we cease defining ourselves primarily through work and start categorizing ourselves by what we consume. A culture of production gives way to one of consumption.

The conjunction of utopian literature and economic and social change is, according to some scholars, hardly a coincidence. Even as these transformations were occurring, researchers noted that responses such as populism, progressivism and socialism were overt political campaigns promoting specific visions aimed at directing rapid and troubling transformation. As early as 1922, the urban sociologist Lewis Mumford argued in his *Story of Utopias* that 'modern utopias were inseparable from the rise of technology'.[11]

Bellamy's optimistic *Looking Backward* finds 'technology and cooperation have banished the harsh inequities so oppressive to Bellamy's contemporaries'.[12] In opening his story, the narrator, Julian West, describes to his audience in the year 2000 the misery and squalor parts of humanity endured in 1887. By Chapter 3, West's miraculous awakening concludes with his first sight of the future. Refusing to believe it is some 113 years later, West is taken by his companions to the rooftop and asked, 'if this is the Boston of the nineteenth century'. Bellamy writes:

> At my feet lay a great city. Miles of broad streets, shaded by trees and lined with fine buildings, for the most part not in continuous blocks but set in larger or smaller enclosures stretched in every direction. Every quarter contained large open squares filled with trees, along which statues glistened and fountains flashed in the late-afternoon sun. Public buildings of a colossal size and architectural grandeur unparalled in my day raised their stately piles on every side. Surely I had never seen this city nor one comparable to it before. Raising my eyes at last toward the horizon, I looked westward. That blue ribbon winding away to the sunset – was it not the sinuous Charles. I looked east – Boston harbor stretched before me within its headlands, not one of its green islets missing. I knew then that I had been told the truth concerning the prodigious thing which had befallen me.[13]

As suggested earlier, the science-fiction effect works through the device of rewriting a known city. More importantly, Bellamy's vision is literally first of all that of a cityscape and an architectural style. Subsequently, analogies between this physical world and an invisible but real social formation will be drawn out.

Walker describes another utopian novel, Bradford Peck's *The World a Department Store* (1900), in which 'Peck united producer and consumer in one great cooperative headquartered in buildings designed to produce both efficiency and unquestioning respect.'[14] But perhaps the best known – and most influential – science-fiction writer of the period was H.G. Wells. Wells's writings might be considered to fall into both utopian and dystopian categories (at times for the same novel), but his 1905 book, *A Modern Utopia*, suggests Wells's more confident vision. As Mark R. Hillegas puts it, this utopia is the 'archetypal welfare state'.[15] The city represented here, however, is alarmingly similar to a bleaker variation in Wells's earlier story *When the Sleeper Awakes* (1899): 'the symbol in much twentieth-century utopian fantasy of the "interdependence of science, technology, industrialization, mass population, and social organization"'.[16] And what are the features of this ambiguously positive and negative Wellsian 'Super-City'? The protagonist's 'first impression was of overwhelming architecture'. The city was roofed in by glass, permitting control of climate. Surrounded by advertisements, people in the streets were treated to 'babble machines' which provided constant news. Although the Sanitary Company burned books, people could watch 'kineto-tele-photographs'. Furthermore, despite a governmental ordering of social services, hierarchies continued to exist, with labourers – living and working underground – separated physically from the nobility.

I am assuming you are already anticipating my drawing linkages between Wells's city and films such as *Metropolis*, *Fahrenheit 451*, *1984*, as well as *Blade Runner*, *Brazil* and *Max Headroom*. In fact, a major similarity in plot structure between *Blade Runner* and *Brazil* ironically reverses that of Wells's earlier 'A Story of the Days to Come' (1897). The love story of Elizabeth and Denton is contrasted with the 'oppressive tyranny of life in the super-city'.[17] To escape, the couple flee beyond the edge of the city into the countryside. In Wells's tale, however, survival becomes a problem, and the lovers choose to return. Such irony does not occur in *Blade Runner*, for any potential problems in coping with the wilderness are masked by Deckard's proposition that the length of one's life is uncertain. Satire returns in *Brazil*, where the trip to the countryside is revealed to be the hallucination of protagonist Sam Lowry. Consequently although the motif of escape to nature circulates between the texts, functionally it serves both utopian and dystopian purposes. Semantically, it provides a 'happy ending' in *Blade Runner*, but it can also be inverted, as in *Brazil*, to connote psychosis.

The connections between Wells and cinema are obviously not necessarily direct, since much anti-utopian fiction has intervened.[18] Hillegas, however, points to the importance of Wells's writings as predecessors of numerous motifs in modern literary science fiction. In particular, he locates Zamyatin's *We* (1924), Huxley's *Brave New World* (1932) and Orwell's *Nineteen Eighty-Four* (1949) as anti-Wellsian tracts. What all three writers objected to in Wells's welfare utopias were the implications that in spite of their 'planned, ideal, and perfected' social systems, people 'are conditioned to obedience, freedom is eliminated, and individuality crushed; … the past is systematically destroyed and men are isolated from nature; … science and technology are employed, not to enrich human life, but to maintain the state's surveillance and control of its slave citizens'.[19] Such propositions, I would argue, lead to specific dominant connotations for features of fictional cityscapes. Wellsian high-rise, climate-controlled, mass-mediated and sanitized megalopolises adduce the benefits of welfare socialism, but they can also imply state surveillance and individual alienation. Yet literary science fiction is not the only venue for such iconic motifs. They also derive from twentieth-century urban planning and certain theories of architecture for modern cities.

Although utopias created by writers like Bellamy, Peck and Wells describe supercities with distinctive features, architects were also susceptible to visionary speculation. Furthermore, the same economic and social forces operating to shape literary utopias functioned to foster idealist urban design. Donald M. Lowe argues that while earlier planning might consider visual aesthetics, transportation concerns and hygiene needs, a major transformation is marked by individuals projecting future economic, regional, and demographic developments.[20]

Certainly the turn of the twentieth century saw the proposal of a number of utopian cities, some of which have provided the basis for actual town plans. Robert Fishman looks at three detailed designs for ideal cities in relation to 'the economic and political organization of the city, which could not be easily shown in drawings [but which] was worked out in the voluminous writings which each planner appended to his designs': Ebenezer Howard's 'Garden City', Frank Lloyd Wright's 'Broadacres', and Le Corbusier's 'Radiant City'. As he argues, 'in the three ideal cities, the transformation of the physical environment is the outward sign of an inner transformation in the social structure'.[21]

While Ebenezer Howard's 1902 vision may be relatively unfamiliar to us today, his notion of small communities of limited size – thirty thousand or fewer people – surrounded by a 'greenbelt' is perhaps closest to the present state of affairs in major inland cities of the United States. Branched off the hub of the central city are smaller towns joined by railway lines running into the metropolitan focal point. Howard was directly influenced by *Looking Backward*, and constructed a city complex that might handle large numbers of urban dwellers while struggling to maintain older traditions of small-scale cooperation and direct democracy. As Fishman points out, Howard's plan was a nostalgic attempt to retain the city/country structure of a pastoral England.[22]

On the other hand, Frank Lloyd Wright's 'Broadacres' (1945) becomes the antithesis of Le Corbusier's 'Radiant City'.[23] Wright rejected any concentration of population: for him the notion of separating town and country was inconceivable. Hoping for no population concentration larger than a county seat, Wright planned thousands of homesteads, with everyone having a minimum of one acre of land and transportation occurring by car rather than by rail. His utopia is certainly not a city, as it spreads across plains of prairie countryside. 'Organic' architecture permeates not only the houses but the world, as interiors and exteriors are 'opened up'. As with Howard, Wright's Broadacres was designed so as to promote a specific social formation: individual ownership and decentralization. But if the separated houses indicated self-reliance, they also endorsed privacy. Stephen Kern notes that the homes' entrances are hidden by stone parapets and porch walls. Walker connects some of today's urban planning – such as James Rouse's New Town, Columbia, Maryland (1963) – to Wright's work; but clearly strands of Howard's Garden City influence it, as well as Victor Gruen's city planning. In the mid 1950s, Gruen advocated what is now a popular renovation procedure for town centres: pedestrian precincts in the inner areas, intercept parking lots further out, and beltline freeways circling the core area.[24]

If Howard's Garden City most closely anticipates actual characteristics of today's less than orderly urban sprawl, and Wright's Broadacres illustrates a plan almost lacking in instances of contemporary use, Le Corbusier's Radiant City, as well as his other proposals, stands for what are arguably the most widely implemented properties of modernist architecture, with its attendant implications for social planning. Although Le Corbusier's work differs from the most extreme high modernist skyscrapers, the extent to which his design style has symbolized an 'official' approach in contemporary architecture is evident in Wolf Von Eckardt's 1977 pronouncement:

> Modern architecture died on April 21, 1972. Few architects noticed. The public did not care. No one mourned. It was never popular. The end was not unexpected. The International Style – as the architecture conceived by Walter Gropius at the Bauhaus in Weimar and by Corbusier in his atelier in Paris, came to be known – had long been feverish, erratic and contradictory. But no one got at the basic affliction, which was that Modern architecture is an abstract art – an abstraction that failed to meet practical human needs. This affliction caused the authorities in St. Louis, that April morning five years ago, to do the only thing left to do with the modern highrise slabs of the Pruitt–Igoe public housing project. They blew them up. With dynamite. The first of the 33 identical human filing cabinets collapsed in 20 seconds flat.[25]

Von Eckardt links the utopian sources of the International Style to a twentieth-century avant-garde sensibility which was appalled by the squalor, chaos and outright mess of the modern city. Additionally, these designers considered nineteenth-century architectural styles to be 'hypocritical, bourgeois

Victorian gimcrackery. They wanted "honest" structures without ornament'.[26] If their plans included the social action of liberating people from slums and crowded streets, their goals also demanded new styles of buildings, cityscapes and roadways. Le Corbusier's famous maxim, 'a house is a machine to live in', expresses this group's pleasure in and hopes for technology. Consequently, Le Corbusier's blueprints for his 1922 'Contemporary City' stress orderliness, symmetry, space and vistas among twenty-four high-rises which would house and office three million people. An elaborate transportation system becomes the nerve centre of the city, but no monuments recall a dead past. 'Corridor streets' are gone, as wide, open boulevards stretch towards a perceivable linear perspective horizon line. These are the very features that future noir dystopias will mock.

Furthermore, as Fishman points out, Le Corbusier hardly envisioned an egalitarian democracy as this city's political and social system.[27] Rather, a technocracy dominated, with hierarchies of planners and workers. Those close to the centre of the city were higher in the social scale than the labourers living further out. A sort of pyramid of living space and social caste operated in synchronization. This implied splitting of people into categories shows up also in sharp distinctions between city and country: the boundaries between the two are readily distinguishable in Le Corbusier's drawings.

The International Style of Le Corbusier and others seems the closest visual approximation to Bellamy's and Wells's literary utopias of planned societies; and Le Corbusier's own writings suggest that the affinities are also conceptual. It is also the case that the dense high-rise connected by roadways quickly appears in art as a vision of the future. Paul Citroen produces *Metropolis* in photomontage in 1923, while Norman Bel Geddes shows City of 1960 at the 1939 New York World Fair.

In cinema of the 1920s and 1930s, set designs and storylines respond to this version of modernism and its utopian themes. Visually, both Fritz Lang's 1926 *Metropolis* and the British film *Things to Come* (1936) duplicate the high-rises and transportation systems of Wells's supercities and Le Corbusier's

1

Contemporary City. In *Metropolis*, the city's orderliness and symmetry above ground are perhaps more visible in Erich Kettelhut's set design, but balance and uniformity between parts are emphasized for the factory scenes (through camera framing) and for the workers (via blocking of actors' movements). Additionally, *Metropolis*'s poster provides a strong concentration of pertinent motifs – sleek skyscrapers, critical arteries, and pyramid peaks. The linkages of *Things to Come* (Figure 1) to this system of visualizing the future are scarcely tenuous, based as the film is on Wells's 1934 novel *The Shape of Things to Come*. Here the modern city of 2036, Everytown, is characterized by multi-storey buildings, moving sidewalks, and a domed glass shell protecting the climate, marking off city from exterior countryside and diffusing light to an even glow.

Besides the visual similarities to Wells's and Le Corbusier's utopias in these films' mise-en-scene, narrative propositions also connect to these antecedents. A major recurring postulate in both films is the necessity of a division and rationalization of labour. This is most pronounced in *Metropolis*, where the planners reside above ground in an Edenic natureland while the workers toil on gigantic underground machinery, surviving despite backbreaking labour and regimented assembly-line work. The conflict of *Metropolis* is easily – though some believe implausibly and unsatisfactorily – resolved through the fortuitous acceptance by the CEO of the necessity to join the head (the planners above ground) and the hands (the workers below earth) via the heart. Through such a conclusion, the hierarchy and paternalism of a social formation similar to that accepted by Le Corbusier is asserted and reinforced.

Similarities to *Metropolis*'s symbolism and plot conflict can also be found in Wells's *The Time Machine* (1895). In the year 802,701 the Eloi live above ground in a kind of paradise while Morlocks exist below the surface, running the machinery necessary for the Eloi to survive. At night, though, the Morlocks emerge, eating the Eloi. Despite narrative and visual comparisons, such a bleak spectre in the Wells story should act as a caution against assuming that recurrent motifs reference similar political positions. As I have argued, in discursive formations motifs can be employed both in admiration of their antecedents and oppositionally, inverting (or twisting) the dominant semantics.

If *Metropolis* accepts divided labour as a prerequisite for a successful future, in *Things to Come* the final narrative crisis ironically (through its probable unintentionality) asserts its necessity. After a devastating world war in which humanity is reduced to regressive barbarism, the use of massive machinery and giant turbines rebuilds civilization. Yet this technological progress and its attendant social harmony are nearly halted once again when one individual incites masses of people to prevent space travel. 'Halt. Stop this progress' becomes the villainous intervention. Wellsian socialism and planned economy, using technology for alleviating the poverty and misery of labourers, wins for 'a whole world peace', but to accomplish this the intellectual ruling class ignores the voices raised in opposition, and pursues its dream.

The economic conservatism of Le Corbusier and *Metropolis* versus the radical visions of Wells and *Things to Come*: these instances are certainly different in their political analysis of a proper utopia. Yet in such diverse anticipations of the future, similarities occur in the features of architecture (slab-block high-rises and peaked skyscrapers, breathtaking vistas from the more significant buildings, diffused lighting); symmetry and balance in the cityscapes; orderly and rational mass transportation systems; and efficient, immediate, and extensive methods of communication (both films visualize television and computer screens as signal media for mass information).

These patterns will also occur in future noir films. However, these films have taken positive images of the future as signifiers for more troubled notions of how maladjusted and distorted the visions might become. By parodically inverting those motifs' semantics, future noir films question the economic and political status quo that would generate such a future. For if the utopias of Wells and Le Corbusier, *Metropolis* and *Things to Come* are bright, optimistic views of possibilities for tomorrow, future noir dystopias seek to establish an opposing proposition.

The dynamics of social reform, Walker maintains, progress through a five-step sequence: (1) random negative (unorganized protest); (2) structured negative (organized protest); (3) random positive (various remedies); (4) structured positive (organized movement with a constructive aim); and (5) watchdog (surveillance of institutionalized reform).[28] Obviously, not all attempts at reform succeed. Consequently, some criticisms of the social formation never move much beyond steps (1) or (2).

I find this outline helpful, however, in characterizing the political action of dystopian texts since the phrasing 'random negative', or unorganized protest, strikes me as particularly apt. The advantage dystopias have is that they do not have to provide alternate visions of tomorrow: they can merely exaggerate or invert utopias, suggesting that aspects of the fantasy ideal future will eventually produce distortions or contradictions. Considered as negations of specific fantasies of the future and as unorganized protests about social tendencies, dystopian fictions criticize specific utopias and function as warning messages about the present day: this is tomorrow – if we don't watch out.

How soon tomorrow may occur is part of each dystopia's alarm. For our future noirs, *Max Headroom* is probably the bleakest, as it is set 'twenty minutes into the future'; although *Brazil* might have already transpired, since it takes place at 8:49 p.m. 'somewhere in the twentieth century'. *Blade Runner* is set in Los Angeles, November 2019. Moreover, as predictions of the future, these texts are consistent in their notions of the city, even if their criticisms of the implications of those cities' social systems differ slightly. In particular, variant attacks on modern architecture as representing twentieth-century late capitalism, commodity fetishism and a class system cross these texts, along with fear of an age of information and of multinationalism. However, as mentioned earlier, *Blade Runner* and *Max Headroom* link these problems more specifically to multinational capitalism, while *Brazil* suggests they are symptomatic of an advanced liberal welfare state bureaucracy.

One of the most immediate experiences of *Brazil*, *Blade Runner* and *Max Headroom* is their kindred presentations of the urban area. Most obviously, the skyscraper and high-rise do not necessarily ensure either peaceful work surroundings or harmonious family habitations. The very privileged and significant inhabitants of the future noir buildings – all powerful multinational corporations – seem to be the sources for disruption of lives. In *Blade Runner* the most magisterial of the pyramids to which Deckard flies houses the headquarters of the Tyrell Corporation, a leading manufacturer of the replicants who revolt against their makers and whom the ruling class insists that Deckard 'retire'. It is Deckard's conflict with these directives that motivates both the film's action and its implicit social criticism. This is a society that has so commodified human labour and animal life that it engineers it genetically, perfecting it to the

point that only the most sophisticated devices can distinguish real from simulacrum. Deckard is unsure of the borderlines between human and humanoid, but paranoia over its own accomplishments requires that this society keep the distinction viable. As with elitist paternalism and divided labour technocracies, classes must be maintained.

In *Brazil*, the impressive and oppressive lobby to the Ministry of Information leads to absolutely uniform corridors and closet offices in which desks are shared through walls. References to *Brave New World* and *Nineteen Eighty-four* abound as Lowry works for an institution that habitually invades private homes because 'suspicion breeds confidence'. Classes and hierarchies abound isomorphically with the architecture: police are stationed in the ministry's sub-basement and the CEO's office is on the top floor. A member of the privileged class, Sam's mother lives in an apartment whose design contrasts markedly with that of victimized Harry Buttle. A criticism less of capitalism than of a post-industrial, commodified, bureaucratic information society, *Brazil* works in dialogue with its British literary utopic predecessors. Furthermore, it evokes Le Corbusier's 'machine to live in' as a literalized metaphor – although the habitations may be said to be more 'alive' than the inhabitants. On the one hand, snaking behind the walls of the rooms are the intestines of the social system: breathing, pulsating tubes transport food, heat, air conditioning, waste products, information and, if one counts the subways, people. On the other hand, surrounded by manufactured women (teeth are straightened, faces lifted, fat dissolved), Lowry fantasizes and then hallucinates escape with a dream woman to a green countryside.

For *Max Headroom*, the semantic analogies between mise-en-scene and plot are crystallized in the prominence of the opening titles locating in the skyscraper the corporate headquarters for Channel 23 – a leading contender in the television ratings wars. In the series, protagonist Edison Carter works as a top-rated investigative reporter, often discovering that the cause of social and economic injustices is his own industry's drive for profit maximization. Before the television series was cancelled in the USA because of low ratings in Autumn 1987 (and then revived in Spring 1988), one of its fictional episodes suggested that a competitor's ratings were being artificially increased through subliminal electronic stimulation of viewers. Another episode traced to the CEO of an officially sanctioned information monopoly the evil plot to exploit for its own profit computerized data which were being fed through the firm's networks. And an early episode uncovered members of Channel 23's board of directors as perpetrators of criminal acts which bolstered ratings. Closer to *Blade Runner* in its criticism of capitalism, *Max Headroom* echoes *Brazil*'s post-industrial age-of-information theme. And, as with *Brazil* and *Blade Runner*, *Max Headroom*'s architecture employs a degraded 'Contemporary City' as its target. For all three texts, modern architecture houses corrupt institutions which are pivotal sources for a failing social formation.

Thus the dominant thrust of these future noirs is to use the signifier of the international high-rise or the nostalgic pyramid-peaked skyscraper as a method of marking out the dangers of the hierarchies and elitism that a late capitalist class system or a Weberian bureaucracy produces. Yet, additionally, in each of these texts the signifiers of the cityscape develop bleak semantic connotations not only through intertextuality but via their special contextual and parodic permutations.

For one thing, if high modernist internationalism hoped to erase the vulgarity and ugliness of the nineteenth century, it has apparently failed, partially as a result of what it brought with it: its own notions of class and elitism. The dialectic of the utopian sources of the style's meaning produces its own critique. For how are categorical distinctions between individuals to be maintained if they are not visually perceivable and commercially exploited? Advertising and product differentiation in monopoly capitalism construct 'lifestyles' with which individuals seek identification as they sort out their own self-image in relation to possible purchasable ones. To buy a beer requires knowing, or deciding, whether you are a party animal, a tough but sensitive buddy, or a gourmet. Contemporary consumer culture requires the buyer to consider who she or he is in relation to the array of products available. Thus, added to the product's original use value is a new one: constructing self-identity. Consequently, in this consumer society, these cities become mixtures of styles and cultures, tied together by threads of advertising.

The postmodern city is the result: to high modernists, a chunky stew of architectural 'monstrosities' rather than a smooth broth of sleek uniformity; Venturi's strip rather than Le Corbusier's boulevard. Furthermore, if the ruling class inhabit the monoliths and pyramids of modernism, *hoi polloi* drift among an ahistorical potpourri of 'theme' architecture ranging from colonial and Victorian to modernist and pop. In *Brazil*, for instance, Lowry's home is most reminiscent of the international style, with the exterior similar to Le Corbusier-influenced 'Silver Towers', home for New York University faculty and staff. Deckard also lives in such a cubical space, with a small balcony, built-in appliances, and diffused lighting sources. Mrs Lowry's apartment suggests late Victorian bric-a-brac, with antique tables and chintz antimacassars scattered around the living room. The Buttles inhabit a clearly working-class domicile, a chainstore version of Mrs Lowry's home. J.F. Sebastian resides amidst his android toys in a nearly empty grand hotel, 'The Bradbury'.

Fredric Jameson argues in one of his studies of postmodernism that such a figuration of mise-en-scene is indicative of a historical shift. 'I have mentioned', he writes, 'the populist aspect of the rhetorical defense of postmodernism against the elite (and Utopian) austerities of the great architectural modernisms.'[29] Indeed, a populism may inhabit advocacies of postmodernist architecture, but in these films the strategy is more of a deliberate contrast to modernist aesthetics of beauty and order as the dystopias use 'ugliness' and urban bricolage to indicate the impact of capitalist commodification. Or again, as in *Brazil*, the criticism may be of false appearance of options in a choiceless social order, for although the guests at a fancy hotel can order various meals, they are all served three scoops of – admittedly different coloured – glop, along with a picture of their 'filet mignon'. In either case, commodification is attacked as fetish and alienating, and postmodernist 'choice' of style is false consciousness.[30] The satire is vicious.

This postmodern mix is not only of product styles but, in a xenophobic move, also of cultures. An earlier implementation of this device occurs in Stanley Kubrick's *A Clockwork Orange* (1971). Here, Russian and English languages mingle for the gang of mod streetwise brutes that Alex heads. Such multilingualism and cultural plurality is evident in future noir texts as well, but with an ominous shift of connotation. *Blade Runner*, for instance, describes 'Cityspeak' as a combination of five languages, while advertising montages constructed from Japanese and English become ideograms spreading across Times Square-style billboards. Eastern electronics meets Western electricity to produce gigantic display ads.

As with the mix of lifestyles, this concoction of cultures is a result of monopoly capitalism, now that the world is an international marketplace. Furthermore, *what* is bought and sold seems less and less important. For instance, in *A Clockwork Orange* the range of homes Alex and his droogs visit plays out the variety of lifestyles possible in an England of the early 1970s. As Robert Hughes puts it in an article neatly entitled 'The Décor of Tomorrow's Hell', 'The impression, a very deliberate one, is of cultural objects cut loose from any power to communicate, or even to be noticed.'[31] That this is supposedly the age of information produces a fine irony.

The pervasiveness of advertising and lack of communicative content are potent subtexts for all three future noirs. In *Blade Runner*, Wellsian 'babble machines' float along streets dispensing not news but ads. The route from Lowry's office to the Buttles' home is a corridor (not a boulevard) of billboard jammed up against billboard. As the camera pans upwards, a bleak, nearly desert horizon with factory chimneys fleshes out an almost vacant landscape. Carter's programme is constantly monitored in the news station central for its ratings, since the function of television programmes is to deliver consumers to advertisers, not information to viewers. Carter's texts only fill the empty air between commercials.

Postmodernism, then, in these future noir texts is not a necessary transition in history. Instead, a more political bite lies within the function of this style for these films. The criticism is of commodification of modes of living, of (sometimes approved) divisions between styles and culture, of elitism, and of surfaces emptied of meaning despite utopian hopes. The major economic and political institutions may reside in modern architectural monuments, but their offspring are postmodern urban strips nostalgically imitating design styles that only convey the content of 'product'.

While postmodernism is perhaps the most obvious of the characteristics of future noirs, the subgenre's name emphasizes a second feature: dusk or darkness. Intriguingly, the role of glass and light in literary and film utopias distinguishes these films from their predecessors. Glass domes protect super-cities and an even light glows everywhere. But such choices also result in the loss of something else: natural climates and sunshine. As humanity controls its urban environment, even something so basically natural as light becomes artificial.

Additionally, shutting in also means shutting out – although the implications of glass structures might originally relate to beauty of design and enhancement of visual pleasure. In architectural history, glass has operated contradictorily. In a 1914 manifesto, futurist architect Antonio Sant'Elia called for new materials responsive to the times: 'steel, glass, cardboard, reinforced concrete, and textile fibers…. Elevators must no longer be hidden like tape worms in the bowels of buildings but be accessible and visible on the outside of facades.'[32] Glass becomes part of the side and visual texture of buildings. Yet as Reyner Banham observes:

> The sheer abundance of light in conjunction with large areas of transparent or trans-lucent material effectively reversed all established visual habits by which buildings were seen. For the first time [as a result of glass and electricity] it was possible to conceive of buildings whose true nature could only be perceived after dark, when artificial light blazed out through their structure.[33]

The paradox, however, is that if a glass structure is built in an unpicturesque part of town, its users end up looking over factories and urban sprawl – the by-products of that firm's own participation in industrialization. Apparently when Frank Lloyd Wright designed the Johnson factory complex in downtown Racine, Wisconsin, he solved such visual nastiness by turning all windows in towards the centre of the environs, and by using translucent rather than transparent glass materials. Fredric Jameson hypothesizes that the Bonaventura Hotel obscures entries because it 'aspires to being a total space, a complete world, a kind of miniature city.' Indeed, it leaves a 'degraded and fallen city fabric' to its own devices.[34]

Consequently, the darkness of the future noirs serves to draw forth visually the geometrical block designs of the brown and grey buildings, sprinkled with smaller rectangles of incandescent and neon light. But no natural light greets the individual travelling through the interiors of homes and along the avenues of city streets. Blocks of glass permit diffused light to enter: they prevent gazes outwards, but what would one see? *Brazil*'s urban transport system is built of blocks of translucent glass. In *Blade Runner*, fluorescent tubing is pervasive, even serving as an umbrella handle.

Postmodern urban sprawl and convoluted or artificial sources of light contribute to a general semantics of decline, and connect to a third aspect of these future noirs: the labyrinthine character of space. In all cases, overhead schematics supplied by 'omnipotent' computers are necessary for travel. Transportation systems may merge in the centre of the city, but multi-storey pathways now outstrip humanity's ability to navigate by eye-level perspective. In a more exaggerated case, Carter scouts his subjects via short-wave linkages to the home news centre, where his 'controller' has access (via a computer that somehow accesses up-to-date sensory input) to subjects' movements. Programmed much like the source of his information, Edison receives his directions in a form which matches his eye-level perspective, while he must rely on those sequenced commands to reach his destination. Deckard's travels are similarly through crowded streets rather than long avenues. Lowry cannot look beyond billboards or through glass walls as he travels. As suggested at the beginning of this chapter, one implication of capitalism is the commodification of space, with attendant value placed on vistas. Yet Le Corbusier's twenty-four skyscrapers have yielded to hundreds of structures obscuring visions beyond the neighbouring building. Indeed, the external skeleton of high modernism becomes a labyrinth of industrialization. If 100 United Nations Plaza promises views that go on and on, future noir films question who is able to share in that hope, and how.

Seeing this labyrinthine view of space slightly differently, but in a complementary way, Jameson notes that due to the 'absolute symmetry of the [Bonaventura's] four towers it is quite impossible to get your bearings in [its] lobby'. For him, we are in a new 'hyperspace' – a 'disjunction' finally exists 'between the body and its built environment ... [which] can stand as the symbol and analogue of that even sharper dilemma which is the incapacity of our minds, at least at present, to map the great global multinational and decentered communication network in which we find ourselves caught as individual subjects.'[35] Thus, with space as either labyrinthine or 'hyper', humanity's senses, particularly the privileged one of sight, are no longer guarantors of ability to negotiate space and determine perspective.

Finally, and consequently, entropy as randomness and disorder increases, and predictions for the future are not of a hopeful change for the better. The spills of waste and garbage, the graffiti-covered walls, the breakdown of appliances, are constants of set design for future noir movies. Rain, probably from car emissions and smog, falls continually in the Los Angeles of the replicants. Urban hoodlums trash Lowry's car within minutes of his parking it outside the Buttles' home. Carter often scouts around the edges of his city, near where 'blanks' – those on the margins of society and without identity cards – warm themselves by barrel fires.

In 'The Imagination of Disaster', Susan Sontag makes a worthy observation about science fiction. She writes:

> Science fiction films are not about science. They are about disaster, which is one of the oldest subjects of art.... Thus, the science fiction film ... is concerned with the aesthetics of destruction, with the peculiar beauties to be found in wreaking havoc, making a mess.[36]

If this is the case, dystopias surely must have the upper hand over utopian fiction, for the ways humanity can allow its own civilization to self-destruct are clearly the challenge for set designers.

As indicated earlier, four characteristics – postmodernism, indirect lighting, labyrinthine space, and an entropic civilization – seem common to the mise-en-scene of future noir films; and these yield part of the texts' signification of protest. The grievances are numerous and certainly do not cohere around a central plan for reform. Rather, they seem random shots at deficiencies in present-day life. Integral to all these dystopias is a bleak criticism of utopian versions of high modernist architecture and modern cityscapes, structures which harbour corrupt economic and social institutions. The semiotic operation, however, is apparent: transform, through context and intertextuality, the signifiers of modern life so that they become the signs of a troubled society.

NOTES

1. *New York Times*, 21 June 1987.
2. Anthony Giddens, *Sociology: A Brief but Critical Introduction*, 2nd edn, San Diego, CA: Harcourt Brace Jovanovich, 1987, p. 101, italics in original. The present chapter is a slightly shortened version of an essay that appeared under the same title in *East–West Film Journal*, vol. 3, no. 1, 1988, pp. 20–44.
3. *New York Times*, 21 June 1987, pp. 4–5.
4. *American Way*, 15 November 1987, p. 52.
5. Samuel Delany, 'Generic Protocols: Science Fiction and Mundance', in Teresa de Lauretis, Andreas Huyssen and Kathleen Woodward, eds, *The Technological Imagination: Theories and Fictions*, Madison, WI: Coda Press, 1980, p. 179.
6. I find it significant in a period of postmodernism that, while I am not the creator of the term 'future noir', I cannot supply its origin. One of my students, Bert Greene, used the term to describe these films, but he said he heard it from another student whose last name he did not know. I rather like the fact that in an essay about postmodern science fiction, I cannot properly attribute my source except to say it is a circulating discourse in Austin, Texas.
7. Donald M. Lowe, *History of Bourgeois Perception*, Chicago: University of Chicago Press, 1982, p. 46.
8. Robert H. Walker, *Reform in America: The Continuing Frontier*, Lexington, KY: University

Press of Kentucky, 1985, p. 132.

9. Ibid., p. 20.

10. Ibid., p. 121.

11. Cited in ibid., p. 132n.

12. Ibid., p. 136.

13. Edward Bellamy, *Looking Backward: 2000–1887* (reprint of 1888 edition), New York: New American Library, 1960, p. 43.

14. Walker, *Reform in America*, p. 134.

15. Mark R. Hillegas, *The Future as Nightmare: H.G. Wells and the Anti-Utopians*, New York: Oxford University Press, 1967, p. 71.

16. Ibid., p. 43, citing Richard Gerber.

17. Ibid., pp. 49–50.

18. However, Méliès's *A Trip to the Moon* (1903) bears many similarities to Wells's *The First Men in the Moon* (1901).

19. Hillegas, *The Future as Nightmare*, p. 3.

20. Lowe, *History of Bourgeois Perception*, pp. 66–70.

21. Robert Fishman, *Urban Utopias in the Twentieth Century*, New York: Basic Books, 1977, pp. 3, 6.

22. Ibid., pp. 8–10, 32–6.

23. Robert Venturi makes the opposition explicitly in his chart contrasting urban sprawl with the megastructure, 'Broadacre City' versus 'Ville Radieuse'. See Robert Venturi, Denise Scott Brown and Steven Izenour, *Learning from Las Vegas: The Forgotten Symbolism of Architectural Form*, revised edn, Cambridge, MA: MIT Press, 1977, p. 118.

24. Stephen Kern, *The Culture of Time and Space, 1880–1918*, Cambridge, MA: Harvard University Press, 1983, pp. 186–7; Walker, *Reform in America*, p. 117; Grady Clay, *Close-Up: How to Read the American City*, Chicago: University of Chicago Press, 1973, p. 62.

25. Wolf von Eckardt, 'The Death of the Moderns (I)', *The New Republic*, no. 6/7, 6 and 13 August 1977, pp. 31–3.

26. Ibid., p. 31.

27. Fishman, *Urban Utopias in the Twentieth Century*, pp. 188–93.

28. Walker, *Reform in America*, p. 12.

29. Fredric Jameson, 'Postmodernism, or the Cultural Logic of Late Capitalism', *New Left Review*, no. 146, 1984, pp. 80–81.

30. This is possible since the films themselves are not of a postmodern aesthetic; that is, these future noir films may display a postmodern mise-en-scene, taking the value of spectacle associated with that style, but since that mise-en-scene is represented as the environment for the characters, the filmic effect is that of criticizing that environment. In every regard, these movies are quite traditional in their narrative form and style.

31. Robert Hughes, 'The Decor of Tomorrow's Hell', *Time*, 27 December 1971, p. 59.

32. Kern, *The Culture of Time and Space*, p. 99. Always quick to observe a trend, *Time* magazine reported in 1968 that one feature of new architectural shapes was 'Honesty…. Today architects like to show how buildings stand by calling attention to the structural system…. Another school of architects feels that a building ought to tell what is going on beneath its skin' ('To Cherish Rather than Destroy', *Time*, 2 August 1968, p. 40).

33. Cited in Kern, *The Culture of Time and Space*, p. 186.

34. Jameson, 'Postmodernism', p. 81.

35. Ibid., pp. 82–4.

36. Susan Sontag, 'The Imagination of Disaster', in *Against Interpretation*, New York: Dell, 1968, p. 213.

6

CITIES ON THE EDGE OF TIME:
THE URBAN SCIENCE-FICTION FILM

VIVIAN SOBCHACK

In 1952, science-fiction writer Clifford Simak published *City*, a loosely related collection of short stories unified by their location in a metropolis that – over thousands of narrative years – radically changes its shape, its functions, and its citizenry. This episodic and millennial history of urban transformation is framed by its narration as a 'bedtime story' – told by a golden robot to a pack of articulate young dogs gathered around a blazing hearth, wondering if it is really true that once, and very long ago, the nearby city (and the world) was populated by animate, two-legged beings called 'humans'.[1]

Like most of the cities in science-fiction literature and film, Simak's city with its fabulous transformations over time is clearly a city of the imagination. Owing no necessary allegiance to representational verisimilitude, such a metropolis serves as a hypnogogic site where the anxieties, desires and fetishes of a culture's waking world and dream world converge and are resolved into a substantial and systemic architecture. This imaginary architecture – particularly as it is concretely hallucinated in American science-fiction film images – is more than mere background. Indeed, the science-fiction film city's spatial articulations provide the literal premises for the possibilities and trajectory of narrative action – inscribing, describing and circumscribing an extrapolative or speculative urban world and giving that fantasized world a significant and visibly signifying shape and temporal dimension. That is, enjoying particular representational freedom as a genre of the fantastic, the science-fiction film concretely 'real-izes' the imaginary and the speculative in the visible spectacle of a concrete image. Thus, it could be argued that because it offers us the most explicitly poetic figuration of the literal grounds of contemporary urban existence, the science-fiction city and its concrete realization in US cinema also offers the most appropriate representational grounds for a phenomenological history of the spatial and temporal transformation of the city as it has been culturally experienced from the 1950s (when the American science-fiction film first emerged as a genre) to the present (in which the genre enjoys unprecedented popularity). Indeed, although not as radical in its transformations as Simak's *City* (nor as long-lived), the imaginary city of the American science-fiction film from the 1950s to the 1990s offers us a historically qualified and qualifying site that might be explored as both literal ground and metaphoric figure of the transformation of contemporary urban experience and its narratives in that period now associated with 'postmodernism'.[2] This, then, is a historical trajectory – one we pick up at a generic moment that marks the failure of modernism's aspirations in images that speak of urban destruction and emptiness and that leads to more contemporary moments marked by urban exhaustion, postmodern exhilaration, and millennial vertigo.

The following analysis of the cityscapes in American science-fiction film refuses the perspective of classical urbanism, which looks at the city as an 'object' distinct from the subjects who inhabit it. My project is best summed up as a desire to 'let "the city" emerge, in the complex and shifting fashion proper to it, as a specific power to affect both people and materials – a power that modifies the relations between them'.[3] Thus I wish to describe the nature of this affective power as it appears historically in a dominant set of poetic science-fiction film images, and then to thematize these images as they emerge from and co-constitute a phenomenology of urban experience. That is, these historically shifting urban images express a lived structure of meanings and affects experienced by the embodied social subjects who inhabited, endured and dreamed them.

Given this historical as well as phenomenological project, it might seem strange to begin by focusing on a series of 'detached' images – images of the science-fiction city described and given importance 'out of context' and not in relation to the specific texts and narratives in which they play a major or minor part. However, as Gaston Bachelard tells us in *The Poetics of Space*, the poetic image 'has touched the depths before it stirs the surface', and by its very novelty it 'sets in motion the entire linguistic mechanism'.[4] Thus the poetic image can be seen as *constitutive* of its narrative context. It generates, coalesces, condenses, embodies, 'troubles' and transforms the more elaborated text of which it is ultimately a part, and is itself open to transformation as it performs the semiotic and affective work of adjusting the systems of representation and narrative and the demands of the psyche and culture to each other.[5] The following 'detached' images of the American science-fiction film city, then, are not to be seen as ahistorical or absolute and essential. They are not really taken 'out of context', abstracted from the 'text'. Rather, it could be said that their poetic reverberations generate and configure not only the discretion of their individual texts, but also a larger historical narrative – one that generally dramatizes the transformational character of the American city and its shifting affective significance for us. It is that larger narrative which is of ultimate concern here. To *configure* that larger narrative, however, we must first grasp its *figures* and treat each of them phenomenologically – as Bachelard says, 'not as an object and even less as the substitute for an object', but rather in 'its specific reality'.[6] That is, prior to narrativizing the poetic image, we should be receptive to its reverberations within us, to its compelling originality – understood not only as immediately significant but also as strangely familiar. Indeed, the poetic image is an image that we have already deeply lived but never before imaginatively projected.

As mentioned previously, the American science-fiction film emerges as a genre with a marked corpus only in the 1950s. Yet to appreciate the poetic significance of this postwar and postmodern genre's various spatial and temporal transformations of the city from the 1950s to the present, we need briefly to evoke an image of the city as it was figured in American film fantasies before the 1950s. This fantasized city, one must remark, reverberates quite differently from the city figured as 'contemporary' in the popular genres of the musical or gangster films of the 1930s or in the urban melodramas and films noirs of the 1940s.

First, there is *Just Imagine* (1930), a bizarre wedding of science-fiction futurism and musical comedy. Set in 1980, the film shows New York City as a high rise of skyscrapers intricately connected by a network of aerial thoroughfares and bridges. Here, one sees no base and pedestrian street level. The hero and heroine stop their little one-seater planes and hover in mid-air to rendezvous – the city around them busy with traffic that, however quotidian, is nonetheless emphatically and literally 'uplifted'. Although this rather loony film posits a repressive – if café – society, its concrete imagination reverberates as soaring aspiration. Indeed, finding its poetic source in Fritz Lang's *Metropolis* (1926), whose futuristic bi-level city was inspired by Bauhaus architecture and the German director's 1924 visit to New York, *Just Imagine* is selective in what it borrows. It does not visualize a New York whose architecture is as oppressive as it is also liberating and beautiful – a cityscape that, for Lang, also evoked confusion, exploitation and 'living in perpetual anxiety'.[7] Ignoring the baseness of Lang's lower city, and drawing only upon *Metropolis*'s most affirmative modernist architecture, the New York of *Just Imagine* seems – to quote Lang in a moment of positive description – 'a vertical veil, shimmering, almost weightless'.[8] In sum, *Just Imagine*'s New York poetically reverberates only with the vertical power, vast size and ethereal delicacy of Lang's upper city (Figure 1).

Three other fantastic images of the city dominate the 1930s, but they do not appear in science-fiction films (although one is frequently associated with the genre). Each is so strong as to have gained lasting iconic status – and, indeed, one was explicitly acknowledged by the filmmaker as the generative force informing the narrative. Meriam C. Cooper, co-director of *King Kong*

(1933), claims that his 'first idea was of the giant ape on top of a building battling a fleet of planes'.[9] In the image, the fifty-foot-tall great ape 'towers' over Manhattan, momentarily triumphant and forever poetically transcendent atop what once could be called 'New York's tallest phallus', the Empire State Building – officially opened on 1 May 1931, only two years before the film's release.[10] Despite Kong's fall and death on the street below the world's then tallest building, it is this *ascendant* image that we remember – Kong's anarchic and 'primitive' natural presence surrealistically at ease (as well as at odds) with Western culture's most modern and 'civilized' architectural presence by virtue of their shared transcendent scope, the imaginative monumentality and aspiration they so differently (but yet so similarly) embody.

The two other major fantasy images of the city in 1930s films neither signify *aspiration towards the future* (as in *Just Imagine*) nor celebrate *transcendence in the present* (as in *King Kong*). Instead, their utopian impulses represent the city as *eternal ideal*. Both cities are visualized in aspiring architecture and explicitly located in transcendent space – for one film, in the highest reaches of the Himalayas, and for the other, 'somewhere over the rainbow'. In each, however, the temporal nature of the 'eternal' is encoded differently. The Shangri-la of the aptly titled *Lost Horizon* (1937) seems a mirage of aspiration, shimmering in an eternal nostalgia that has nothing to do with modernity – either present or future. This idealized and lofty city signifies a utopian reach always in excess of modern man's venal grasp, an eternal ideal always already ephemeral and lost. However, appearing in the same year as the microcosmic, utopian and modern city that was the 1939 New York World's Fair (marked by the idealist geometry of the Trylon and the Perisphere) was the emerald city of *The Wizard of Oz*. Given to our sight for the first time, Oz is set off in the distance, framed by a foreground field of poppies (the stuff of dreams). Standing as both eternal and modern, it is aspiring, atemporal, ethereal, and yet evergreen and contemporary, its softened skyscrapers giving the lie to the term since they have no sharp rectilinear edges and, belonging to the sky, have no need to assault it.

The dominant theme of these few fantastic images of the city stands apart from more contemporaneous, realist and 'grounded' visualizations of urban life in the 1930s. With the exception of Shangri-la (its perpetual evocation of loss prescient about the 'down' side of modernity, aspiration and urbanism), they concretely construct 'modernity' in an architecture of 'aspiration' that has commerce with the 'transcendent'. These images emphasize the vertical, lofty and aerial quality of the city rather than its pedestrian and base horizontality. Indeed, equating 'height' with the active reach of human aspiration, the 'loftiness' of the city stands concretely as its most aesthetically significant social value. Here, cultural geographer Yi-Fu Tuan is apposite:

The vertical versus the horizontal dimension? ... [A] common response is to see them symbolically as the antithesis between transcendence and immanence, between the ideal of the disembodied consciousness (a skyward spirituality) and the ideal of earth-bound identification. Vertical elements ... evoke a sense of striving, a defiance of gravity, while the horizontal elements call to mind acceptance and rest.[11]

As we shall see in science-fiction films of the 1970s and 1980s, however, horizontal elements can call to mind less positive modes of passive being: resignation, stasis, asphyxiation and death – as well as more active modes of being: expansion, dispersion and play.

Traditionally, America's spatial mythology has privileged the non-urban and has been, indeed, anti-urban (the paradise of the New World symbolically located in the garden, the West, the frontier, the wilderness, and now – after Steven Spielberg – on the lawns of suburbia). Nonetheless, as we have seen in these few images from the 1930s, the fantasy of the imaginary city constitutes it in a positive image of highness and fullness, envisions it as the site of human aspiration – its vertical projection pointing towards spiritual transcendence and, perhaps, a better and fuller (that is, a materially expanded and more 'civilized') future. In an extremely popularized and 'softened' way, then, the positive image of the 1930s city has its roots in the earlier urban and techno-logical visions of Futurism and Modernism.

Given that social events in the 1940s were not conducive to continuing this utopian fantasy of the city, it is not surprising that, but for the nightmarish and labyrinthine 'low' life hyperbolically figured in the urban introspections of film noir, most film images of the city during this period are neither extrapolative nor speculative. We must move into the 1950s for our next set of explicitly fantastic urban images. It is during this decade marked by nuclear fear and Cold War tensions, by a growing dependence upon electronic technology, by the emergence of new global information and communications systems, and by increasing consumerism and suburbanism, that the American science-fiction film coalesces as a recognized genre that, more often than not, poeticizes the city through what Susan Sontag has called the 'imagination of disaster'.[12] Two poetically powerful images reverberate through the 1950s – each spectacularly and concretely articulating a loss of faith in previous utopian and futurist visions of the modern city as the architectural and transcendent embodiment of human aspiration. Although quite differently, both address the failure of concrete verticality and 'highness' spiritually to sustain and uplift modern existence. And, as aspiration and 'highness' are lost or neutralized, so too is the sense of a future.

The first image is an angry, destructive one, and it appears in a great many films of the period – clearly generating its simple and repetitive narratives as a ritual context in which it serves as centre. The elements of the image are all the same, although their specific articulations may change. The mise-en-scene is urban and given to our sight in long shot. The city in this image is identifiable: New York, Washington DC, San Francisco. Culturally symbolic and discrete architectural features like the Statue of Liberty, the Coney Island rollercoaster, the Washington Monument, and the Golden Gate Bridge place and 'name' the urban scene and give it a specificity that makes its imminent destruction seem an immediate, contemporaneous event. Into this scene comes a destructive force which may take any of three forms: an apocalyptic natural force like a tidal wave or comet; a primal Beast or Creature; or a technologically superior alien war machine. In each instance, however, the result is the same – the razing of the city and, most particularly, the bringing low of those monuments that stand as symbols of modern civilization's aspiration and pride. In *When Worlds Collide* (1951), New York is inundated by a tidal wave and its buildings topple; in *The Beast from 20,000 Fathoms* (1953), an atomically awakened prehistoric creature stomps cars and fleeing people, smashes the New York skyline, and tangles with the Coney Island rollercoaster as it mindlessly seeks its ancient breeding ground; in *Earth vs the Flying Saucers* (1956), the sleek and quick alien craft of technologically superior extraterrestrials castrate the Washington Monument and bring the nation's capitol low.

It might seem that the affective power of this image is similar to that of primal Kong atop the Empire State Building swatting planes as if they were flies. Yet fascination with the poetry of destruction is not quite what the image of Kong is about: rather, it touches us deeply with the visible – if brief – resolution of a monumental social and psychic desire, of both the building and Kong's impossibly epic aspirations. The 1950s science-fiction image I am describing here is not about resolution, but about dissolution. Its poetic reverberations have nothing to do with aspiration and ascendancy and everything to do with, as Sontag puts it, 'the fantasy of living through one's own death and more, the death of cities, the destruction of humanity itself'.[13] Thus the failure of modern and urban civilization and its aspirations is poetically represented in appropriately monumental images which constitute an 'aesthetics of destruction' whose peculiar beauty is found in 'wreaking havoc, making a mess'.[14] The city's aspiring verticality, its lofty architecture, its positive 'highness' that thrusts civilization towards transcendence and the future is – through privileged special effects – debased and brought low, in a mise-en-scene that is bustling with contemporary activity and traffic and emphatically temporalized as 'now'.

The second image of the failure of the aspiring city is equally powerful, yet quite different – retaining the city's highness, but temporizing its value as 'past'. Here, the city's lofty architecture is not destroyed; rather, the originally positive and transcendent value of architectural 'highness' becomes dominated by the negative and nihilistic value of '*emptiness*'. Highness thus remains an ideal value but now has little to do with human beings. As Philip Strick reminds us: 'Science fiction writers like Simak, Bradbury, and Kuttner, with varying degrees of irony, have frequently recognized … the ideal city contains no citizens whatever.'[15] Again, the basic elements of this poetic response to concrete human aspiration remain the same across a variety of science-fiction elaborations. In *Five* (1951), we see two characters enter New York City – an empty concrete canyon whose walls are skyscrapers, whose floor is punctuated by static and forlorn automobiles distraughtly angled: nothing moves but the car in which they slowly ride, and a skeleton stares out at them from a window. In *On the Beach* (1959), trying to find the source of a signal from a radioactively dead USA, submarine crewmen wander about an empty San Francisco. And in *The World, the Flesh, and the Devil* (1959), the image of deadly stillness and emptiness overwhelms one with a sense of irrevocable loss as a single character roams through New York, into a vacant Times Square, down an abandoned Wall Street, around an aseptic United Nations building. Cars eternally stalled on a bridge, newspaper blowing down a city street caught up in some ill-begotten wind, street lights and neon blinking on and off in a mockery of animate existence – this is the iconography of emptiness and stillness that marks the American cinematic imagination of the post-holocaust city in the 1950s until the mid 1970s. And this imagination is nostalgic – always already fixed on an irrecoverable past rather than on a future that has not yet occurred.

One of the elements of our lived experience of the modern city is its immediate vitality: its present-tense and up-to-the-minute activity, its busyness, its people and traffic always in motion. To see the city empty and still emphasizes its concrete 'loftiness', but also temporally codes the value of such architectural aspiration as 'past'. Marking the death of the city as an actively functional structure, skyscrapers in these films stand as monumental grave-stones. Although this image of urban emptiness lingers on into the 1980s – in films like *Dawn of the Dead* (1979) and *Night of the Comet* (1984) – it appears less as this nostalgic response to the city's original loftiness and the failure of its aspiration than as a positive opportunity to dramatize the ultimate consumer fantasy of having a shopping mall all to oneself (barring a few extremist shoppers in the form of ghouls and mutants).

The destruction of the city and its symbolic architecture and the city as empty graveyard – these two powerful poetic responses to the failure of the city's aspiration (and to the failure of 'modern' civilization) mourn the out-moded value of loftiness, the ineffectual outcome of aspiration; but they still hold aspiration as a positive value and offer no alternative to its failure. Things get even worse in the 1960s and most of the 1970s. If the utopian vision of the imaginary city emphasizes concrete loftiness and spiritual fullness as positive

values, then 1950s science-fiction film kept at least one of these values operative – even if only in a literal way. That is, in those films where the city's
architecture is destroyed and brought low, its literal fullness is asserted in busy
human activity and an emphasis on the 'masses' (whether they are screaming
beneath the behemoth's scaly feet or 'cooperating' with the 'authorities'). And
in those films in which the city's utopian plenitude is challenged by its literal
emptiness, at least its concrete loftiness remains. However, from the late 1960s
to 1977 (the year that marks the release of both *Close Encounters of the Third
Kind* and *Star Wars*), the science-fiction city poeticized neither highness nor
fullness as positive values. Rather, both were imagined negatively – and turned
in on themselves to become *lowering oppressiveness* and *overcrowdedness*. Indeed, if
the utopian science-fiction city is perceived as *aspiring*, then the science-fiction
city during this period is dystopian and perceived as *asphyxiating*.

Pointing to the despair of a country involved in both domestic and international contestation, Joan Dean describes the science-fiction films of the late
1960s and most of the 1970s as articulating a 'diminishing fear of nuclear
apocalypse' and 'a growing concern with domestic, terrestrial issues – most of
which are related to totalitarian government control of people's lives or overpopulation, food shortages, pollution, and ecology'. Indeed, the 'single theme'
that 'dominated the science-fiction imagination between 1970 and 1977 was
overpopulation and its concomitant problems of food shortage and old age'.[16]
The image of the city that generates science-fiction film narratives of this
period emerges most forcefully in *Soylent Green* (1973), which visualizes a New
York City that no longer aspires but suffocates and expires. Emphasis is not
on the height of buildings but on their baseness. Verticality is no longer significant – and the city's horizontal dimension stresses its limitations, not its openness. In 2022, New York is not seen in its positive fullness. Rather, it is
impossibly overcrowded: its population is forty million. People overflow the
streets and most live and huddle in dark masses and clots on the sidewalks, in
the alleys, and stairwells of buildings that all look like slum tenements. Their
whispering and overlapping cries and coughs and sobs sound like the sighing

of some desolate wind. This New York City has no monumental centre, no moral centre. Indeed, it is all corrupted and base, all suddenly inner city. The mise-en-scene is dark, claustrophobic, polluted and dirty; as Robert Cumbow points out, in 'its crumbling buildings and rotting cars were the beginnings of … junkyard futurism'.[17] But this is a futurist image that imagines no future. This New York is literally a *concentration* camp, and the temporality its constraining spaces construct cannot stretch and stream forward, has nothing to do with positive notions of spatial progression or expansion. All is decay and entropy. In the late 1960s to the mid 1970s, the science-fiction city has no positive values to sustain it – and so it falls down and apart. Indeed, many of the period's films – from *Planet of the Apes* (1968) to *Logan's Run* (1978) – imagine cities such as New York and Washington DC in a fantasy of 'the body in pieces', monuments and buildings now fragments strewn on an abandoned landscape on a radically altered planet. The aspiring city, once the centre and architectural symbol of civilization, has fallen in ruins, is no longer functional, no longer the centre of civilized human activity.

By the 1980s, the idealized and lofty science-fiction city is imagined as completely decentred and marginalized. The citizens of dominant bourgeois culture are either 'offworld' in outer space or in the suburbs.[18] In 1977, with *Star Wars* and *Close Encounters*, George Lucas and Steven Spielberg provided the mainstream and nostalgic routes by which to *Escape From New York* – the entire city in that 1981 film imagined literally as a prison. *Star Wars* and *Close Encounters* rally a cinematic exodus from the constraints, pollution and crime of the failed city – and those who leave are all those upstanding and economically franchised folks who believed (and rightly so) that the 'Force' was with them, or (wrongly so) that 'when you wish upon a star, it makes no difference who you are'. What results from this mass bourgeois abandonment of the city, however, is a peculiar and hallucinatory screen liberation for those 'others' left behind. They are the dregs of bourgeois society: punks, winos, crazies, gays, druggies, Blacks, Latinos, new Asians, the homeless, the hipsters, the poor – in sum, everyone previously marginalized and disenfranchised in bourgeois urban culture. Let loose and left to their own devices in a city which now has no centre and no constraints, which has been 'junked' rather than urbanly 'renewed', this newly dominant and diverse population energizes and reformulates the negative and nihilistic urban values of the 1960s and 1970s as sublimely positive. In a complete reversal, the imaginary science-fiction city's lowness, baseness, horizontality; its overcrowdedness, overpopulatedness and overstuffedness, are celebrated and aestheticized. That is, the old imaginary and centred science-fiction metropolis is totally resigned to its ruination, its displacement to its own edges, its concrete transformation from city as centre to city as inner, from aspiring city to city dump. But this total and concrete resignation to the city's debasement results in a positive symbolic re-signing. The junkyard, the dump, the trashy edges of town are culturally reinscribed as a novel and exotic urban space that eroticizes and fetishizes material culture, that is valued for its marvellously unselective acquisitive power, its expansive capacity to accumulate, consume and contain 'things', *any*thing, and its existential status as irrefutable testimony to the success of material production. The omnipresence of waste serves as a sign that the digestive tract of advanced capital's body politic must still be working, indeed working 'overtime' and at full capacity. The city is thus re-energized – finding both a new function and a new aesthetic. It is imagined explicitly as the most monumental and concrete *consumer* and, with its unselective juxtapositions and conservation of material artefacts, as the most eclectic 'pop' *collector*. Fredric Jameson writes of this re-signed city:

> The exhilaration of these new surfaces is … paradoxical in that their essential content – the city itself – has deteriorated or disintegrated to a degree surely still inconceivable in the early years of the 20th century.… How urban squalor can be a delight to the eyes, when expressed in commodification, and how an unparalleled quantum leap in the alienation of daily life in the city can now be experienced in the form of a strange new hallucinatory exhilaration – these are some of the questions that confront us.[19]

Within the context of this new urban exoticism and its erotics of commodification and consumerism, two new images of the science-fiction city emerge. And, given that the postmodernist city is experienced as having no centre –

being all centre or decentred, dispersing its activities in every direction – it is hardly surprising that the site of both of them is Los Angeles. The first and most aestheticized comes, of course, from *Blade Runner* (1982). Its Los Angeles of 2019 is a crowded and polyglot megalopolis filled with a multinational and marginal populace, additive architecture, sensuous 'clutter', and highly atmospheric pollution. This is a city experienced less as base and degraded than as dense, complex and heterogeneous: it stimulates and exhausts the eyes, for there is always – literally – more to see. (Indeed, the eye is a crucial narrative motif.) This imaginary Los Angeles is concretely constructed from 'layers of texture':

> visual information is imparted in every square inch of screen. Details proliferate. The umbrellas carried by extras have lighted tips because the streets are so murky. The television monitors that have replaced traffic signals provide deliberately poor pictures. Skyscrapers are built on top of existing structures – and are shown ... in their hundreds of stories.[20]

Despite the skyscrapers, the visual experience of this Los Angeles has little to do with verticality and lofty aspiration. Rather, the trajectory of our attention tends to stay grounded – fascinated by the city's retrofitted transformation of its ruins, its 'spaces and objects whose original purpose has been lost, due not to obsolescence but rather to an overinvestment brought about by constant recycling'.[21] It is not surprising that industrial pipes and ducts figure prominently in the mise-en-scene (as they would even more explicitly in 1985's *Brazil*). This Los Angeles is literally exhausted – generating that strange blend of hysteria and euphoria that comes with utter fatigue.

The emphasis of the second science-fiction image of Los Angeles is less on design than on random, discontinuous and dispersed movement. It seems no accident that the company that made *Repo Man* (1984) refers to itself as Edge City Productions. The Los Angeles of *Blade Runner* is decentred by being all centre, whereas the Los Angeles of *Repo Man* is centred by being all margin. The Los Angeles of *Blade Runner* unifies its outmoded and vastly disparate material signifiers into new 'retrofitted' and eroticized architectural forms, whereas the Edge City of *Repo Man* celebrates convulsive spatial discontinuities in a constantly moving culture: its mise-en-scene is not cluttered, merely littered (occasional newspapers, strange people, garbage, drunks, dead derelicts and abandoned sofas punctuating otherwise empty and unwalked streets). Indeed, in *Repo Man* the city is perceived as a set of discrete and unconnected spatial rather than architectural fragments – framed by the windscreen of a moving car that, in this city of repossessions, is always changing hands and drivers and points of view.

This is the city in a schizophrenic representation – 'reduced to an experience of pure *material* Signifiers, ... of a series of pure and *unrelated presents* in time'.[22] The city does not cohere, has no causal logic to unify it. Discussing Los Angeles as the 'automobile city', Yi-Fu Tuan points out: 'Driving on a freeway can be disorienting. A sign, for example, may direct one to the far left lane for an objective that is clearly visible to the right.'[23] But repo men find sublime pleasure in these discontinuities, automotively 'troping' the city's streets and freeways – that is, rhetorically swerving from expected trajectories to create new relations of meaning, or, as the film's philosopher Miller would say, new 'lattices of coincidence'. The Los Angeles of *Repo Man* is a city whose spatiality is not bound by architecture but rather by trajectories of movement which, no matter how seemingly random, will – like the freeway system – eventually intersect. Thus, no matter how they disperse themselves, repo men, vicious LA punks, a nuclear physicist, a pair of car thieves, and a Chevy Malibu with a trunk full of extraterrestrial weaponry keep meeting up again. Whereas in *Blade Runner* the pastiche of new and old genres, recycled aesthetic styles, and eclectic material objects constituted Los Angeles' temporal mode as literal and increasingly *collective present*, *Repo Man*'s Edge City is temporally encoded as an eternally *recurrent present*.

Thus the science-fiction city of the 1980s, while not mourning the failed aspirations of its past, was not really capable of envisioning its future but, rather, was euphorically lost in erotic play with its material present. The imaginary Los Angeles of *Blade Runner* and *Repo Man*, the New York of *Liquid*

Sky (1983), only dream their complete reversal of bourgeois utopian values, only hallucinate their liberation from the bourgeoisie who have gone off to live in Spielberg films or gone *Back to the Future* (1985). These cities, in visible fact, eroticize consumption and fetishize material culture in scenographic paeans to advanced capitalism. And, while these cities celebrate their counter-cultural funkiness, their heterogeneity, horizontality and cultural levelling, their alienated terrestrials and terrestrialized aliens whose differences supposedly make no difference in this dispersed and marginalized culture (1984's *Moscow on the Hudson* and *Brother from Another Planet* are, after all, the same movie), they function as virtual ghettoes – or, wishing upon that bourgeois star, effectively efface those differences that *do* make a difference who you are. Positing, on the one hand, a new and liberating model of the city and, on the other, buying back into its failed model by merely reversing (rather than altering) its terms and values, the imaginary postmodernist science-fiction film city of the 1980s is truly a city on the edge, offering us a hallucinatory future we might want to visit, but a present in which – unless we just happen to be bourgeois cinema-goers and 'slumming' – we would not want to live.

Indeed, if the urban mise-en-scene of the 1980s science-fiction film is both intensified and compacted as all 'inner' city, and diffused and dispersed as all 'marginal' city, future urban experience would hardly appear to accommodate normative 'middle-class' life at all. Thus, looking at the 1990s, we might ask whether (and, if so, in what manner) the bourgeois cinematic imagination has effected some form of 'urban renewal'? What can the imagination construct in or beyond a city 'on the edge'? In the last decade of the twentieth century, the cinematic response to these questions has been cities imagined spatially (and tonally) in an urban experience of going 'over the top' or plunging 'over the edge'. That is, although manifest in two quite different modes, the current science-fiction film city has been figured as *groundless*, lacking both logically secure and spatially stable premises for its – and our – existence. This is a city virtually 'bottomed out' and literally fathomless: its inhabitants suffer from giddiness or vertigo and, rootless, they 'free fall' in both space and time.

One contemporary mode of imagining this groundless or bottomed-out city is so cinematically reflexive as to be comic or 'safe' – and thus without much consequence or poetic resonance. This mode returns us in a fashion to 1950s science fiction: to the image of the city brought low, its identifiable architecture destroyed by catastrophic 'natural' disaster or 'alien' attack. Nevertheless, while *Independence Day* and *Mars Attacks!* (both 1996), *Godzilla*, *Deep Impact* and *Armageddon* (all 1998) draw upon older science-fiction movie tropes, they seem themselves temporally rootless and spatially disaffected.

In *Independence Day*, alien flying saucers blow up the White House and the Empire State Building, visibly reducing the USA's major cities to rubble. Nonetheless, while there is panic in the streets, there is no Cold War fear and anxiety here to inform and historically ground it – merely cinematic nostalgia and the imperatives of the latest special effects. And, while one might want to link the urban destruction in *Independence Day* and the films that follow it with recent and explosive acts of urban terrorism in New York and Oklahoma City, there seems to be no human affect or real consequence attached to it. The cities in these films appear to have little meaning; they seem hardly to matter at all. As Roger Ebert notes of *Independence Day*: 'The news comes that New York, Washington and Los Angeles have been destroyed, and is there grief? Anguish? … Not a bit.'[24] Indeed, in the comedy *Mars Attacks!*, manic Martians decimate not only Washington but also Las Vegas in what is less an apocalypse than a wacky celebration. In *Godzilla*, taking on the functions of nearly every 1950s city-stomping giant reptile or insect, Godzilla tromps Manhattan – but lacks the affect generated by Atomic Age anxieties about nuclear annihilation, mutation, and a return to the world as 'primal sink'. And, in both *Deep Impact* and *Armageddon*, in which meteors and asteroids threaten Earth and tidal waves and flames engulf the urban cityscape, the cultural stakes seem remarkably low. What these films have in common (besides a penchant for decapitating the Art-Deco Chrysler Building) is an astonishing – and itself historical – lack of care. Their cities, however familiar, are not 'grounded' or substantial: they seem to exist only for destruction.

Reviewing *Mars Attacks!*, Jonathan Rosenbaum might well be summarizing this mode of urban imagination when he writes of a

> postmodernist free fall through the iconography of 50s and 60s science-fiction in rela-
> tion to the present: a singular sense of giddy displacement that clearly locates the movie
> in the 90s, but a 90s largely made up of images and clichés from previous decades that
> are subtly turned against themselves, made into a form of camp, affectionately mocked,
> yet still revered as if they had a particular purchase on the truth.[25]

There is, however, a second and more affectively engaged mode of imagining the science-fiction city in the 1990s. This urban imagination borrows heavily from the film noir roots and urban mise-en-scene of *Blade Runner*, but its poetic resonance is less eroticized and much bleaker; and, in at least one of its latest expressions, *Dark City* (1998), the entire narrative explicitly foregrounds and visually concretizes the rootless, vertiginous and insecure sense that the city is groundless in both time and place. The cinematic experience of this city is not of the free fall or giddy displacement of going 'over the top', of campy exaggeration or nostalgic pastiche. No longer merely '*on* the edge', this urban imagery takes us literally '*over* the edge'. The city's inhabitants (if, indeed, they still can be called such) are increasingly dislocated in space – and, dislocated, their very identities shift and become displaced and ungrounded. Thus, it is not coincidental that this mode of urban science-fiction film is as concerned with time and memory as it is with space and place. Its correlations between the ungrounding of urban space and the ungrounding of identity begin with *Blade Runner* and are followed by *The Terminator* (1984), *Robocop* (1987), *Total Recall* (1990), and more recently by *Strange Days* (1995) and *Twelve Monkeys* (1996). In these films, we see the city of the future as what Roger Ebert has succinctly described as 'a grunge pit'.[26] The word 'pit' here is telling.

Increasingly, urban science-fiction space seems not only grungy but also bottomless and, in various ways, unfathomable. In the mid twenty-third century New York of *The Fifth Element* (1997), for example, the protagonist is literally located in mid-air: he is a cab driver in a vehicle vulnerable from above and below (the heroine, leaping from a building whose top and bottom recede into invisibility, falls through the roof into his back seat; later, he is chased by vehicles beneath him). Radically different from the ordered urban airways envisioned by both *Metropolis* and *Just Imagine*, this city is a dizzying and densely layered labyrinth of architecture and motion: it has neither skyscrapers (there is no visible sky as such) nor ground. This is a city that seems to have no boundaries and yet, at the same time, is peculiarly hermetic.[27]

These unstable, boundless, and yet hermetic qualities become the very stuff of narrative in the aptly named *Dark City*. Through the use of digital morphing and warping, the very ground of urban and cinematic space and time is destabilized by digital effects and the effects of the digital. Both literally and metaphorically, the city's premisses no longer hold. *Dark City* is some perpetually nocturnal and hermetic metropolis that combines the urban visions of German Expressionism, Edward Hopper and film noir; and its human inhabitants never seem to know where they are, where they are going, or how to get anywhere. The film's alien 'Strangers' are responsible: they literally and metaphorically keep both the city and its inhabitants 'in the dark'. Furthermore each midnight, through a communal act of will, they literally warp, expand, shrink, and shift buildings and streets to transform the entire cityscape architecturally and spatially – which is nonetheless bounded as a finite and hermetic world. Correlatively, in secret experiments, the Strangers also literally re-member and relocate the memories of the city's inhabitants. There is nothing in this city, then, that holds or is stable – except for a recurrent, if also suspect, postcard-like image of a 'perfect' (and decidedly non-urban) seaside town.

Ultimately, Shell Beach in *Dark City* is a postcard construction of the protagonist's wish and will – as unstable and hermetic as the city he escapes. It is at this point that the contemporary science-fiction film departs from the unfathomable and ungrounded experience of urban life. But where cinematically does it go? Most recently, it has fled – in full awareness of its own desires and devices – to the allied genre of fantasy where variations on the Edenic small-town alternative to the groundless city only 'appear' more hospitable to human existence. In recent paranoid fantasies such as *The Truman Show* or

Pleasantville (both 1998), the small town offers no satisfactory escape from science fiction's urban nightmares. Indeed, it offers merely a sunnier imagination of inhospitable space – replacing the science-fiction film city's incoherence with an utterly scripted order, and containing its dizzying boundlessness in the small and hermetic frame of a television set.

NOTES

1. This chapter is revised and expanded from its initial publication in *East–West Film Journal*, vol. 3, no. 1, 1988, pp. 4–19.
2. Since there have been many debates surrounding the concept and definition of 'postmodernism', for the purposes of this essay I refer the reader to Fredric Jameson, 'Postmodernism or The Cultural Logic of Late Capitalism,' *New Left Review*, no. 146, 1984, pp. 53–94; and to my use of Jameson's work in *Screening Space: The American Science Fiction Film*, New Brunswick, NJ: Rutgers University Press, 1997, ch. 4.
3. 'Forward', *Zone*, nos 1/2, 1987, p. 11.
4. Gaston Bachelard, *The Poetics of Space*, trans. Maria Jolas, Boston, MA: Beacon Press, 1964, p. xix.
5. On this issue, see the chapter on 'Figuration' in Dudley Andrew, *Concepts in Film Theory*, New York: Oxford University Press, 1984.
6. Bachelard, *The Poetics of Space*, p. xv.
7. Michael Webb, 'The City in Film', *Design Quarterly*, no. 136, 1987, p. 9. Reading Lang's description of New York, one is reminded more of *Blade Runner*'s imaginative science-fiction cityscape than of any other – including Lang's own *Metropolis*.
8. Ibid., p. 8.
9. John Brosnan, *Future Tense: The Cinema of Science Fiction*, New York: St. Martin's Press, 1978, p. 48.
10. Ibid., p. 47. See also Webb's description of the building's 'phallic crown, designed as a mooring for dirigibles' ('The City in Film', p. 11).
11. Yi-Fu Tuan, *Topophilia: A Study of Environmental Perception, Attitudes and Values*, Englewood Cliffs, NJ: Prentice-Hall, 1974, p. 28.
12. Susan Sontag, 'The Imagination of Disaster', *Commentary*, October 1965, pp. 42–8.
13. Ibid., p. 44.
14. Ibid.
15. Philip Strick, 'Metropolis Wars: The City as Character in Science Fiction Films', in Danny Peary, ed., *Omni's Screen Flights/Screen Fantasies: The Future According to Science Fiction Cinema*, Garden City, NY: Dolphin/Doubleday, 1984, p. 47.

16. Joan F. Dean, 'Between *2001* and *Star Wars*', *Journal of Popular Film and Television*, vol. 7, no. 1, 1978, pp. 36–7.

17. Robert Cumbow, 'Survivors: The Day After Doomsday', in Peary, ed., *Omni's Screen Flights/Screen Fantasies*, p. 41.

18. In relation to Steven Spielberg's oeuvre, see Yi-Fu Tuan's discussion of suburban values and ideals in *Topophilia*, pp. 236–40.

19. Jameson, 'Postmodernism', p. 76.

20. Bart Mills, 'The Brave New World of Production Design', *American Film,* vol. 7, no. 4, 1982, p. 45.

21. Eric Alliez and Michel Feher, 'Notes on the Sophisticated City', *Zone*, nos. 1/2, 1987, p. 44.

22. Jameson, 'Postmodernism', p. 72. Emphasis added.

23. Tuan, *Topophilia*, p. 190.

24. Roger Ebert, *Chicago Sun-Times* (online), n.d.

25. Jonathan Rosenbaum, *Chicago Reader* (online), n.d.

26. Roger Ebert, *Chicago-Sun Times*, 5 January 1996.

27. This image of the city to some degree draws upon contemporary Japanese *anime* and postmodern comics, but it also recalls a singular image from 1950s science-fiction film: namely, the Krel city revealed in *Forbidden Planet* (1956). However, unlike the contemporary vision, and more in keeping with urban themes of its own period, that city was shown as empty and signified the hubris of technological aspiration.

PART III

CORPOREAL SPACES

INTRODUCTION

Because the virtual places of science fiction seem to invite comparison with the 'real' world, social commentary and ideological analysis constitute significant features of science-fiction criticism. Ideological criticism, which came to prominence as an offshoot of structuralist and semiotic film theory, has consequently been deployed primarily and most systematically in relation to cinematic science fiction. With its emphasis on the production and circulation of social meanings through cinema's processes of signification, ideological film criticism's key *topos* is the nature of the relationship between representations and the real world of which they are part. This relationship assumes special significance with regard to cinema, because film appears to possess a peculiar capacity to present itself as uncoded, as transparent in its (re)presentation of the 'real world'.

While ideological criticism would reject any simplistic notion that films mirror reality, it is materialist to the degree that it assumes a relationship of some sort between cultural texts and the 'real' world: the relationship posited, however, is one of mediation, overdetermination, even of contradiction. Ideological criticism aims to expose, and so make available for critique and transformation, the relations of power embedded within the ideological workings of cultural texts. The object of analysis here, then, is the text itself; and the method is textual interpretation. Hence ideological film analysis is characterized by a detailed attention to the internal workings of film texts: not only, nor even predominantly, the overt contents of films but rather formal signifying processes whose operations and effectivities might not even be visible on the surface of the film.[1] If ideological film analysis is political, or at least cultural-political, in its purpose, its most significant political motivator has arguably been feminism. Feminist ideological criticism aims to lay bare the workings of patriarchal ideology in and through cultural texts in general, and films in particular.

Cultural studies, with its attention to questions of hegemony and popular culture, shares a cultural-political agenda with ideological film criticism, though the two differ in their objects and methods of analysis. For example, cultural studies tends to concern itself with the uses consumers make of popular cultural texts rather than with these texts' internal ideological workings, and has been less interested in cinema than in other popular media forms. Nonetheless, some recent feminist scholarship has attempted to combine the approaches of cultural studies and ideological film analysis. This move has proved especially productive in readings of cultural texts which explore overt and subtextual themes and images relating to gender and sexual difference as these are produced through figurations of the body.[2]

In 'Action Bodies in Futurist Spaces: Bodybuilder Stardom as Special Effect', Linda Mizejewski takes up this strand of feminist cultural criticism and extends it into analysis of the cultural meanings of the 'built' male body in cinema. She looks at these meanings in relation both to stardom (an institutional feature of cinema) and to textual markers, such as iconographies and special effects, peculiar to science-fiction films. Stardom, special effects and science-fiction iconographies are condensed in a recurrent figure in recent science-fiction/action cinema: the cyborg, invincible armoured hybrid of man and machine associated with performances by male bodybuilt stars such as Arnold Schwarzenegger and Jean-Claude Van Damme. With the assistance of cinematic special effects technologies, these performances push the 'impossible' and 'unnatural' to the limit, argues Mizejewski:

> The contended boundaries between technology and the body, nature and artifice – the oldest themes of science fiction – are … repositioned through the ambiguous status of the bodybuilder star, who is both natural and unnatural, biological and constructed.

All the films Mizejewski discusses combine generic features of science fiction with those of another genre, the action movie; and it may be of some cultural significance that Catherine Constable's 'Becoming the Monster's Mother: Morphologies of Identity in the *Alien* Series' also deals with a generic hybrid – here the science-fiction/horror film, specifically *Alien* and its sequels. With their reiterated thematics of procreation, birth and maternity and their enduring female superhero, the films in the *Alien* series have attracted considerable attention from feminist film scholars and cultural critics.[3] Constable pursues the feminist debate and, through analyses of *Alien* and its three sequels to date, challenges and extends Barbara Creed's Kristevan readings of the original film.[4] Drawing on current feminist philosophical debates around embodiment, Constable argues that all the *Alien* films – and the recent *Alien Resurrection* in particular – posit a dissolution of bodily boundaries between human and alien in images which render corporeal permeability fully visible. If Mizejewski's bodies are hard and machine-like, Constable's are soft and leaky: but both forms of cultural embodiment arguably express, at the levels of both story and spectacle, primal desires and fears concerning bodily separation and merging.

In 'Psycho-cybernetics in Films of the 1990s', Claudia Springer looks at another science-fiction hybrid, the 'cyberthriller', which, she says, narrativizes a desire to escape the body and be free of corporeal imprisonment and the fractured instability of a subjectivity confined by the skin. In cyberthrillers like *Johnny Mnemonic*, cyberspace figures at the levels of narrative and spectacle as metaphor for a merging of body, mind and machine. *Pace* Donna Haraway,[5] Springer contends that 'Human beings and their technologies become increasingly indistinguishable'; and argues that the cyberthriller posits the merging of body, mind and machine as potentially healing and redemptive.

In cyberthrillers, much like the 'cities on the edge of time' discussed by Vivian Sobchack in Part II, cyberspace figures as visible, sensuous space: as both mise-en-scene for narrative action and virtual space entered and experienced by the spectator. The cyberthriller's cyberspace is singular, however, in that entry into and exit from it constitute at one and the same moment a key narrative move and a particular kinetic experience for the spectator. Specifically, in an enactment of the mobilized and virtual gaze[6] which recalls the celebrated Stargate sequence in *2001: A Space Odyssey*, the activity of 'diving into cyberspace' is rendered visible, audible and sensuous. Cyberspace thus figures as a place, a setting for narratives of embodiment and disembodiment on the part of characters in the film. But also, and in many ways more importantly, cyberspace works like the 'cinema of attractions' of the earliest days of the medium: it seizes the spectator's body in shocks, sensuous experiences which may well begin, but certainly do not end, with vision: experiences, in other words, which render the gaze fully corporeal.

NOTES

1. For more detailed discussion of ideological film analysis, see Annette Kuhn, ed., *Alien Zone: Cultural Theory and Contemporary Science Fiction Cinema*, London: Verso, 1990, pp. 53–7; and for examples of ideological criticism of science-fiction films, see ibid., chs 4 to 7.
2. See, for example, Yvonne Tasker, *Spectacular Bodies: Gender, Genre, and the Action Cinema*, London: Routledge, 1993; Chris Holmlund, 'Masculinity as Multiple Masquerade: The "Mature" Stallone and the Stallone Clone', in Steven Cohan and Ina Rae Hark, eds, *Screening the Male: Exploring Masculinities in Hollywood Cinema*, New York: Routledge, 1993.
3. See, for example, Kuhn, ed., *Alien Zone*, chs 6, 7, 11 and 17. On science-fiction cinema and genre hybridity, see Barry Keith Grant, '"Sensuous Elaboration": Reason and the Visible in the Science-Fiction Film', in this volume. In 'Internet Fandom and the Continuing Narratives of *Star Wars*, *Blade Runner* and *Alien*', also in this volume, Will Brooker notes that *Alien* fans, unlike those of *Blade Runner*, made no reference to scholarly work on the film: could this be because scholarly writing on *Alien* is motivated more by feminist interest in this particular film and its sequels than by an interest in science-fiction cinema?

4. Barbara Creed, '*Alien* and the Monstrous-Feminine', *Screen*, vol. 27, no. 1, 1986; 'From Here to Modernity: Feminism and Postmodernism', *Screen*, vol. 28, no. 2, 1987.

5. Donna Haraway, 'A Manifesto for Cyborgs: Science, Technology and Socialist Feminism in the 1980s', *Socialist Review*, no. 80, 1985.

6. See Anne Friedberg, *Window Shopping: Cinema and the Postmodern*, Berkeley: University of California Press, 1993, ch. 1.

7

ACTION BODIES IN FUTURIST SPACES: BODYBUILDER STARDOM AS SPECIAL EFFECT

LINDA MIZEJEWSKI

In Marco Brambilla's futuristic 1993 film *Demolition Man*, the LA cop hero, played by Sylvester Stallone, is deep frozen in the 1990s and defrosted in the year 2032 to learn that, through a special amendment to the Constitution, Arnold Schwarzenegger has been elected president. 'Wasn't he an actor once?' his perky young colleague asks. In light of Schwarzenegger's real-life campaigns for health and fitness, the joke in *Demolition Man* is his association with a distinctly 'unnatural' future in which the government tampers with biology, gender and sexuality. Dense with references to *Total Recall* (Paul Verhoeven, 1990) and both *Terminator* films (James Cameron, 1984 and 1991) – that is, to Schwarzenegger's most prestigious science-fiction roles – *Demolition Man* wittily posits The Arnold as one of the bad political choices of the nightmarish coming century, but also hints at the ambivalences of his stardom and its resonances in camp humour.

Schwarzenegger may inhabit the White House only in science-fiction cinema, but his habitation of the latter has prompted a great deal of critical attention to his status as political body and icon. Given his real-life Republicanism and godlike poses in popular iconographies, Schwarzennegger has been identified by cinema scholars and cultural critics as embodying meanings ranging from nationalism to fascism, and from hypermasculinity to failed paternity and queer eroticism.[1] *Demolition Man*, on the other hand, features Stallone as a less ambiguous star whose muscular iconography represents traditional masculinity in a feminine-fascist future.[2] Doubling its bulked-up super-bodies, this film also stars Wesley Snipes as the grand, formidable villain; so the bodybuilder hero's racial identity and its continuities in future worlds spring to comic-book life.

The action hero is in fact a target of self-referential humour in *Demolition Man*, which both satirizes and replicates 1980s/1990s mega-action, mega-special-effect science-fiction films. While their camp values are less semiotically loaded than Schwarzenegger's, Stallone and Snipes deliver good-natured self-parodies. The film was marketed, however, as action-adventure rather than spoof: designed by David L. Snyder of *Blade Runner* fame (Ridley Scott, 1982) and produced by Joel Silver of the *Lethal Weapon* series (Richard Donner, 1987, 1989, 1992), it smoothly offers the virtuosity and pleasures of high-tech science-fiction action cinema, making it an appropriate point of entry for my discussion of this hybrid genre. Likewise, Schwarzenegger's role in both these cultural sites – bodybuilding and science-fiction – serves not as my primary topic but as an example of my question: why and how has the male super-body figured in the futuristic cinematic genre which reimagines and transforms the body and its genders?

In a 1993 essay about *Total Recall*, I noted that the postmodern dissolutions and decentrings of identity and narrative in that film are strikingly at odds with its masculinist concerns for the coherent male body of action cinema.[3] However, this reading may be extended in several directions. First, my question about Schwarzenegger in *Total Recall* is repositioned as one concerning the male bodybuilt star in relationship to science-fiction cinema's special effects. In both the film genre and in bodybuilder performance, 'the impossible' and 'the unnatural' are visualized and pushed to their limits. Cinematic technology further fictionalizes the capacities and strength of the star body by enabling ever more impossible stunts and feats. The contended boundaries between technology and the body, nature and artifice – the oldest themes of science fiction – are thus repositioned through the ambiguous status of the bodybuilder star, who is both natural and unnatural, biological and constructed. The roles of Schwarzenegger in *Total Recall*, Stallone and Snipes in *Demolition Man*, and Jean-Claude Van Damme in *Timecop* (Peter Hyams, 1994) are my test cases for reconsidering science fiction around issues of stardom and physical performance, and their impact on narrative. In each case, racial identification emerges as a key ideological issue through which traditional masculinity is measured and tested. In this sense, my questions focus on a specific genre to amplify current feminist criticism describing 'spectacular' cinematic tough guys as articulations of crises around masculinity in culture.[4]

My aim is to connect the biological/constructed status of the male bodybuilder with the ambiguous politics of these films, notably the ways in which they shirk questions of ideology through recourse to 'the natural'. Critical attention has focused mainly on the myriad meanings of the Schwarzenegger body in *Total Recall* and the *Terminator* texts and on the related political incoherencies of these texts, which bundle together progressive and conservative fantasies and trajectories, or render these political positions as empty categories. On the one hand, masculinity as a traditional, coherent entity – specifically, as white, aggressive, heterosexual – persists in the images and trajectories of these films, as well as in *Timecop* and *Demolition Man*. On the other hand, the very fact of its persistence is a clue to its nervous self-consciousness: while all three films suggest the instabilities of this invincible male self, *Demolition Man* most blatantly (and comically) suggests its precariousness as a posture or fiction. Masculinity itself is at stake ultimately as a special effect. My concluding questions, then, concern the latent campness of science-fiction cinema preoccupied with questions of the male body and nature, beginning with James Whale's *Frankenstein* (1931) and *Bride of Frankenstein* (1935), both of them early film visualizations of a 'special' body and its excessive meanings.

The hero of *Total Recall*, construction worker Douglas Quaid (Arnold Schwarzenegger) begins his adventure – or psychosis – at Rekall, Inc., a memory-implantation business where a person can buy recollections of a remarkable or adventurous vacation, even another identity for the trip. The Rekall sales clerk suggests that all vacations are tediously alike because 'no matter where you go, there you are'. In a sense, this comment sums up how Schwarzenegger's coding as star operates in any film: no matter what the narrative, there it is – the spectacle of the incredible body that calls attention to itself. In an interview, the director of *Total Recall* has commented on the cause-and-effect relationship of the film's narrative and the Schwarzenegger body. 'He has this kind of physique that is bigger than life, isn't it?' said Verhoeven, explaining that, after the casting, 'we had to rewrite the script completely'.[5] This is a clue about the contradiction between *Total Recall*'s postmodern concept of character and its far more traditional, coherent characterization coded by the Schwarzenegger body itself.

In the course of this film, Quaid faces a video image of his body in a previous identity, utilizes a hologram body that can be riddled with bullets for a fake death, and passes through a detector screen that projects his body as skeleton. In addition to these tactics that foreground the question of the body itself – how it is represented, where it is located, how it materializes – the film's narrative revolves around the question of who in fact is inside this body, which is actually that of the double character Houser/Quaid as played by Schwarzenegger. The adventure/schizophrenia is made possible by Rekall's futuristic memory-reprogramming technology, which creates virtually 'new' subjects inside the same physique. As Robert Miklitsch points out, this technology slyly alludes to and reifies the technology of cinema itself, and the power of cinematic fantasy.[6] Thus the plotline, already haunted by the double status of hero and villain in the same body, may also be a understood as a vivid Hollywood dream about its own medium. In the interview in which he discusses the certainties or determining effects of casting Schwarzenegger, Paul Verhoeven describes the doubleness of the adventure/dream as the use of 'the principle of uncertainty, Heisenberg's principle.… That means, of course, that there are different realities possible at the same moment. What I wanted to do in *Total Recall* is to do a movie where both levels are true.'[7]

Such self-reflexive, postmodern strategies of narrative and character typically challenge and decentre concepts of the self: what, after all, constitutes the
subject if its ways of knowing, its stories, its fantasies and desires, do not
match or are not aligned with a knowable body, mind, gender? Yet this crisis
– or positing – of a postmodern subject which should take us 'beyond gender'
is reconstituted in *Total Recall* precisely as a gender-related crisis: specifically,
around the anatomy of the male body and the threat of its dissolution into the
feminized and the maternal. While classic notions of narrative and character
are questioned and even foregrounded as illusion in this film, the text repeatedly valorizes and posits as triumphant a particular male body as an essentially
autonomous and unified entity despite its constant encounters with its own
ghostly, feminine, maternal, treacherous Others.

The Schwarzenegger physique operates as one of the film's iconographic
features: moreover, as a construct of bodybuilding technologies, it can be
understood as a special effect, 'bigger than life', as startling as the film's hologram battle-scene or its wall-size television set. In its massive imperishability,
the Schwarzenegger body survives whole and sound despite being punched,
mauled, crunched, stabbed, shot, thrown, or kicked in every key scene. These
physical blows include punches and kicks to the crotch, with the double implication that the masculinity of this body is as indestructible as its triceps or
biceps. Because Quaid/Houser has been programmed with a microchip implant, cyborg-style, Claudia Springer aligns this body and character with the
'invincible armored cyborgs' evident in the *Terminator* films as well as in *RoboCop*
(Verhoeven, 1987) and *RoboCop 2* (Irvin Kershner, 1990). In *Total Recall*, she
says, the hero's fragmented 'psychological instability has no visual signifier; he
is undeniably present and solid as a rock as played by Arnold Schwarzenegger'.[8]

While the Schwarzenegger physique is indeed a constant signifier in *Total
Recall*, the film renders visual representations of the split subject by means of
two special effects that are remarkable for their relationship to the star physique.
They not only produce two amazing illusions and spectacles but also serve to
emphasize the specialness of the massive/masculine/muscular Schwarzenegger

body as another, parallel amazing spectacle, 'solid as a rock'. These special effects are the female cyborg and the stunning 'interior' scene of 'recall' which takes us into Quaid's memory.

The female cyborg is a high-tech version of a very old 'special effect' – cross-dressing – and it occurs when Quaid hides inside a female robotic form in order to get through passport control on Mars.[9] At the crucial moment of 'passing', the shell or disguise inexplicably begins to malfunction and then explodes, revealing Quaid inside, and suggesting that the huge Schwarzenegger body simply cannot be contained by the feminine masquerade. The visual dynamics also clearly represent the male giving birth to himself through the machine of his own construction – certainly a metonymic reference to Schwarzenegger's real-life bodybuilding.

The storyline reinforces this trajectory of male birth, for 'Quaid' is himself a construct of the evil colonial agency: in a later scene, Quaid actually comes face to face with a videotape of his 'parents': the agency chief Cohaagen and Quaid's former self, Houser. Thus the postmodern strategy here, the play with split subjectivity or the multiply constructed self, is a particularly masculinist one, envisioning self-creation as the male-constructed self. The play of identity and fictionality is suspiciously linked to the video image of two male parents smiling back at their son. The absence of the mother is openly flaunted in this scene. When told there is someone (his 'real' or former self) who wants to meet him, Quaid says sarcastically, 'Who is it this time? My mother?'

Curiously enough, had this narrative followed the Oedipal path it originally invokes – the man in search of who he has been – the key identification would indeed be recognition of the mother: the ultimate 'recall' would acknowledge the mother's body. 'Total recall' would be nothing less than the emergence of the entire subconscious, the acknowledgement of a sexual biology in which there is actually a woman (as opposed to the male triad Quaid–Houser–Cohaagen), and acknowledgement of the symbiotic merging with the mother. But the trajectory recoils from this recollection: the fantasy of *Total Recall* seems to be the possibility of male self-reproduction, of never having been part of a woman's body at all. This is the memory that can be totally repressed in an action film centred on the Schwarzenegger body, a text in which 'a man is defined by his actions', as Quaid is told by the guru – underground leader Kuato. Kuato serves as the hypnotist who triggers the second special effect, which may be contextualized within the question of coherent male identity: a dazzling continuous shot that takes us 'into' Quaid's memory and 'into' the interior of the planet.[10] The shot begins as a close-up of Quaid's forehead, dissolving to one of the walls of the Mars interior. Within this space, the camera/memory recovers the visual presence of three men, Cohaagen and two henchmen, repeating the image of the all-male family.

However, Kuato's agency in this recall is a threatening reminder of boundary transgression through symbiosis. The product of a peculiar Martian mutation, Kuato is an embryo-like creature contained within the body of another man, who must go into a brief 'labour' to produce the miniature guru (both child and adult, sexed and sexless) from the space of his abdomen. As an astonishing special effect himself, Kuato as feminized man and as a visual representation of symbiosis is a shocking reminder that every male body as hard-edged as Quaid's was once merged with a woman's – though Kuato's male parent in one sense disavows female maternity altogether. The contrast with the Quaid body is also important: Kuato as special effect is a gooey, grotesque and helpless figure of merger and symbiosis in contrast to the specialness and power of Quaid's body and its own 'impossible' strength.

To begin the journey/hypnosis, Kuato asks Quaid to hold both his hands; and while the close-up of Quaid's forehead is the entrance to the continuous shot beginning the sequence, the exit is a dissolve into the iris of Kuato's eye, suggesting a particular symbiotic connection. If in fact a *man* is defined by his actions rather than by interior exploration or 'recall', then this sequence may signify the danger the text otherwise seeks to disavow – the feminization of Quaid/Houser/Schwarzenegger, which is always the threat posed by the male bodybuilder on display.[11]

Yet my argument here is that the threat to the male body in *Total Recall* is not feminization as castration, effeminacy or homosexuality, but the trans-gression of autonomy and coherence as represented in symbiosis, the pre-Oedipal merging in which gendered identity is lost. The threat is the threat of becoming, of process, of the possibility that the body is not separate and stable, but could at any moment turn into or merge with something else. Maternity as the site of mutation and merger is the sight from which this particular action-hero turns away in total recoil.

Critics often comment on the special effect as the hallmark of science-fiction cinema, but special effects are also crucial in the action/adventure genre. The technology of the composite matte shot, for example, used to create space-station attacks, is also used to enable breathtaking escapes for Indiana Jones – that is, to construct physical feats of a superlative, indestructible body. In science fiction, special effects create amazing, impossible machines and amaz-ing, impossible bodies: monstrous organisms such as Kuato, 'invincible ar-mored cyborgs' such as those in the *Terminator* and *Robocop* films; but also – in conjunction with the action genre – a Douglas Quaid in *Total Recall* or a John Spartan in *Demolition Man* who can outleap explosions and bullets. The difference is the extent to which these technologies call attention to them-selves, announcing themselves as 'special' or effacing themselves as 'natural'. The spectacular male body amplified through special effects – the muscular body rolling deftly out of the collapsing building – evokes a different level of marvel and disavowal (belief and disbelief) than does the marvel of Kuato or of Martian landscapes.

Bodybuilder stardom, the network of references to real ability and perform-ance, creates an especially resonant signifier in science fiction, investing its otherwise unbelievable worlds with a powerful material and cultural urgency. The spectacular physical performance refers to and celebrates the bodybuilder–star's talents and strengths, even as it refers to the hype and the glossy technologies of stardom. As a result, this performance effaces easy differenti-ations between the levels of reference in the film text: stardom, performance, cinematic technology, and the imaginary universe of the film's fiction. In *Total Recall*, this levelling of effects glamorizes the Schwarzenegger body as both impossible and true, special but credible, a 'solid' anchor for the plotline's twists, doublings and illusions.

Making the distinction between marked and unmarked special effects, Michael Stern argues that in spite of the artifice and technology of *every* cinematic shot, certain special effects in science-fiction cinema – usually the 'ones that enact the possibilities, delights, and terrors of glamorous new technologies' – create the illusion that the textual features around them are 'natural objects'.[12] This distinction and, more importantly, its resulting delineations of nature and artifice, have particular relevance to the male bodybuilder as signifier in this genre. Beginning with Mary Shelley's *Frankenstein*, science fiction's productive tension between nature and technology has always been specifically gendered. In an early description of this genre, Vivian Sobchak describes its trajectory in what could be a capsule description of *Total Recall*: 'the male desire to break free from biological dependence on the female as Mother and Other, and to mark the male self as separate and autonomous'.[13]

However, the muscular hero/star embodies *both* nature and the 'glamorous technologies' of cinema and bodybuilding. Schwarzenegger performs as Quaid, who, despite the microchip in his head, is construction worker, husband, dreamer – a 'natural' man. But Schwarzenegger also performs his own stardom, which involves at least three obviously 'unnatural' postmodern technologies: the transparent devices of celebrity, the self-creation of bodybuilding, and the editing and cinematographic processes which have become cinematic attractions in their own right. As a result, this bivalent body recuperates traditional masculinity as a 'naturally' superior category, but also manifests it in self-consciously artificial, postmodern mechanisms, so that masculinity can be read in ironic, contradictory ways.

Stern claims that science fiction 'foregrounds technology as a special effect – magical, socially ungrounded – while naturalizing the technologies of domination themselves'.[14] Readings of the multiple political agendas of *Total Recall*

reveal how slippery the 'technologies of domination' are rendered, through the film's ironic reversals and self-reflexive 'recallings' of its own racist and misogynist traces.[15] The masculine superbody, both identical to and distinct from the 'magical' special effects of this film, renders 'the natural' as an empty signifier, so that questions of ideology (as naturalizations of assumptions and power) become blurred – or are reworked, revised, 'recalled'.

The distinctly masculinist and racially specific inclinations of this body as special effect can be traced in *Timecop* and *Demolition Man*, science-fiction films in which the borderline status of the bodybuilder-hero ensures the survival of the 'natural' or 'human' as white/heterosexual/male. In their respective narratives, the Jean-Claude Van Damme character and the Stallone character end their adventures by reasserting biological norms as social/ideological ones: white heterosexuality. In *Demolition Man*, the Stallone character must recuperate physical sexuality itself, which has been forbidden as too dangerous in an age of sexual-contact viruses even more deadly than AIDS. The film's final scene features the traditional kiss with the female adventure partner, just as corny and possibly camp-ironic as the closure of *Total Recall*, significant here because kissing itself is *verboten* in this dangerous future. In *Timecop*, the closure revisits and corrects history by bringing back to life the hero's pregnant wife who has been killed by the bad guys in one version of the past. The final shot of the film includes the traditional couple's kiss, and also the embrace of their son who, à la *Terminator*, would never have been born if the 'bad' past had persisted. Unlike the closure of *Total Recall*, which wavers between schizoid fantasy and superheroism, the closure of *Timecop* in front of a restored Victorian house (the couple's 'dream' house) has little ironic overtone and instead restates the film's general trajectory about restoration of a traditional past.

Max Walker, the Van Damme character of *Timecop*, rescues his murdered wife and unborn son through the technologies of time travel and his own superior physical swiftness and discipline. While the time travel is marked as constructed and special (with warped screens, fiery spacemobiles and liquid morphing), the impossible physical feats of Walker (constructed through cinematography and editing) are masked as moments of masculine heroics. The significance of this masked technology is suggested in the attempted assassination scene in Walker's apartment, where he is sleeping on the sofa and wearing only gym shorts, the better to exhibit his gleaming torso in the imminent foray. A tracking shot reveals an assemblage of computers, monitors, videoscreens and scanners recognizable as the ordinary machineries of modernity: but here they also promise extraordinary effects, for this is the year 2004, and Walker's job is the policing of time travel. Despite this postmodern occupation and the accumulated whizz-bang equipment, Walker has fallen asleep with one of the homeliest and most familiar technologies of the twentieth century: the home movie, a video recording of his dead wife. Walker/Van Damme as timecop and 'natural' man (half-naked, watching home videos of a beautiful wife) literally embodies a borderline or boundary between these family/familiar, traditional masculine identities and a more disparate identity posed by a plotline in which the self can be split and doubled in various pasts.

The awakening of Walker by the assassins signals a fight scene that has become a setpiece of the genre, juxtaposing high-tech gadgetry and hand-to-hand combat involving knives, muscles, laser and/or traditional artillery, and some version of the martial arts. Attacked by a whirling, kick-boxing, knife-wielding Oriental, and also by a bureaucratic goon with a death-ray gun, Walker kills both in a ballet of machinery and machismo, finally saving himself from electrocution through a special effect, a fantastic/fantasy leap that lands him in a perfect leg-splaying split (the form that cheerleaders ache to attain) on two kitchen counters. Van Damme's split is real enough, but the leap is accomplished by two matching shots that are impossible to discern on first viewing. In the shot that flaunts the feat's accomplishment, the Van Damme body, laterally suspended in mid-air, divides the screen space (Figure 1). The split also visualizes the position of Walker/Van Damme between actual physical agility (he can perform the perfect acrobatic contortion) and technological artifice (only an editing process could have materialized the speed of his reaction).

I

Like Houser in *Total Recall*, Walker is later split onscreen to confront a former self in the time-loop gymnastics of the narrative, with its unsettling insinuations about manipulated personal and national histories. The interface of these split selves, as in the Schwarzenegger film, is the powerful male embodiment of performances ambiguously situated between artifice and biology. An acrobatic split is precisely such a performance, entailing the shocking sight of the legs tortured into opposite angles, directing attention to the crotch. And in the long run, the association of this feat with female cheerleading pushes its absurdity: the spectacle of Walker so earnestly and seriously splayed across his kitchen counters is richly readable as camp.

At this moment in the plotline the police arrive in the figure of a black female timecop, Fielding (Gloria Reuben). Fielding is assigned to be Walker's new partner, and is also an internal affairs watchdog. Not surprisingly, Fielding as foil embodies all the incoherences resisted by the Walker/Van Damme character: she is treacherous, unreliable, and physically vulnerable to the time-travel process easily weathered by Walker. In a film heavily indebted to its predecessors, *Timecop* suggests in the Fielding character a reworking of two racially marked characters from *Total Recall*: Quaid's partner/romantic interest Melina and the treacherous/victimized African-American taxi driver Benny. And, as in *Total Recall*, the racial politics are slippery to the point of un-readability.[16] Is Fletcher's position as timecop a triumph of her own talents or an affirmative-action appointment, the contempt for which we read in a snide remark by the agency director during the time-travel scene? Is her betrayal of Walker a subversive move characterizing her independence within the white power structures, or is it a racist characterization of unreliability? The narrative in some ways positions her sympathetically. As Walker's double, for example, she is similarly aligned with an absent family by means of an oldfashioned technology, a photograph of her parents and little brother that she carries as a talisman. Eventually, the plotline erases her betrayal and even her death as part of a 'bad' past that can be rewritten. Although we never see them work as a team again, a scene near the end of the film posits Fielding and Walker as future timecop partners and buddies.

Because the film identifies body as character in this way, Fielding's body (and hence her character) simply does not count as much as the heroic Van Damme body, even though she is supposedly his partner-timecop. Certainly she does not count in the narrative except as physical foil. After her murder, Walker alone must triumph over the villains and correct the past in order to undo the murder of his wife. The fact that this action also undoes Fielding's murder is presented as an afterthought: Walker (and likewise the audience) is truly surprised to find Fielding alive again at timecop head-quarters in 2004.

Moreover, Walker's physical superiority is intrinsic to the accomplishment of this narrative line because it operates parallel to other special effects in the climactic battle scene: his 2004 self returns to his 1994 self and faces it in the same shot; the villain self-destructs (morphs and melts); and the 1994/2004 Walker body enacts superheroic deflections of artillery, falling building pieces, and fiery explosions. These special effects render this battle scene as preposterous as any comic-book cartoon, but the scene is also grounded in more serious references. His pregnant wife is present and endangered, for one thing, and the athleticism of Van Damme as he whirls and kicks to defend her is impressive. This climactic fight occurs on the roofs and grounds of the restored Victorian house, so the entire postmodern time-loop narrative is literally grounded in a middlebrow dream of a perfect house and family. The racial specificity of this dream is suggested by the image of white parents and toddler son in the closing shots, an image displacing Fielding's photograph of her black parents and small brother.

My argument here is that this concluding scenario, with its class and racial inflections, and even its hammy excesses, is a highly constructed Hollywood effect. However, it is composed as an inevitable, recognizable, 'real' scenario coexisting in a future world with time travel, time loops, and multiple selves available in concurrent histories. The Walker character, as constituted by the Van Damme body, functions to efface the status of this Victorian home and family in 2004 as 'special' – that is, artifically and technically constructed – because his body/character interfaces so seamlessly with the unnatural and even absurd features of this fictive world. Its real-life performative talents extended by cinematic technologies, this body's obvious superiority is also obviously a cartoon or fantasy. Thus its racial constitution, foregrounded by the casting of Fielding, can be dismissed as an artificial surface feature without ideological implications. Likewise, the identities of the anonymous Oriental assassin and the villainous Jewish senator Aaron McComb (Ron Silver) can be attributed to the multicultural randomness of the text rather than to a pattern of enemies as racial or ethnic Others. When we move to the racial double in

Demolition Man, however, the stakes are raised considerably. For facing John Spartan/Stallone – the white, crazy outsider cop familiar from the *Lethal Weapon* and *Die Hard* series – is no female buddy or mutant taxi driver, but a formidable black enemy who is his physical equal, the psychotic criminal Simon Phoenix played by Wesley Snipes.

As even this much implies, Stallone and Snipes in *Demolition Man* enact parodies of their own super-macho Hollywood stereotypes. As enemies flash-frozen in 1996 and thawed in the year 2032, their characters are retrieved not only from the lawless, primitive last decades of the twentieth century, but also from the films of those decades. In addition to the joke about President Schwarzenegger, characters refer to Rambo, Luke Skywalker and Jackie Chan movies; a *Lethal Weapon* poster is visible on an office wall. With comic-book names and tongue-in-cheek posturings, the Phoenix and Spartan characters mock the 1990s-style, super-violent bodybuilder action star, but they valorize this star and style as well. Scene after thrilling scene of muscle, carnage, car chases and explosions confirm the entertainment value of this venue. The plotline twist carries these characters from contemporary action (the historical era and the genre) to science fiction and a brave new future; the term is never used, but the satirical target is obviously 'political correctness'.

As Lenina explains, 'anything that's bad for you' in this dystopia has been banned: tobacco, alcohol, drugs, violence, physical sex, contact sports, spicy food and 'uneducational toys'. A 'verbal morality code' prohibits vulgar language, which is overheard and punished by the all-seeing state machinery, so Spartan is issued demerit tickets every time he says 'shit' or 'fuck'. The joke here, besides the comedy of the hulky Stallone being treated like a foul-mouthed schoolchild, is that these terms refer to oldfashioned body functions refashioned in the twenty-first century: sex has been replaced by virtual-reality machines, and toilet paper has been less explicably replaced by 'the three sea shells'. In addition, the mise-en-scene is packed with a multicultural future populace of Los Angeles (a crime-free San Angeles in 2032) whose robes, capes and saris could easily be read as feminine.

An enforced, artificial homogeneity ensures the non-violence of this multi-cultural paradise. Differences in the citizens' costume and ethnicities are super-ficial: no matter what people look like, they think the same way and have the same desires. In the 'franchise wars' earlier in the century, Taco Bell won, so now 'all restaurants are Taco Bell', Lenina tells us. Actual differences of desire (taste) and class have been driven underground, where the starving rebels still look and act like Los Angeles street people and action-movie heroes from 1996: they sweat, they grunt, they use guns. (They also closely resemble the Martian underground of *Total Recall* and the street-level population of *Blade Runner*.) But they are unable to liberate themselves until two 'real men' come back from 1996 to introduce oldfashioned kick-ass violence and racial and gender difference.

John Spartan is several times referred to as an 'animal', a 'Neanderthal', and 'a muscle-bound grotesque'; but he and Phoenix are posited as more human than their future counterparts, so that masculinity is again naturalized in comparison to the special-effect gadgetry of the nightmare future. Masculine gender stereotypes are validated through satirical humour. Seeking to tone down his machismo, the state machinery has secretly encoded Spartan with sewing and knitting skills, and he impulsively whips up a sweater when he comes across some needles and yarn. After Spartan shocks the police with his foul language, Lenina explains to them that talking dirty 'used to be a bonding device for insecure heterosexual males'. With the latter comment, *Demolition Man* makes the familiar move (from *Lethal Weapon* and recent James Bond films, for example) of citing its own macho excessiveness, joking about it, and then enacting it with a clearer conscience.

In contrast, the racial dynamic, the triumph of the white cop over the black thug, is positioned more precariously within the comic-book superheroics, with more variable potential readings. The script contains no references to racism as a bonding device for insecure whites, but the film's visual depictions of 'Neanderthal' white cop and 'super-bad' black criminal can be read as a demystifying joke, sanctioning the dynamic as a send-up of stereotypes. 'Real' difference bursts upon the hyper-clean surface of San Angeles with Simon Phoenix's rap irreverence, punky dyed-blonde hair, and politically incorrect body, sculpted into muscles not needed in the non-violent future. Thus his menacing gangsta excesses are delivered with a big wink towards the audience – although the wink, and even the target audience, are conveniently ambiguous.[17] For example, when Phoenix finds machine guns and Uzis displayed as museum pieces, he smashes the pristine glass exhibit cases and restores the use value of the guns by blowing away the white guards and police. The possible spectatorial pleasures of this sequence range from the subversive (a gleeful rampage against white uptight museum culture) to the racist (a gleeful rampage demonstrating primitive blackness). Phoenix himself is destined eventually to be electrocuted, incinerated and detonated by the white cop, who escapes the same explosion, gets the girl, redeems the future, and liberates the repressed underground. Given the film's self-referential humour, this clichéd resolution may be read as a snide reminder that white Hollywood is in charge of creating these future worlds, where even in science fiction the black dude does not get a break. But the film can also be read as an in-your-face triumph over politically correct agendas, plotlines and representations.

However, perhaps the most suggestive reading of this film's relationship between body politics and racial politics is offered in the credit sequence early in the film. The racial tensions of *Demolition Man* are clearly invoked in its remarkable opening scenes, which introduce the characters and conflicts as contemporary referents. The establishing shots show buildings on fire in a 1996 Los Angeles, alluding to the openings of *Blade Runner* and *Terminator*, and also to Los Angeles's tense history of fiery racial incidents, including the riots after the Rodney King decision in 1992, the year before the film was released.

Given this racial allusion, I want to emphasize the figuring of the Stallone super-body as conduit to and bond with the disavowing satire of multiculturalism that follows. The tone of the film switches to comic-book punchiness only after it shifts to its 2032 scene, the transition being nude shots of Stallone over which we see the credits. These shots reveal the John Spartan character frozen in a blue liquid, composing an erotic and aestheticized visualization of the famous Stallone physique. His body is literally the bridge between a contemporary scene of racial violence and a science-fiction future which 'fixes' the racism and the violence through satire and self-referential irony. Super-muscular, frozen, poised for action but floating in passive self-exhibition, the Stallone body as channel here is the bodybuilder/science-fiction device *par excellence*, in that the entire plotline rests on its collusion with a fictive technology (flash-frozen and revived nearly four decades later) and its star status (authentically powerful but also hyped). This is also a body destined to meet its match, its equally gorgeous black Other. 'I've been dreaming about killing you for forty years', Phoenix tells him in the future. Dreaming of each other, Spartan and Phoenix are bonded together in a passion that crosses genres and decades in Hollywood's versions of Los Angeles and San Angeles.

I am suggesting, of course, that *Demolition Man*'s excessive representations of gender and race – the two 'naturally different' super-bodies within an 'unnatural' future world – also expose and offer the multiple *sexual* readings of these super-bodies. The over-the-top male iconicity also functions within the recent cinematic history of black–white buddy films and their homoerotic overtones.[18] In *Demolition Man*, the implications are spelled out by Lenina's malapropisms that garble twentieth-century clichés: she gushes that Phoenix has 'matched his meet' in Spartan, who really 'licked his ass'. 'Let's go blow this guy', she cheers. Spartan rolls his eyes and corrects her: '*met* his match, *kicked* his ass, blow him *away*'. Too late. The slips of the tongue register the unspoken or the unspeakable.

The self-consciousness of bodybuilder stardom in *Demolition Man* – the title itself poised between parody and a more earnest flexing of muscle – raises a wider question about the uses of the male body in science-fiction cinema and its subsequent camp appeal. The in-the-know campness of this film ranges from its broad satire (advertising jingles from the twentieth century are now pop tunes) to more subtle allusions: the future police chief is costumed and made up to look like Erich von Stroheim, 'The Man You Love to Hate', in

Griffith's *Hearts of the World* (1918); and the virtual-sex scene is borrowed from Roger Vadim's *Barbarella* (1968). However, the nuances of the male posing and flexing, beginning with Stallone's provocative, frozen nudity, also suggest camp's queer, more radical, dimensions and politics.[19] After all, my argument in this chapter has been that science fiction's bodybuilder star, as a special effect, destabilizes binary concepts of 'nature' and 'the unnatural' already contended in this genre. Given queer theory's positing of masculinity as performance, science fiction visualizes masculinity as an even more fantastic illusion and special effect.

The founding text of science fiction, Mary Shelley's *Frankenstein*, illustrates how these radical underminings of category have always hovered around the genre's 'built' male body. The category at stake is often described as human nature itself, but the embodiment of this crisis or anxiety is male/masculine. J.P. Telotte points out that in such films as *Blade Runner*, *Robocop* and *Total Recall*, the 'image of a generally empty human nature' is 'a generally *masculine* empty nature' (stress in original). Telotte's analyses of bodily representation in science-fiction cinema emphasize the tensions between surface and depth, between the private body and the body on public display as self-aware image. Looking at the two *Terminator* films and their male robotic forms, he discusses the difficulties of reading the body and judging bodies by appearances, noting that 'When the body is all surface, exposed, a visible function, there is little point to motivations or special knowledge … scant space left for human identity.'[20] Telotte's topic is 'human identity' as a site of anxiety in these films, but the conflicts he cites (surface versus depth, private versus public, appearance versus 'special knowledge') also constitute the tropes and contradictions expressed in camp. In camp humour, the artificial cultural definitions of 'nature' beg impersonation, drag, exaggeration and posturing. We can consider Van Damme's 'split' across kitchen counters and Schwarzenegger's burst from the female robot as excessive bodies and outrageous performances with pointedly humorous overtones. The 'emptiness' of the super-built male body as signifier suggests the emptiness of its gendered and sexual identities, but also – for a

more radical, queer camp – its infinite plenitude of meanings.[21] What boundaries are evoked or demolished by Stallone's exposed, sculpted body, floating
in blue ether? Connecting representations of 1990s' masculinity and the science-
fiction future, his body is impossible, spectacular, a special effect.

NOTES

1. See Claudia Springer, 'Muscular Circuitry: The Invincible Armored Cyborg in Cinema',
   Genders, no. 18, 1993. This characterization of the Schwarzenegger physique as the re-
   gressive, fascist hardbody has been contested and debated by Albert Liu, for example,
   in 'The Last Days of Arnold Schwarzenegger', *Genders*, no. 18, 1993. See also Doran
   Larson, 'Machine as Messiah: Cyborgs, Morphs, and the American Body Politic', *Cinema
   Journal* vol. 36, no. 4, p. 199. Jonathan Goldberg in 'Recalling Totalities: The Mirrored
   Stages of Arnold Schwarzenegger', *Differences: A Journal of Feminist Cultural Studies*, vol.
   4, no. 1, 1992, comments that, 'With Schwarzenegger politics is science fiction (Star
   Wars taught us to take this seriously). He embodies an unnatural sex, too' (p. 177).
2. See Yvonne Tasker's discussion of Stallone and Schwarzenegger as the primary exam-
   ples of stardom in 'muscle culture' and the action film in *Spectacular Bodies: Gender,
   Genre, and the Action Cinema*, London: Routledge, 1993, pp. 80–87. Also see Chris
   Holmlund, 'Masculinity as Multiple Masquerade: The "Mature" Stallone and the Stallone
   Clone', in Steven Cohan and Ina Rae Hark, eds, *Screening the Male: Exploring Masculinities
   in Hollywood Cinema*, London and New York: Routledge, 1993.
3. Linda Mizejewski, 'Total Recoil: The Schwarzenegger Body on Postmodern Mars', *Post
   Script*, vol. 12, no. 3, 1993. Parts of the middle section of 'Total Recoil' are excerpted in
   the present chapter.
4. See, for example, Barbara Creed, 'From Here to Modernity: Feminism and Postmodernism', *Screen*, vol. 28, no. 2, 1987, for a psychoanalytic description of these excessive
   masculine figures as 'a casualty of the failure of the paternal signifier' (p. 65). More
   relevant to my study here is Yvonne Tasker's work, which emphasizes the instabilities
   of super-masculinities onscreen: see especially 'Tough Guys and Wise Guys: Masculinities
   and Star Images in the Action Cinema', in *Spectacular Bodies*, pp. 73–90. My work is also
   aligned with that of Sharon Willis, who, like Tasker, is especially concerned with the
   intersection of racial and gender concerns in the action movie. See *High Contrast: Race
   and Gender in Contemporary Hollywood Film*, Durham, NC: Duke University Press, 1997,
   especially 'Mutilated Masculinities and Their Prostheses: Die Hards and Lethal Weapons',
   pp. 27–59. See also Cohan and Hark, eds, *Screening the Male*, especially Susan Jeffords,
   'Can Masculinity be Terminated?'
5. Chris Shea and Wade Jennings, 'Paul Verhoeven: An Interview', *Post Script*, vol. 12, no.
   3, 1993, p. 9.

6. '*Total Recall*: Production, Revolution, Simulation-Alienation Effect', *Camera Obscura*, no. 32, 1993–94, p. 10.
7. Shea and Jennings, 'Paul Verhoeven: An Interview', pp. 18–19.
8. Springer, 'Muscular Circuitry', p. 95.
9. Jonathan Goldberg points out that the cross-dressing 'transforms him into a latter-day Divine', and connects the cross-gendering to the plotline's 'attempt to suture identities'. See 'Recalling Totalities', p. 193.
10. Fred Glass comments that female genital space is powerfully suggested in this shot: see 'Totally Recalling Arnold: Sex and Violence in the New Bad Future', *Film Quarterly*, vol. 44, no. 1, 1990, p. 8.
11. Yvonne Tasker points out that the action film partially allays this threat of feminization by avoiding pin-up 'poses' by the bodybuilder hero and keeping him in constant motion. See *Spectacular Bodies*, p. 77.
12. Michael Stern, 'Making Culture into Nature' (1980), in Annette Kuhn, ed., *Alien Zone: Cultural Theory and Contemporary Science Fiction Cinema*, London: Verso, 1990, p. 69.
13. Vivian Sobchack, 'The Virginity of Astronauts: Sex and the Science Fiction Film', 1985, in ibid., p. 108.
14. Stern, 'Making Culture into Nature', p. 70.
15. See Goldberg, 'Recalling Totalities', pp. 193–6. See also Johanna Schmertz, 'On Reading the Politics of *Total Recall*', *Post Script*, vol. 12, no. 3. Schmertz argues for 'the political polyvalence' of *Total Recall*, even while conceding the film's classic masculine narrative. Robert Miklitsch, however, interprets the film's sexual politics as subservient to its 'explicitly revolutionary context'. See '*Total Recall*', p. 16.
16. Johanna Schmertz describes the dual liberatory or racist readings of the Benny character in *Total Recall* in 'On Reading the Politics of *Total Recall*' (p. 38).
17. Discussing similarly diverse audiences and readings of *Die Hard*, Sharon Willis in *High Contrast* points out that the Hollywood market 'demands such layers of audiences as a prerequisite of a film's success', p. 40.
18. Ibid., pp. 28–31.
19. *Demolition Man*, with its bodybuilder aesthetic, homoerotic overtones, but conservative satire, demonstrates the difficulty of clearly distinguishing a 'popular' camp from a more radically queer camp. See Moe Meyer's overview of the politics of this debate in 'Introduction: Reclaiming the Discourse of Camp', in Moe Meyer, ed., *The Politics and Poetics of Camp*, London and New York: Routledge, 1994.
20. These quotations come, respectively, from 'The Tremulous Public Body: Robots, Change, and the Science Fiction Film', *Journal of Popular Film and Television*, vol. 19, no. 1, 1991, p. 16; and 'The *Terminator*, *Terminator 2*, and the Exposed Body', *Journal of Popular Film and Television*, vol. 20, no. 2, 1992, p. 30.
21. See Jonathan Goldberg's analysis of the erotics of the Schwarzenegger body, in 'Recalling Totalities', p. 176.

8

BECOMING THE MONSTER'S MOTHER: MORPHOLOGIES OF IDENTITY IN THE *ALIEN* SERIES

CATHERINE CONSTABLE

This chapter will analyse the representation of maternality and the maternal body in the *Alien* series, focusing on *Alien* (1979); *Aliens* (1986) and *Alien Resurrection* (1997), with a very brief reference to *Alien3*. Beginning with a discussion of Barbara Creed's well-known reading of *Alien*, which uses Julia Kristeva's model of abjection, I shall proceed to address the protagonist Ripley's (Sigourney Weaver) relation to the alien queen in *Aliens* and *Alien Resurrection*. I shall argue that Kristeva's model can be applied to the representation of maternality and matter in *Alien* and *Aliens*. Both films present the alien in ways that emphasize its visceral qualities: from the pulsating flesh of the pods to the mucus-secreting double jaw of the fully grown monster. In these films, human reproduction is represented as scientific or sterile, in clear contrast with the alien's physical materiality, thus setting up an opposition between the human and the monstrous. This corresponds to Kristeva's analysis of the structures of abjection, in which the subject rejects the flux of physical matter in order to secure the boundaries of its own identity. I shall demonstrate that the presentation of the human in *Alien* can be seen to conform to a traditional Freudian/Lacanian model of identity that is secured through opposing, and ultimately subjugating, the threat of the Other. *Aliens* can also be seen to use the model of opposition, but simultaneously to undermine it.[1]

I shall argue that the traditional psychoanalytic model of opposition and subjugation is rendered defunct by the re/presentation of Ripley in *Alien Resurrection* as a clone who has given birth to the alien queen. Becoming the monster's mother involves a breakdown of traditional models of identity, because these models never analyse the position of the mother as a subject position. I will therefore argue that the complex structures of intersecting identities presented in *Alien Resurrection* correspond to a new and different model of subjectivity. This will involve using Christine Battersby's *The Phenomenal Woman*, which argues for a model of female identity that encompasses the capacity to give birth. The crossing of DNA from Ripley and the alien queen has a considerable impact on the lived embodiment of each character. Both gain different physical attributes, and their newfound materiality constitutes their new identities. I will use Battersby's model in order to theorize the ways in which becoming the monster's mother also involves rethinking physical matter as a site of subjectivity.

In her article on *Alien*, Creed argues that the film offers a number of versions of the primal scene. She borrows the term from Freud, defining primal scenes as fantasmatic reconstructions of parental copulation and birth. According to Creed, the first representation in *Alien* occurs at the beginning of the film when the crew of the *Nostromo* are awakened from hypersleep. There is a long tracking shot down one of the ship's corridors: this differs from the other corridors because it has white padding covering the piping and ventilation on the walls. The camera tracks forward towards an octagonal white door. To the left of the door hang two white coats, indicating a human presence. The colour of the padding and the coats suggests a sanitized region of the ship. The door opens, revealing a circular inner chamber, and the track in provides a long shot of seven containers arranged in a geometric star shape. Their clean, clear plastic lids rise as the lights flicker on. The light shines down the walls of the chamber, backlighting the opening sleep capsules and creating a contrast between layers of whiteness (Figure 1). There is a dissolve to a medium long shot taken from Kane's capsule as he reaches to remove two

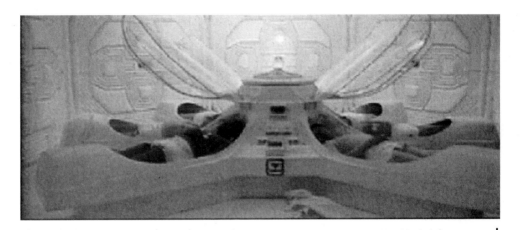

white discs attached to his torso. He and the other visible figures are clothed in white shorts which cover their genitalia like swaddling clothes. Creed comments that 'the re-birthing scene ... is marked by a fresh, antiseptic atmosphere. In outer space, birth is a well-controlled, clean, painless affair. There is no blood, trauma or terror.'[2] The subjects spring to life fully formed, their bodies already decently covered.

Creed contrasts the first 're-birthing scene' with the second version of the primal scene, in which Dallas, Kane and Lambert investigate the alien spacecraft. The horseshoe-shaped craft is first seen from the left in long shots. Later there is a cut to another long shot facing the centre of the horseshoe as if between the legs of the craft. This is followed by a long shot of the three crew members who clamber in through one of two rounded openings. Creed argues that the topography of the ship suggests a female body, its outstretched legs positioned either side of a vaginal entrance. The long shot also serves to establish the vastness of the body: it appears to engulf the crew as they disappear inside. Once inside, a travelling shot reveals an organic structure. Black bone-like structures run vertically up the walls, glistening slightly in the light as if moist. The patterns of the skeletal corridor differ greatly from the horizontal metallic piping seen on the *Nostromo*. The darkness of the alien ship also contrasts with the bright whiteness of the sleep chamber and its hallway. Creed describes the alien craft as 'dark, dank and mysterious'.[3]

While agreeing with Creed's description of the contrast between the spaces, I want to expand on her analysis and challenge aspects of her reading by looking more closely at the film itself. The diverse structures of the alien ship are associated with organic life in a variety of ways. The crew climb out of the inner corridors onto a vast, curved parapet constructed from long black ridges, like spines, which are interconnected horizontally by short black ribs. The camera cranes backwards and upwards to reveal a central, circular dais with a large, almost telescopic, protrusion in the middle. It seems to conjoin a number of large circular pipes like the remnants of the main veins and arteries that once fed into a vast heart. There is a cut to a long shot taken level with the dais as the crew begin to investigate its structure. Dallas moves to investigate the underside and comments that it is attached to a fossilized body. Later, there is a medium shot of Dallas and Lambert viewing some skeletal remains. These are pinky-beige in colour as though the bones had not yet been completely bleached. The skeleton consists of a series of thick ribs attached to a central spinal column. The repetition of the patterning from the parapet reinforces the visual suggestion that the entire craft is a fossilized body and thus explicitly associates the alien craft with death and decay.

In the next part of the scene, Kane is lowered into a vast inner chamber which he describes as 'some sort of cave' whose atmosphere is 'almost tropical'. Creed reads his exploration of the moist warm space as an extreme version of the primal scene in which 'the subject imagines travelling back inside the womb to watch her/his parents having sexual intercourse, perhaps to watch her/himself being conceived'.[4] The film provides a single establishing shot of the vast space as Kane is lowered in. The cave exhibits the same organic structures as the rest of the ship. The spinal columns run down the walls and across the floor space, dividing it into a series of channels. The front two are scarcely illuminated, but can be seen to contain a number of circular mounds.

Kane's torch lights up the middle section, picking out a layer of blue mist which covers it. Later, there is a medium long shot of Kane walking along one of the ridges that separate the channels, his torch illuminating a blue line of light that runs level with his feet. As he kneels down, the sound of the electrical hum changes to a higher pitch. There is a cut to a medium close-up of his arm as he lowers his hand through the beam twice, and the electrical pitch gains in frequency on both occasions. The forcefield operates as a protective layer which Kane penetrates when he falls off the ridge. He goes on to discover that the pods also carry an electrical charge when he receives a shock as he touches one. The electrical fields are clearly designed to repel intruders, indicating that Kane has entered a hostile environment.

I have described the presentation of the alien craft in some detail in order to establish that it is already presented as a hostile and dangerous space prior to the attack on Kane. This is important because Creed reads 'the womb-like imagery, the long winding tunnels leading to inner chambers, the rows of hatching eggs'[5] as positive images of a parthenogenetic mother figure. She argues that these images and those of the first sleeping chamber represent an archaic mother figure who gives birth to all life by herself. Creed draws on myths of the mother goddess, from the Greek figure of Gaia, the earth from whom all life springs, to the South American figure of the spider woman, who is said to create the universe through her spinning.[6] Importantly, these reproductive maternal figures are not presented in relation to a male partner. Creed comments that 'the womb signifies "fullness" or "emptiness" but always it is its own point of reference'.[7] The use of the womb as a key reference point clearly provides a break from the Freudian system in which the mother is encoded in relation to a phallic standard.

Creed's move beyond Freud's Oedipal and pre-Oedipal eras is an attempt to generate new images of the maternal figure. For Freud, the boy's love of the pre-Oedipal mother is the result of his mapping her as an all-powerful, phallic figure. This is later destroyed by the 'discovery' of maternal castration, which leads the boy to construct the Oedipal mother as mutilated and lacking. Creed

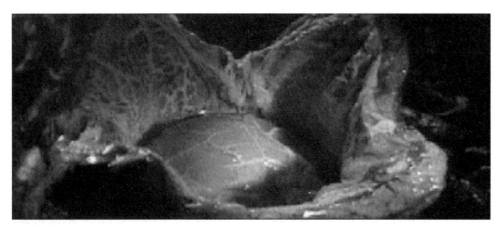

2

pits her image of the reproductive mother against the Freudian images of the phallic or mutilated mother. However, she does suggest that the figure of the archaic mother can be recuperated when it is constructed negatively as death-dealing. The reconstruction of the womb as tomb is a patriarchal appropriation of the figure of the archaic mother, which Creed argues often occurs in horror films.[8] I think that detailed textual analysis of *Alien* shows that the presentation of the alien craft as a fossilized structure clearly corresponds to the image of tomb rather than womb.[9]

Creed argues that the maternal characterization of the alien craft changes after Kane is attacked, moving from archaic mother to pre-Oedipal phallic mother. The face-hugger is viewed as phallic because it attacks through an aggressive act of penetration. However, I want to offer a different reading of the attack, using Kristeva's work on abjection and matter. After receiving an electric shock from one of the pods, Kane investigates its structure. The second close-up of the pod is the clearest: it is backlit so that the outer skin appears to be a translucent blue/white, and the curved shape of a dark pink organic structure can be clearly seen fluttering inside it. The internal life form has a central darker curve which appears to extend into a series of less dense

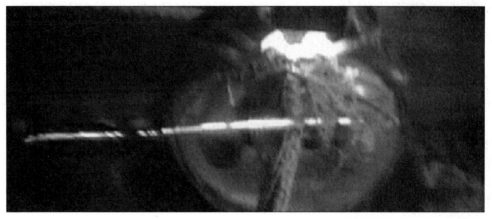

3

'fingers'. The dense curve resembles the curve of a foetus's spine when viewed on a scanner. Kane comments: 'It seems to have life, organic life.' There is a cut to a medium close-up of Kane and the camera travels back and up, providing a medium shot of him viewing the top of the pod as it opens with a creaking sound. This is followed by a subjective shot of the inside of the pod, and the handheld camera moves forward to provide a more direct view into the gaping hole. The four newly opened leaves are deep pink with white veining, and the centre is a pulsating pink mound of flesh which glistens in the light (Figure 2). The curve of flesh resembles a womb lining, its colour suggesting it is composed of interior tissue rather than an external skin. The moist heaving flesh makes a rhythmical squelching sound as if breathing. There is a cut to a shot of Kane as he reaches into the pod, rapidly followed by another subjective shot as the creature propels itself towards his face, its tail uncoiling rapidly. There follows a cut to a medium shot of Kane as he staggers and falls with the face-hugger attached to his helmet. The central cord hangs down from behind it as the monster appears to ingest his face. Its shape resembles a placenta with an umbilical cord (Figure 3). This is followed by a return to the long shot of the alien craft in which the camera is positioned parallel to the space between the legs of the craft. The positioning of the shot clearly suggests that the monstrous craft has given birth.

I have emphasized the visceral qualities of the attack on Kane in order to demonstrate the way in which the representation of *matter* is crucial to the structures of horror in this film. For Creed, the attack on Kane is horrific because the character is threatened by the prospect of reabsorption into the figure of the pre-Oedipal mother.[10] Within the Freudian model, the child's first psychic organization, the pre-Oedipal, is that of a state of undifferentiated union with the mother. Subjectivity is created and secured through a complete separation from the maternal figure. For Freud, the boy must pass through the Oedipus and castration complexes, ultimately rejecting the mother for a substitute love object. Lacan argues that the intervention of a third term, the Name of the Father, splits the mother–child dyad and acts as a cut that separates the pair. In this model, it is the acquisition of language that forcibly splits the child from the mother. Furthermore, once the child has acquired language, it is situated within the Symbolic and the mother is relegated to the Imaginary. Creed borrows from Kristeva in arguing that the threat posed by the horror film is that of the dissolution of the subject.[11] The representation of the figure of the mother is the return of that which has to be rejected and suppressed in order for the subject to exist at all.

Creed's account of the abjection of the maternal figure is problematic, however, in that she fails to trace it back to the child's earliest development and therefore to comment on the mother's relation to matter. Kristeva traces the process of abjection to the pre-Oedipal:

> The abject confronts us … with our earliest attempts to release the hold of the *maternal* entity even before ex-isting [sic] outside of her, thanks to the autonomy of language. It is a violent, clumsy breaking away, with the constant risk of falling back under the sway of a power as securing as it is stifling.[12]

The process of abjection does not secure the split between subject and object; it merely establishes a 'defensive *position*', setting up permeable borders which constitute gestures towards subjectivity.[13] These primary borders are said to create the foundations of binary structures: 'As if the fundamental opposition were between I and the Other, or in more archaic fashion, between Inside and Outside.'[14] Importantly, the establishment of this first border between inside and outside involves the expulsion and rejection of physical matter such as food and bodily waste products. This expulsion establishes the contours of the body itself and sets up a further division between the living, contained body and dead matter:

> These bodily fluids, this defilement, this shit are what life withstands, hardly and with difficulty, on the part of death. There I am at the border of my condition as a living being. My body extricates itself, as being alive, from that border.[15]

Kristeva's account of the processes of abjection links the maternal body to physical matter in two ways. First, the child establishes a bodily contour through acts of expulsion which form that which is to be considered 'outside' the boundary, typically the mother's body and dead matter. Second, the bodily division between inside and outside sets up the skin as a container which holds in the palpable stuff of physicality like muscles and blood.[16] The maternal body operates as the privileged trope for the visceral flows of the inside.[17] Within this framework the attack on Kane is horrific because the monster engulfs his helmet, covering his face (the privileged site of individuation) within its own physical structures. It is also horrific because it presents the spectacle of inside as outside, the skinless palpitating flesh of the pods raising the spectre of a viscous physicality that has been rejected. For Kristeva, the re-emergence of the maternal 'inside' is horrific rather than uncanny because the processes of abjection involve expulsion and ultimately suppression.[18]

I am not arguing that Kristeva's conception of abjection is the universal structure of all horror films. Indeed, as I shall show, *Alien Resurrection* does not conform to these structures. However, the Kristevan framework is appropriate to *Alien* because of the contrasts drawn between the mother ship and the alien craft. The opening sequence in which the crew spring to life fully formed within an utterly cleansed, sanitized environment is clearly opposed to the visceral birth of the face-hugger within the organic body of the alien craft. While Creed recognizes the differences between the two birth scenes, she is concerned to present them as fundamentally similar in that both are said to construct different images of the archaic mother.[19] My analysis builds on the contrast in order to position the mother ship as a traditional Symbolic space in which codes of cleanliness and decency are already operative, in opposition to the alien craft which constitutes the abjected maternal body. I would therefore argue that the female voice-over of the computer on the mother ship cannot be constructed as a maternal voice. She simply mouths the commands that comply with the aims and objectives of the Company.[20]

Within *Alien* the initial presentation of cleanliness and sterility creates and sustains that which is to be designated abject. The threat posed by the alien is explicitly presented as one of contamination. Ripley refuses to allow Kane to be brought back on board, arguing that the crew must observe quarantine procedures. She is outmanoeuvred by Ash, whose apparent disregard for protocol positions him as a threat to the secure space. The scene in which the chest-buster is born enacts the complete destruction of this space. The establishing shot of the scene shows the crew gathered around a white table having dinner. All the food containers are made of clear plastic and the crockery is white. The crew are clothed in a combination of pastel shades and white. The predominance of whiteness in the mise-en-scene suggests sterility and cleanliness. Once Kane begins to suffer from convulsions the crew clear the table, spilling some of the containers, and try to hold him down onto its surface. There follow several medium shots of Kane's face and torso, taken from a high angle at the edge of the table. The fourth shows blood spurting from his chest cavity, the fifth shows the fluid seeping through and staining his white T-shirt. The blood is presented against the surrounding surfaces, the dark stain contaminating their whiteness. The creature finally bursts through Kane's chest and there is a rapid cut to a medium shot of Parker, Ripley, Brett and Dallas stepping back, and then to a medium shot of Lambert against a white wall as she is splattered with blood. Later, there is a close-up of the creature emerging

4

from Kane's body, its ridged pink flesh covered with blood. Its shape resembles intestinal tissue. The camera travels up as it pulls free of the body. Kane's arms twitch convulsively in death, his face a motionless mask of blood. The monster stands erect, gazing sightlessly from side to side, jaws snapping (Figure 4).

This second monstrous birth replays the horror of the first in so far as it, too, constitutes the inside become outside. The contour of containment which establishes the subject/character is violently eroded by an explosion from within. It is as if Kane's intestinal coils had taken on a life of their own. The later horror of the full-grown monster's attacks can also be compared with this drama. The monster emerges from the shadows, slicing and pulverizing the characters, reducing them to frescos of flesh. Parker is sliced in half, his legs dripping blood and his torso slumped forwards on the floor. In the film's final scene on the escape craft, Ripley's semi-clad body clearly forms a contrast to these presentations of mutilated flesh. Becoming aware of the monster's presence on board, she backs into a cupboard and proceeds to dress in an astronaut's suit. The film cuts from a low-angle shot of Ripley stepping into the suit to a close-up of the monster's doubled jaw, and then between medium close-ups of Ripley and close-ups of the jaw as it elongates to its full extent, dripping mucus: these cuts juxtapose a body re-barriered through the pristine white suit with the viscous physicality of the monster. Ripley then proceeds to secure the space of the ship by forcibly ejecting the monster and pulverizing it within the heat of the engines. The twin processes of abjection – barricading the body and ejecting the monster – serve to secure the space.[21]

Alien offers a representation of the human as a sterile community forcibly confronted by a physicality it has rejected. The structures of horror in *Alien* conform to Kristeva's model of an inside that erupts and disrupts the body as container. The ending of the film secures the Symbolic space of the escape craft through the ejection and destruction of the monster. The space of the human is thus guaranteed through the abjection of the Other. In *Aliens*, however, the presentation of the opposition between human and monstrous is more complicated. While the dialectic ultimately conforms to a model in which the Other is rejected and subjugated, *Aliens* is complicated by the presentation of divisions within the human community. The film also sets up an interesting structure of mirroring by pitting Ripley and Newt against the alien queen. The final battles can therefore be read as confrontations between two parthenogenetic mother figures, a doubling that disrupts the structures of abjection.

Alien and *Aliens* offer very different representations of the human community, and this feeds into their distinctive presentations of Ripley's character. James Kavanagh argues that *Alien* can be read as 'almost post-feminist' because of its obliteration of the issue of sexual difference within the crew. 'There are strong and weak women and men on the ship, but the women's right to assume authority is not even an issue; authority and power are ceded to persons irrespective of sex, solely in regard to their position and function.'[22] In *Alien*, Ripley is first and foremost a science officer, a fully integrated member of the crew of the *Nostromo*. She is fleetingly feminized when she undresses in the escape pod, a glimpse of sexual difference at odds with the impersonal egalitarian structure of the rest of the film. In *Aliens*, however, Ripley is an outsider, a civilian advisor on a military expedition. Her positioning outside the marine corps is clearly conveyed in the waking scene en route to the planet LB426. Ripley's

costume of grey vest top and pants contrasts with the regulation khaki under-
wear worn by the other waking figures. On seeing her, Vasquez asks 'Who's
Snow White?' The question explicitly feminizes Ripley's outsider status in that
a fairy-tale princess is clearly out of place on a military mission. This labelling
also adds a humorous dimension to the opening scene, in which Ripley is
discovered sleeping in an ice-encrusted glass capsule. In this case, however, the
handsome prince turns out to be a salvage crew. Ripley's unusually long hypersleep also parallels another fairy-tale princess in distress, Sleeping Beauty.

Ripley's feminization is completed by the discovery of Newt on LB426. She
is now positioned as surrogate mother to the civilian child. Constance Penley
argues that Ripley's new-found maternal instinct means that *Aliens* presents a
traditional construction of sexual difference which is a regressive move away
from the egalitarianism of *Alien*.[23] I would argue that the presentation of
Ripley and Newt diverges from patriarchal tradition in so far as both are
transformed from outsider figures to key combatants in the battle against the
aliens. This reconfiguring clearly changes Ripley's positioning as Snow White.
Instead of waiting to be rescued – the fate of most fairy-tale princesses –
Ripley rescues the marines. The reversal is also a joke, in that the figures of
the surrogate mother and daughter act as a trope for the helpless women and
children the military are supposed to protect. The inversion begins when Ripley
challenges Gorman and commandeers a tank in order to rescue the marines
from the alien craft, and is completed in the scene in which the craft that
constitutes their link back to the ship crashes.

The rescue craft spirals out of control, scattering burning wreckage over a
wide area. Hudson panics while Hicks searches among the wreckage. There is
a long shot in which the two marines are positioned at frame left with Burke
in the centre in the background. Ripley is positioned frame right in the
midground, and Newt takes centre screen. The camera travels upwards and
towards Newt as she climbs up onto a rock. Ripley moves alongside her,
giving her a reassuring hug, and the pair stand together, equal in height, in
centre frame, while the others continue moving at a lower level in the back-

ground. Hudson can be seen wandering aimlessly, lamenting their fate. The camera tracks forwards and finally closes in on a two-shot of the pair. The similarity of their facial structures presents an image of female–female mirroring. Newt calmly suggests they go back because the monsters usually come at night. Her voice and stillness contrast with Hudson's mounting panic. There is a cut to a long shot, taken from behind, in which they are positioned on the left of the frame, looking across a bleak, dark landscape towards a distant silver moon. This shot links the image of the surrogate mother and daughter with a horizon that symbolizes the future. Ripley and Newt will be crucial to the construction of future survival strategies.

The presentation of Ripley and Newt as an image of generational continuity enables the pair to function as a trope for the entire human species. The conflict between human and monstrous presented in *Aliens* is a battle between two species types. The differences between the first and the second films of the series can be seen by comparing the scenes in which the face-hugger appears. I have argued that the face-hugger in *Alien* is presented as a foetus/placenta. It evokes horror because it is the image of a visceral inside. In *Aliens*, the face-hugger appears after Newt has been captured and cocooned. There are several medium close-ups of her face surrounded by thick white opaque strands. These appear slightly foamy at the bottom as if in the process of congealing. Newt is trapped in a viscous spider's web (Figure 5). Once the pod opens, there is a medium shot of its palpitating contents which consist of white, foaming strands. There are two shots of the face-hugger as it emerges, its elongated legs feeling their way over the edge of the pod. The creature's skin is stretched taut, each limb displaying two bony joints. Its six-legged structure and wavering movements clearly resemble a spider (Figure 6). The conflict between human and monstrous is that of humanity versus insects. Importantly, this changes the structures of horror. If the threat of *Alien* is that of a visceral *inside*, the threat of *Aliens* is that of a viscous materiality that must be designated *outside*. The congealing web functions like Kristeva's skin on the top of the milk, its palpable viscosity designating it abject.

5

6

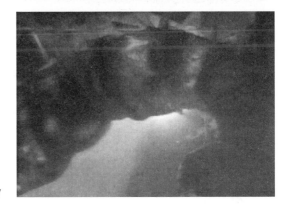

7

In *Aliens*, differentiation between species types takes the form of an opposition between cerebral replication and physical reproduction. This contrast is built up in the scene in which Ripley and Newt find the queen. Newt is balanced on Ripley's hip at first, and there follow cuts between medium close-ups of their two faces and shots of the queen. Their faces mirror each other, acting as a symbol of continuity but, importantly, a continuity achieved through shared experiences of being sole survivors rather than by physical reproduction. The first shot of the queen shows the end of her abdominal sac as she lays a pod. The translucent sac rises up, leaving the pod in place and covering it with a thick veil of mucus. The second image is a subjective shot which travels along the swollen abdominal sac. The dense, rounded shapes of the pods are clearly visible inside it, and the sac moves rhythmically as if pushing them along (Figure 7). The piecemeal presentation of the queen conveys a sense of her size. The cuts between Ripley's and Newt's faces and the queen's body also serve to contrast their cerebral mirroring with her mute physicality. The opposition face/body feeds into a traditional dialectical model, sustaining other oppositions such as mind/matter, individuation/undifferentiated physicality. As a representative of matter/maternality, the queen is clearly designated Other.

However, the presentation of the queen as materiality also intersects with her construction as a species type in that she is first presented as a queen bee. Her vast swollen belly renders her immobile while the drones wait at the threshold of her moist, blue inner chamber. The insect references are multiplied in the first shot of the queen's face and body. The camera is positioned behind Ripley and Newt as they gaze up at her. The queen's long mask-like face is presented centre screen, and three sets of what appear to be long black legs run from the edge of her face to the edge of the frame. This composition places her face as the centre of her black web-like body. The later close-ups of the queen's double-toothed jaw repeat the same web-like pattern of composition. She conjoins both the bee and the spider. It is this construction of the queen as another form of life that disrupts some of the structures of abjection in *Aliens*. The queen can be mapped as simply inhuman, a bug that lacks consciousness. However, she can also be mapped as parallel to the human, another form of life.

The battle between the two species types places them in an oppositional relation while drawing attention to the similarity between the two protagonists. Both are parthenogenetic mother figures who are tropes for the perpetuation of their respective species. The conflicts between them take the form of attempting to destroy each other's generative powers. Ripley torches the fields of pods with the flame thrower, rather than launching into a direct attack on the queen. Later, once the escape craft has returned to the main ship, the queen kills Bishop and goes after Newt. Ripley intervenes and manages to deflect her from her purpose. While the representation of motherhood as the instinctive desire to protect one's young does not break with tradition, the use of the mirroring mother figures in the final battle scenes does have a significant impact on the dialectical structures previously presented. Rather than upholding the oppositions between individuation/materiality, human/monstrous, the scenes imply that the desires and motives of both maternal figures are the same. Such a paralleling serves to undermine the Kristevan model of abjection in that it suggests that the Other might have its own desires and motives.

The end of *Aliens* can therefore be seen to offer two radically different constructions of the relation between the human and the monstrous. In so far as the confrontation ends with the queen being blasted into hyperspace by Ripley, the model of abjection is clearly dominant. However, the forcible rejection of the Other intersects with the presentation of resemblances between Ripley and the queen. This intersection means that the structures of horror are continually placed in jeopardy. For Kristeva, the abject is never securely banished. Its return is marked by a 'massive and sudden emergence of uncanniness, which, familiar as it might have been in an opaque and forgotten life, now harries me as radically separate, loathsome. Not me. Not that'.[24] If the structure of abjection is utter repudiation, the not me, it follows that the structure of the uncanny is both that which is familiar and that which the subject recognizes to be the same. The ending of *Aliens* can therefore be seen to play across both of these structures: setting up the queen as the visceral 'outside' to be rejected while also presenting her as a parthenogenetic mother whose motivations mirror Ripley's, swinging between the horror of the abject and the eeriness of the uncanny.

In punctuating the differential structures of abjection with patterns of mirroring, *Aliens* pushes the Kristevan model to its limits. The possibilities of drawing patterns of resemblance between Ripley and the queen are taken up in the rest of the series. In *Alien3*, Ripley is positioned as the feminine outside, the sole woman in an all-male penal colony. She is identified with the monstrous because she brings it into the colony and because she is carrying a future queen inside her. This film remains within traditional dialectics, repositioning Ripley as the abject. In contrast, *Alien Resurrection* abandons an oppositional construction of identity. The presentation of Ripley as the monster's mother does not simply conflate her with the queen, but presents the characters in relation to each other.

The opening of *Alien Resurrection* is set in a laboratory and reworks the mother–daughter relation of *Aliens*. As the camera moves forward, so the frame closes in to provide a medium close-up of the face of a female child. Ripley's voice-over can be heard repeating the words Newt said to her in another medical laboratory in *Aliens*: 'My mommie always said there were no monsters. No real ones. But there are.' The camera moves into a tighter close-up of the child's face, stopping at the word 'ones'. The face morphs into Ripley's and her voice-over then completes the line. The repetition of Newt's words conjoins the surrogate daughter and mother for an instant. However, as the camera pulls back, revealing a ring of scientists staring at Ripley's body, the connotations of the comment change. The 'monsters' may well be human scientists. The final twist is added by Dr Wren's later comments on Ripley's memories. Ripley can remember her past because the DNA from the alien queen has bequeathed her a capacity for instinctual memories. Newt's line is both a reminder of a particular relationship and a species memory. The figures of Newt, Ripley and the alien queen intersect in the morphing figure in the tube.

Ripley's identity is thus set up as an intersection point. She is altered by giving birth to the queen just as the queen will later display the nature of Ripley's bequest to her. Within a traditional psychoanalytic model, these points of intersection would constitute a breakdown of the oppositional structures of identity. On this model, Ripley's new-found memories would indicate a collapse of the division between human and monstrous, conflating Ripley with the alien queen. However, the beginning of *Alien Resurrection* is complicated in that the alien's capacity for instinctual memory also provides Ripley with a means of remembering Newt. The alien DNA is therefore reconfigured within Ripley to provide access to a specific relationship as well as to activate a species memory. The capacity for instinctual memory does not dissolve Ripley into the alien queen, but sets up a point of intersection between two distinct characters. Theorizing the possibility of productive points of intersection between self and Other, human and monstrous, requires an entirely different model of subject formation. The morphing figure in the tube stands for the possibility of change through productive encounters with otherness.

The opening of *Alien Resurrection* breaks away from Kristeva's model of abjection, offering a more Irigarayan account of subject formation. In *The Phenomenal Woman*, Christine Battersby defines Irigaray's project as an attempt to think through 'the formation of a self which can be permeated by otherness, and in which the boundary between the inside and the outside, between self and not-self, has to operate not antagonistically ... but in terms of patterns of flow'.[25] This conception of a subjectivity formed through permeable boundaries clearly contrasts with Kristeva's conception of a subject permanently fighting to maintain its borders. Moreover, the valorization of patterns of flow sets up a very different conception of the body. For Kristeva, the concept of the body as container relies upon the abjection of the viscous physicality of both inside and outside. In Irigaray's model, the body itself becomes a permeable structure, a volume without contours, whose physical fluidity sustains and supports the possibilities of intimate embraces with others.

Importantly, Irigaray's model of the subject as flow arises from a re/conceptualization of the space of the Other. She argues for a model of identity based on mother–daughter relations. The model of the permeable body arises from a re/imagining of the female body.[26] Battersby takes up Irigaray's project of theorizing from the position of the object to argue for a different model of the female subject. She argues that the female subject position exhibits five distinct features: capacity to give birth, being positioned within unequal power relations, lack of a sharp division between self and other, an identity that emerges through embodiment, and an identity linked to the monstrous.[27] In taking the capacity to give birth as a defining feature of a subject position, Battersby clearly challenges psychoanalytic models in which the mother functions only as an object to be rejected/abjected. (The focus on birth is not empirical, is not an attempt to argue that all women should have children.[28]) Importantly, the use of birth as a paradigm for re-thinking identity formation creates a model in which two selves can be mapped as interrelated and yet distinct:

> For the (normalised) 'female' there is no sharp division between 'self' and 'other'. Instead, the 'other' emerges out of the embodied self, but in ways that mean that two selves emerge and one self does not simply dissolve into the other.[29]

It is this possibility of two emergent selves, interrelated yet different, that I want to put into play in considering Ripley's relation to the queen in *Alien Resurrection*. The crossover of characteristics arises because Ripley has given birth to the queen. Their intimate relationality clearly corresponds to Battersby's model of an identity that 'allows the potentiality for otherness to exist within it, as well as alongside it'.[30] The abiding interpenetration of otherness can be seen in Ripley's characterization: she has gained particular motor skills from the queen. She has a significantly increased strength and her senses of hearing and smell are particularly acute. The scene in which Call breaks into her cell displays Ripley's other attributes. As she pushes her assailant's knife into her hand steam rises from the metal, indicating that it is being corroded by her acidic blood. Call asks her who she is. There is a cut to a medium long-shot of the pair kneeling opposite each other. Ripley is still holding her hand onto the steaming knife as she reels off her previous identity: 'Ripley, Ellen, Lieutenant first class, number 36706.' The positioning of the knife at centre frame clearly suggests she is not who she has been. Call tells her that she is 'a thing' grown in a lab and that the alien has been taken out of her. There is a medium close-up of Ripley's face and shoulders as she replies 'I can feel it, behind my eyes. I can hear it moving.' She holds Call's hand by the wrist as she delivers the line, tracing the socket of her eye with Call's fingertips. The use of touch shows the great increase in her tactility. It is as if she can express knowledge of her alien aspects through touch rather than language.

The choreography of Sigourney Weaver's performance serves to sustain the presentation of Ripley as more animal than human. When Call finds her she is lying on the floor, apparently asleep, with her left knee bent. She moves into the kneeling position opposite Call in one fluid roll. Later in the scene there is an over-the-shoulder shot of Ripley in which the camera is level with Call's head. Ripley suddenly rises from her heels, kneeling upwards, and the camera tilts rapidly keeping her in frame. There is a cut to a high-angle shot taken from over Ripley's shoulder as she reaches to grasp Call's frightened face in her hands. The angles of the shots emphasize the latent power displayed by Ripley's sudden movement. However, the gesture itself appears to be one fluid motion resembling a cobra arching upwards to strike. The alien queen has altered the nature of Ripley's lived embodiment. Ripley's new identity as 'the monster's mother' is conveyed through her new-found physical attributes and her fluid bodily gestures. This is important because her new identity can therefore be seen to arise through her materiality: 'it erupts from the flesh'[31] in a non-hylomorphic way. This reverses the Kristevan/Lacanian model in which materiality is that which has to be abjected, placed outside language, in order for the subject to be secured.

If the alien mother bequeaths Ripley a new physicality, the nature of Ripley's bequest to her is made obvious in the birth scene. Ripley is called to witness the birth. There is a series of five shots with fade-outs in which an alien carries

8

her to the birthing place. The fourth shot is a medium close-up in which Ripley's head is positioned directly below her carrier's and she appears to be lying beneath him. This shot clearly suggests a sexual encounter, another metaphor for the crossing of human and alien potentialities that occurs across the film. On arrival at the birthing place, Gediman tells Ripley that the queen has developed a mammalian reproductive system. The long shot of the queen taken from over Ripley's shoulder shows the dense, swollen belly she has developed. Unlike the sac in *Aliens*, which was light and translucent, showing the movement of the eggs as the mother laid them, this belly is dark heaving flesh (Figure 8). The contrast shows the development of the queen as a species type. The insectual image of the queen bee appears to have given way to a human reproductive system. There is a cut to a close-up of the queen's jaw as she throws her head back and screams. The sound is guttural, indicating pain. It is a sharp contrast to the sinister hissing sound directed by her predecessor at Ripley in *Aliens*. Indeed, unlike that earlier confrontation, the queen is hardly aware of Ripley's presence. All her sounds and movements belong to the process of giving birth. A later high-angle shot shows the mother arching her body as she throws her head backwards, imitating the rhythmical movements of human labour.

Ripley's bequest to the queen – the pain of labour – is a gift of a potentiality that has been mythologically encoded as distinctively human. In the story of Genesis, God curses Eve with the pain of childbirth as a punishment for having offered Adam the apple.[32] However, the birth scene in *Alien Resurrection* is an intersection point for both human and alien aspects. The baby is born by splitting the belly in two. It emerges from the dense flesh covered in a translucent layer of mucus. The light, visceral covering is similar to the white covering from which Ripley was seen to emerge after the operation. The image is that of a chrysalis, which re/works the insectual references of *Aliens*. The point is also made by Gediman, who coos 'you beautiful, beautiful butterfly' at the newborn.

The newborn is mapped as monstrous through its first act, the killing of its birth mother. While the presentation of Ripley and the alien queen displays a complex series of intersecting potentialities, their offspring is less diverse. It is the point at which the deadly force of the alien combines with a human infantile sadism. The alien infant has a humanized appearance, possessing an upper torso and a skull-like face. It lacks the double jaw and distinctive clenched-toothed mouth of the alien. The infant's mouth is hinged like the jaw of a skull, providing a width of stretch which enables it to crush Gediman's head between its teeth. The later killing of DiStephano displays the doubled genealogy of the child's ferocity. Having cornered Call in the cargo deck of the freighter, the *Betty*, the infant turns to confront DiStephano. The camera moves into a close-up of the infant, and the strobe lighting effect blanches out its skin, turning its mouth into a dark gash and drawing attention to the baby blue colour of its deep sunken eyes. The strobe lighting, used throughout the attack, facilitates a kind of perverse joke. The baby blue eyes are a reminder of the traditional helplessness of the newborn human child. They contrast with the ferocity it displays and also serve to present its aggression as an alien trait. The attack ends with a medium shot of the infant looking down at the pieces of DiStephano's brain in its hand. As the camera travels forward so the child flattens out its palm and straightens its elongated fingers, allowing the bloody debris to fall to the ground. This shot suggests that the violence may also be read as an expression of curiosity, positioning the attack as a form of infantile sadism.

The way in which the monstrous child is dispatched by Ripley plays into the theme of intersecting identities that structures the film. Ripley enters the cargo deck and demands that the infant release Call. She then moves towards the child, and there is a cut to a close-up of the pair embracing in which the infant's face is positioned in profile in the upper left corner of the screen and Ripley is looking up into his face from the lower right corner. The infant's elongated fingers can be seen stroking her hair. Their shape acts as a visual reminder of the fourth clone which Riply discovered earlier, and emphasizes the infant's genetic link to Ripley. There is a later close-up taken from the same side, but from a different angle, so that Ripley appears to be lying beneath the infant. The camera turns, repositioning them as standing once again. However, the initial angle is a reminder of a previous shot in which Ripley was being transported to the birth place and appeared to be having sex with her carrier. The motif of sexual intercourse compounds the intermingling of alien and human potentialities represented by both participants.

The intimate reunion of mother and child that prefaces the infant's death means that the traditional dispatch of the final monster cannot be regarded as a triumph. The infant's body is gradually destroyed as it is sucked out into hyperspace through a tiny hole in an inversion of human birth. There are three close-ups of Ripley's distraught face as she watches its death throes: in the second she utters the words 'I'm sorry'. The infant's sounds move up a register during its death. The guttural roars of its previous attacks and low moans of pleasure during Ripley's embrace give way to a higher, more human, register as it seems to be struggling to form words. The infant's intestines are sucked out first and its face, its most humanized feature, is left intact until the last moment when the skin is pulled from the skull and the facial bones themselves are finally pulverized. This painful piecemeal destruction clearly contrasts with the orgasmic expulsion of the final monsters in *Alien* and *Aliens*. In *Alien*, Ripley dispatches the threat, securing the Symbolic space of the craft. In *Aliens* the battle between Ripley and the queen is a fight for species survival in which the human is pitted against the insectual. By *Alien Resurrection* the oppositional relation between the human and the inhuman has been completely reconfigured to form a series of intersecting potentialities. The lack of an oppositional relation between self and Other, human and monstrous, means that the final confrontation between Ripley and the alien child is structured around similarity and therefore permeated by a sense of appalling loss.

Alien Resurrection may therefore be said to rework the structures of horror. If the ending of *Aliens* oscillates between the abject and the uncanny, the climax of *Alien Resurrection* completely reworks the uncanny. The final monster cannot be abjected in one swift movement because its appearance emphasizes its links to Ripley. Moreover, the blood relation between the child and its (grand)mother means that the destruction of the monster is an act of infanticide. Within the uncanny, the relations of familiarity and resemblance unsettle the subject because they act as a reminder of an 'opaque and forgotten life',[33] the pre-Oedipal union of the mother–child dyad. The uncanny can therefore be seen to constitute a reminder of maternality which unsettles the structures of opposition that create the subject. However, the finale of *Alien Resurrection* positions the mother as a subject and presents the killing of the child as painful because it constitutes a part of herself. The incestuous embrace that precedes the killing emphasizes this closeness, but does not constitute a disintegration of difference. The embrace shows the fondness that exists on both sides. The terrible inversion of birth that is played out at the end finishes the remarkable play of intersecting potentialities between Ripley and the queen that has structured the text. It is an appalling moment of loss because it seems to negate the trajectory set up by the constant crossings over, leaving Ripley as the sole reminder of the possibility of productive intersections.

9

The structures of resemblance in play at the end of *Alien Resurrection* become most acute in the film's most eerie scene, in which Ripley discovers clones one to seven. This scene expands Battersby's model of two emergent identities into a series of emergent selves. The scene sets up mirrorings across the text and across the *Alien* series. The bodies of the clones are presented floating in green fluid, each in a separate tubular container. The first container is lit by a top light that shines down onto the crown of the head of the floating body. This clone consists of a human head and torso conjoined with an alien tail. The light on the green water gives the flesh a yellow, waxy look as if it had been preserved from decay. As Ripley approaches the second container, there is a cut to a subjective shot of the clone's face. Her long black hair forms a still cloud in the water as the camera moves around the tube showing her two mouths: one with human lips parted in a silent 'o' and the other with the alien's clenched razor-toothed jaw (Figure 9). This close-up is mirrored by a close-up of Ripley towards the end of the swimming scene. She is looking back towards the last human female crew member, who has been grabbed by one of the aliens. Ripley tilts her head from side to side as she gazes, her black hair forming a swirling cloud about her face (Figure 10). The green water

10

blanches her skin tone, emphasizing the contrast between the darkness of her hair and the whiteness of her flesh. The lighting makes her less than human, as does her expression. She is gazing with curiosity rather than looking upset by the death of the crew member. This close-up of Ripley recalls the earlier shot of the clone, emphasizing their relationality.

The third container is shown through a travelling subjective shot which begins at the feet of the clone and moves up its body. The left arm of the third clone is crossed over the body and her hand is positioned on her right shoulder. The posture acts as a reminder of the initial presentation of the young Ripley. However, the clone only has one arm. There is a medium shot of Ripley taken through the contents of the fourth container. The clone's jawline, neck and arm are silhouetted on the left side of the screen. Her elongated hand and finger are positioned on the right side. Ripley's face is presented centre frame. She is side-lit and appears slightly blurry through the density of the green water. The convex tubing distorts her features as she moves off screen right. There is a cut to a medium close-up of the clone, whose clenched, alien jaw mirrors the previous distortion of Ripley's face.

The last clone extends the mirroring across the series as a whole. The establishing shot shows her lying on a metal operating table, her legs splayed outwards and a green cloth covering her pudenda and right thigh. The posture suggests that she has given birth. The camera travels towards her, ending with a medium shot of her upper body drawing attention to the suture in her thorax, showing that she has 'given birth' to the queen. There is a cut to a medium close-up of Ripley followed by a repetition of the medium shot of the clone, who struggles to form the phrase 'Kill me'. The clone stammers on the second word when repeating her request: 'Kill m'me'. The intonation pattern recalls the request of the female colonist found by the commandos in *Aliens*: she begs 'Please k'kill me', stammering on the second word. In *Aliens* the colonist is a mirror image of Ripley's nightmare self: both have been impregnated by the alien. By watching the colonist on the monitor, Ripley is looking at the double of her unconscious self, or the fate she might have had. In *Alien Resurrection* the previous doubles of the colonist and the dream self intersect in the figure of the clone. Ripley obeys the request and torches the operating table.

The clone scene presents the most forceful construction of resemblance between selves. Yet the clones are not simply to be conflated with Ripley: they constitute differential selves in so far as their bodies literally instantiate the possibilities of different kinds of intersections between Ripley and the queen. The collection of bodies constitutes a series of potentialities. If the colonist constitutes the literal manifestation of the fate Ripley feared at the beginning of *Aliens*, so the final clone forcibly materializes the fate of a 'meat by-product' (the term Colonel Perez uses to describe Ripley). The clone's body has clearly been subjected to surgical practices. The positioning of the green cloth reveals patterns of stapling down her abdomen and the incision in her thorax still gapes. She has been left without being stitched up – presumably to die, since the order, earlier in the film, to stitch up Ripley was a decision to allow her to live. Ripley's relation to the clone is the relation to that which she might have been, a relation of potentiality, the fate she did not have. The act of euthanasia enables the clone to escape the cycle of being experimented upon. The destruction of all the clones marks an end to their helpless powerlessness.

The structure of intersecting identities that occurs across *Alien Resurrection* has a doubled temporal aspect. The clones and the infant represent both what Ripley might have been and what she might become. This relation of potentiality expands Ripley's responsibilities. She cannot allow the clones to be used in future medical experiments, just as she cannot allow the sadistic infant to go on killing indiscriminately. While the use of the double in *Aliens* has the same futural aspect – the fate that Ripley might still have – the colonist also represents an unconscious fear that Ripley ceases to have. By the end both she and Newt cease suffering from nightmares. They have successfully dispatched the threat of the Other. This is important because the structures of identity in *Alien Resurrection* are different. Ripley is created through her relationality to the queen, the clones and the infant. Their deaths position her as the final intersection point. Yet as an intersection point she is also permeated by their ghosts, which remain in the present acting as potentialities. The sense of their continued presence is provided by Ripley's later mirroring of the second clone in the swimming scene. The open-endedness of *Alien Resurrection* is the result of an absence of the psychoanalytic frame. Identity is more than recollection and replaying of basic structures: it becomes a series of intersections which have a futural aspect. Ripley may yet become the alien queen, laying her pods in some capital city on Earth; she may be used in further experiments to create dangerous weapons; she may become a psychotic killer: all of these possibilities remain – until the arrival of *Alien 5*.

NOTES

1. Barbara Creed, '*Alien* and the Monstrous-Feminine', in Annette Kuhn, ed., *Alien Zone: Cultural Theory and Contemporary Science Fiction Cinema*, London: Verso, 1990; Julia Kristeva, *Powers of Horror: An Essay on Abjection*, trans. L.S. Roudiez, New York: Columbia University Press, 1982.
2. Creed, '*Alien* and the Monstrous-Feminine', p. 129.

3. Ibid. Creed refers to a single vaginal entrance, although two entrances can be seen.

4. Ibid., p. 130.

5. Ibid., p. 131.

6. Ibid., pp. 131, 133.

7. Ibid., p. 136.

8. Ibid., pp. 135, 136, 140.

9. James H. Kavanagh, 'Feminism, Humanism and Science in *Alien*', in Kuhn, ed., *Alien Zone*, p. 76. Kavanagh reads the body of the craft as combining elements of both womb and tomb.

10. Creed, '*Alien* and the Monstrous-Feminine', pp. 137, 138.

11. Ibid., p. 137.

12. Kristeva, *Powers of Horror*, p. 13.

13. Ibid., p. 7.

14. Ibid.

15. Ibid., p. 3.

16. Ibid., p. 53.

17. Ibid., p. 54.

18. Ibid., p. 5.

19. Creed, '*Alien* and the Monstrous-Feminine', pp. 129–31.

20. Kavanagh, 'Feminism, Humanism and Science in *Alien*', p. 77.

21. See Vivian Sobchack, 'The Virginity of Astronauts: Sex and the Science Fiction Film', in Kuhn, ed., *Alien Zone*, p. 107. Sobchack reads the revelation of Ripley's body as significant, arguing that it strips the character of her 'narrative competence' and reconstructs her as a sex object. I argue that it is Ripley's act of dressing again that is crucial to this scene.

22. Kavanagh, 'Feminism, Humanism and Science in *Alien*', p. 77.

23. Constance Penley, 'Time Travel, Primal Scene and the Critical Dystopia', in Kuhn, ed., *Alien Zone*, p. 125.

24. Kristeva, *Powers of Horror*, p. 2.

25. Christine Battersby, *The Phenomenal Woman: Feminist Metaphysics and the Patterns of Identity*, Cambridge: Polity Press, 1998, p. 49.

26. Irigaray's project can therefore be compared with Creed's attempt to generate new images of the feminine that are not simply the inverse of the phallic standard.

27. Battersby, *The Phenomenal Woman*, pp. 38, 39.

28. Ibid., p. 4.

29. Ibid., p. 8.

30. Ibid., p. 57.

31. Ibid., p. 39.

32. Genesis, iii, 14–19.

33. Kristeva, *Powers of Horror*, p. 2.

9

PSYCHO-CYBERNETICS
IN FILMS OF THE 1990S

CLAUDIA SPRINGER

'I want to get out of this rat hole! I want to get online! I need a computer!' declares Johnny (Keanu Reeves) in the 1995 film *Johnny Mnemonic*. His desire to flee the inhospitable world and take refuge in cyberspace is not unusual in science-fiction films of the mid 1990s. The dark, decrepit, garbage-strewn, plague-infested wasteland in *Johnny Mnemonic* is typical of these films' dystopian vision of humanity on the brink of destruction. Fear that human beings have lost control figures prominently in the millennial anxiety that pervades contemporary science-fiction films. A combination of environmental destruction, late-capitalist corruption, drug-resistant diseases, and increasingly sophisticated electronic technology (not to mention alien invaders) threatens human existence in 1990s science fiction.

Human beings in science-fiction films have already lost their uniqueness to robots, androids, and cyborgs. Replicants – genetically engineered androids – were touted as 'more human than human' by their corporate creators in the 1982 film *Blade Runner*, and the film's contrast between dejected humans resigned to a dreary existence dictated by corporate greed and the replicants' passionate intensity proves the motto depressingly true. During the 1980s and early 1990s, steely hard muscular cyborgs were a science-fiction film mainstay, putting human beings to shame with their indomitable strength and superior logic in the films *The Terminator* (1984), *Terminator II: Judgment Day* (1991), *RoboCop* (1987), *RoboCop 2* (1990), *RoboCop 3* (1993), *Hardware* (1990), *Eve of Destruction* (1991), and others.[1] The T-800 cyborg in *Terminator II* even surpassed humans as a wise and compassionate father figure. But the muscular cyborg's relentlessly destructive power eventually became a predictable cliché and object of parody. Its ability to fascinate had run its course.

In films, rampaging muscle-bound cyborgs were replaced by slim young men and women jacked into cyberspace, inspired by 'console cowboys' in cyberpunk fiction of the 1980s. Cybernetically enhanced existence shifted in films from pumped-up physiques to expanded minds in films that critics labelled cyberthrillers.[2] Influenced by political, cultural, artistic and scientific developments, the new cyberthrillers – *Strange Days*, *Johnny Mnemonic*, *Hackers*, *Virtuosity* and *The Net* (all released in 1995) – place their emphasis on the psychological.[3] Cyberspace in the films is frequently a metaphor for the human mind. Cyberthrillers are fascinated by the extraordinary capabilities of sophisticated technological devices in a future inhospitable to humans, but they revolve in contradictory fashion around resolutely human fears and desires. This contradiction is obscured by the films' erasure of difference between their two dichotomous elements. Human beings and their technological inventions become increasingly indistinguishable in the films as the human mind projects itself into the farthest reaches of the electronic realm.

Science-fiction films join other contemporary discourses in positing an analogy between the workings of computers and of the human mind. For over thirty years, various branches of science have maintained that minds function similarly to computers. The computer–mind analogy is by now a widely known postulate, though not a universally accepted one, but its manifestations in popular culture display anything but scientific methodicalness and precision. Cyberspace in films is typically an unpredictable internal space that delivers intoxicating thrills but also contains treacherous dangers. Lurking within it are the unconscious mind's deeply repressed drives and desires. As Margaret Morse points out, 'Cyberculture is personal rather than impersonal, irrational rather than rational, perceptually elaborate rather than abstract, and so on.'[4]

From their Golden Age in the 1950s, American science-fiction films have combined pseudo-scientific rhetoric with religion and militarism.[5] But while the Cold War-era science-fiction films of the fifties were drenched in paranoia, the post-Cold War-era films exude anxiety, concerned not with protecting a valuable status quo against invading enemies but with trying to make sense of a corrupt world in which there is no longer anything worth protecting. In many cases, science-fiction texts of the 1990s distrust official science, casting doubt on its ability and willingness to provide accurate explanations. Individuals in the texts have come unmoored: they are unable to trust any institutions and have no viable way to understand their own predicaments. Cultural critic McKenzie Wark writes that with the popular television show *The X-Files*,

> science fiction completes a journey, from stories of decimating the world with technology, through the dystopias where people have to battle a technology gone out of control, to the worst-case scenario: We have lost control, and don't even know it.[6]

Loss of control is a central trope of postmodern existence and something that science-fiction films have warned against for decades (for example *Invasion of the Body Snatchers* [1956] and *THX-1138* [1970]). Science-fiction films have been instrumental in visualizing and narrativizing the qualities associated with postmodernism: disorientation, powerlessness, fragmentation, disintegration, loss of boundaries, and hybridization. Warding off these threats was one of the symbolic functions of the iron-clad muscular cyborg in science-fiction films of the 1980s and early 1990s. Despite the irony that the fortified cyborg was itself a man–machine hybrid and could no longer lay claim to a unified identity, it fought hard to resist the postmodern breakdown of gender boundaries and rigid rules pertaining to sexuality. But its own compromised status as a hybrid made its mission futile. Leaving the hard-bodied cyborg behind, Hollywood turned to cyberspace and the expansion of the mind.

There is nothing new in Hollywood's metaphoric use of space: ever since German Expressionism filmmakers have designed their diegetic worlds around psychological projections. And, as Margaret Morse writes, 'The interiors of the home television viewing space, the automobile, the space capsule, and the computer are ultimately associated with the interiority of the human mind.'[7] Facilitating the metaphor is the unsurpassed intimacy of humans with their technologies in the late twentieth century. The virtualities created by the screens in our lives have, for many, become more 'real' than the experience of un-mediated actuality. Responses to the rise of virtuality are polarized between critics who condemn the collapse of 'reality' into simulation and celebrants who applaud what they see as a new freedom to reshape identity.

In 1990s cyberthrillers, cyberspace functions as a device for filmmakers to recreate the self in a depleted and corrupt external world, experimenting with both liberatory and repressive scenarios. Each film acknowledges the capacity of cyberspace to alter human identity. But even though the films experiment with expanded electronic embodiment, they all eventually establish the suprem-acy of 'the real'. Not unlike the hard-bodied cyborg films of the 1980s, the 1990s cyberthrillers work to ward off the instability made possible by elec-tronic existence. An analysis of the cyberthrillers reveals that cyberspace is constructed as an instigator of wild instability, and simultaneously as a thera-peutic device used to restore conventional order.

In *Johnny Mnemonic*, the first of the cyberthrillers to be released and the one that most clearly plays out their contradictions, Johnny has been substantially re-created, and this causes him to lose control of his identity and his life. He has been transformed by surgical means: his head contains 'wet-wired brain implants' into which he can upload data directly through a cranial jack. He is an elite agent in the year 2021 who is paid high prices for smuggling corporate data in a world where information is the most valuable and carefully protected commodity. But Johnny has also paid a price for his transformation into a 'mnemonic courier': he has had to 'dump a chunk of long-term memory', namely, all memory of his childhood. Without personal memories, Johnny has lost access to a coherent identity, to a sense of self attained through the accumulation of remembered experiences. Johnny's lost identity pushes to an extreme the ideas of historical amnesia, fractured subjectivity, and loss of control associated with postmodernism. Its premiss is that human interactions with electronic technology have abolished conventional notions about individual identity.

Johnny's condition in *Johnny Mnemonic* exemplifies postmodern fragmentation, disorientation and powerlessness. He is determined to obtain full memory restoration, but instead finds himself carrying an excess load of data in his head; and unless he finds the download code and removes the data within twenty-four hours he will experience neural failure and death. With his head crammed full of data, his loss of memory, and his confused attempts to understand his predicament and the hostile environment, Johnny literalizes a postmodern subject bombarded with information, disconnected from the past in an eternal present, and spatially disoriented. Johnny is not the film's only symbol of the postmodern condition: the diegetic world is devastated by NAS – Nerve Attenuation Syndrome – which produces palsy and seizures before destroying its victims. NAS is caused by the omnipresence of electronic technology in people's lives: it has overloaded their nervous systems and created a new global plague.

Other 1990s cyberthrillers join *Johnny Mnemonic* in using cyberspace as a metaphor for the mind in order to explore human subjectivity in the electronic age. *The Net* is about computer systems analyst Angela Bennett (Sandra Bullock), whose entire life revolves around her home computer; she has no need to set foot outdoors. Angela's identity is erased by terrorist hackers when she inadvertently gains possession of a disk they want. Once they have wiped out her existence in all computer records, she is, to all intents and purposes, gone. With no way to prove her identity, she cannot get help from the police and must rely on her own resourcefulness to solve the mystery, regain her identity, and apprehend the terrorists.

In *The Net*, the computer, as in *Johnny Mnmonic*, is both deadly and life-affirming. Angela *is* her computer in more ways than one: she lives through it, maintaining connections to others almost exclusively via computer, and is eliminated by it when her on-line identity is erased. Although the film is a cautionary tale about the dangers of human dependence on electronic technology, it also ironically reinforces fears about face-to-face human interactions: Angela becomes vulnerable when she naively falls for the romantic overtures of the dashingly handsome hacker leader at a tropical beach resort. Thus the film's paranoia extends to both electronic and physical contact. Because Angela's vulnerability is linked to her gender and sexuality – which is expressed in a conventional Hollywood version of heterosexuality – the film disavows the computer's ability to reconstruct these attributes. Angela is assumed to have an on-line self identical to an absolute 'actual' self. Her identity certainly does not participate in what Sadie Plant calls 'the new malleability', in which gender and sexual identities exist on a fluctuating continuum, always capable of transforming into another state.[8]

The film *Virtuosity* acknowledges the computer's power to create new identities, but a simulated electronic being is represented as the ultimate in villainy. Sid 6.7 (Russell Crowe), a computer construct, is a ruthless composite of the world's most heinous criminals: Adolf Hitler, Charles Manson, John Wayne Gacy and Jeffrey Dahmer, among others. When Sid 6.7 escapes from the confines of the computer and enters the real world, ex-cop Parker Barnes (Denzel Washington) is recruited to go after him. Barnes is in jail for killing the criminals who murdered his wife and daughter, and while incarcerated he has become a subject of virtual-reality experiments designed to create more effective policemen. After Sid 6.7 – Barnes's chief adversary in virtual reality – escapes, Barnes is told that if he succeeds in stopping the virtual killer's murderous spree, he will be given his freedom. Barnes teams up with a young woman psychologist, Dr Madison Carter (Kelly Lynch), who has a young daughter. In the film's climax, Sid 6.7 has taken Carter's daughter hostage and trapped her in a rooftop air-conditioning cylinder with a bomb attached to a timer, restaging the exact circumstances that destroyed Barnes's wife and daughter when Barnes was unable to rescue them in time. This time, Barnes is able to defuse the bomb before it detonates, thereby saving the new mother and daughter in his life and redeeming his past inadequacy. He also defeats Sid 6.7, returning him to the confines of virtual reality.

In *Virtuosity* the computer houses the mind's demons, and the forces of psychiatry and law enforcement team up to apprehend and contain them. Sid 6.7 is society's unrestrained Id, which has erupted from the depths of cyberspace. On the surface, then, *Virtuosity* condemns cyberspace for unleashing dangerous, destructive powers; but perhaps unintentionally it also enacts a vision of jubilant release from the constraints of a fixed identity. Sid 6.7 is a flamboyant, lively merrymaker who luxuriates in his simulated life. He teases and taunts, struts and leers, as he wreaks havoc. His immaculate blond, blue-eyed visage and brutal violence code him as an Aryan fascist, but there is also a hint of sexual ambiguity in his taunting come-ons to Parker Barnes. Before the film's forces succeed in containing Sid 6.7 in virtual reality, he frolics through actual reality, overturning all norms and conventions and flaunting the freedom of 'the new malleability'.

Strange Days joins *Virtuosity* in condemning cyberspace for its ability to cross boundaries and blur identities. Ralph Fiennes plays Lenny Nero, also an ex-cop, who sells illegal 'playback', digital recordings of other people's experiences. The illicit drug of the future, playback seductively draws users into another person's consciousness, allowing them to escape their own subjectivity and enjoy thirty minutes of someone else's excitement, danger or sex – everything the other person saw, heard and felt. Lenny is inadvertently pulled into criminal intrigue when a killer on the loose starts supplying him with playbacks of brutal murders from the victims' point of view, and implying that Lenny's ex-girlfriend Faith (Juliet Lewis) will be the next victim. With the reluctant help of his friend and bodyguard Mace (Angela Bassett), Lenny protects Faith and searches for the killer, only to discover that he is a close friend, another ex-cop who is also having an affair with Faith. At the end of the film, Lenny kills the murderer, renounces Faith, and, at the stroke of midnight on New Year's Eve 1999, surprises Mace by embracing her and giving her a passionate kiss.

Poised as it is on the eve of the new millennium, *Strange Days* explicitly evokes the possibility of change. Stylistically the film acknowledges that things have already changed: its rapid editing and dizzying hand-held camera movement provide a sensation of electronic-age speed and vertiginous existence. Playback intensifies the feeling with its disorienting sense of disembodied presence. The dizzying style of *Strange Days* provides a more fully articulated vision of electronically altered consciousness than is found in the other cyberthrillers. In *Johnny Mnemonic*, *The Net*, *Virtuosity* and *Hackers*, cyberspace is carefully differentiated from the 'real' world with a distinct cinematic style. Cyberspace is characterized by computer graphics, rapid camera movement, and extreme angles, while the 'real' world is live-action footage shot pedantically in conventional Hollywood style. But, despite its more radical style, *Strange Days* joins *Virtuosity* in discrediting electronically expanded identity and imposing the restrictions of the 'real'. Playback in the film is associated with two types of experience: murder and sex; and the sex is represented as regressive and debilitating. Lenny obsessively uses playback to re-experience his relationship and sexual encounters with Faith, on whom he is fixated in a self-destructive way. When he renounces her, he in effect renounces dwelling mentally in the electronic realm, and kissing Mace represents his return to 'actual' experience.

Ironically, these films often employ cyberspace as a therapeutic device to restore order even after they have implicated it as the cause of dangerous instability. Angela in *The Net* uses her computer skills to outmanoeuvre the hackers and regain her original identity. Parker Barnes and Madison Carter, the psychologist, are able to outwit Sid 6.7 in *Virtuosity* by successfully psychoanalysing his demented electronic mind. *Hackers*, a film about a group of high-school hackers who take on a powerful criminal hacker called The Plague, uses cyberspace as the playing field for elaborate electronic showdowns that culminate in their victory. In *Johnny Mnemonic*, Johnny turns to cyberspace, which functions as externalized mind, to restore order after his life has spun out of control. Cyberspace saves not only Johnny himself but the entire population of the world. In order to succeed, Johnny enters cyberspace, but cyberspace also enters him in the form of the voluminous data jacked into his head.

Entering and exiting, filling up and spewing out: *Johnny Mnemonic* relies heavily on such motifs. The film's most kinetic sequences are the digital representations of data uploading into Johnny's head and Johnny flying through cyberspace and his own mind. In all of these computer-animated sequences, there is an explosive blast into virtuality. The camera careens forward at breath-taking speeds in the digitized sequences of cyberspace, a technique that *Strange Days* duplicates in live-action footage in its representation of playback. *Johnny Mnemonic* heightens the intensity of cyberspace with bright, vivid colours that are in sharp contrast with the greyness of the film's bleak external world. The film's association of technology with exhilarating speed places it in the tradition of 1950s and 1960s youth culture films that celebrate fast cars and motor-cycles. Like the screen rebels played by Marlon Brando, James Dean, Peter Fonda and Dennis Hopper, Johnny responds to a meaningless, hypocritical world by blasting away on a powerful machine – except that his vehicle is a computer console. Speed equals freedom in these films, and the highway – whether actual or virtual – cuts a purifying swath through the confusion. Not coincidentally, Johnny suits up to 'enter' cyberspace, donning data-gloves and eyephones that recall the biker rebels' leather gear and helmets. The steep three-dimensional grids through which Johnny speeds have become the stand-ard cinematic signifier for cyberspace. With its energy and lively colours, cyber-space is the film's antidote to its depleted realm of 'reality'.

A preoccupation with entrances and exits – gorging and disgorging – exists in all of the cyberthrillers and extends beyond their interest in entering and exiting cyberspace. *Virtuosity* revolves around a motif of containment and escape: Parker Barnes from prison, Sid 6.7 from virtual reality and back in again, and Madison Carter's daughter from an air-conditioning cylinder. *The Net* is concerned with Angela's exits from and entrances into houses: she originally confines herself to her house, becomes endangered when she leaves, is unable to return after her house is sold, and sets up housekeeping with her mother in a new house at the end. *Strange Days* contains a motif of corridors, and its frenetic moving camera repeatedly invades narrow spaces. The films' concern with containment creates a tension, since it implies a desire for a pleasure that cyberspace can best provide, and yet cyberspace is simultaneously reproached for causing uncertainty and instability.

In a perceptive analysis of the desire for containment, Margaret Morse identifies it as an 'oral logic of incorporation' that pervades the late-twentieth-century cultural fascination with escaping the body for immersion in the virtual. In what she calls 'the culinary discourses of a culture undergoing transformation to an information society',[9] the oral logic of incorporation 'is a more-than-closeness: it involves introjecting or surrounding the other (or being introjected or surrounded)'.[10] The desire for disembodied immersion is a new cultural fantasy, an escape fantasy that has superseded the idea of space travel: 'The desire for an evolutionary transformation of the human has shifted focus from the preparation for the journey into "outer space" from a dying planet to the virtual "inner space" of the computer.'[11] Containment in the computer's virtual realm provides comforting security in this fantasy, as opposed to the space-travel fantasy's aggressive confidence. The desire for immersion, Morse points out, pervades our culture and exists in even the most sophisticated discourses, but its prototype is the infant's experience of oneness with its mother. Oral logic begins in infancy, in the Lacanian Imaginary, but extends throughout life when it is evoked metaphorically in immersive experiences not necessarily related to food. In fact, when the body is abandoned to enter a computer, food is implicitly relinquished. Morse writes, 'We are in a strange situation when the desire for fusion and wholeness presupposes, at least in representation, the repudiation and disavowal of the body and the negation of food itself.'[12]

Johnny in *Johnny Mnemonic* wants room service, wants his food provided automatically, shouting to the heavens at his lowest moment, 'I want room service!' After he loses access to room service, he turns to the abstemious world of cyberspace. But in fact room service and cyberspace, despite their superficial differences, are fundamentally alike in the film: both evoke a regressive infantile attachment to the mother, whose shadowy presence underlies the logic of incorporation. Room service is a substitute for the mother's plenitude, which fulfils the infant's every need. Cyberspace also functions as a maternal substitute, surrounding the computer user with its all-encompassing embrace. By enveloping the body, cyberspace recalls the powerful sense of unity with the mother experienced by an infant before the disruptive awareness of its own separateness intervenes.

In *Johnny Mnemonic*, the maternal role of cyberspace is in fact explicit: what the spectator learns is that cyberspace is haunted by Johnny's mother. Cyberspace functions as Johnny's mind; and deep in Johnny's unconscious, beyond his awareness, is his mother. The film takes Johnny from fragmentation to unification, and defines the process only in conventional terms of a resolution of the Oedipal crisis and attainment of heterosexual romance, scenarios that are entirely dependent on a coherent subject to do the resolving and attaining. The possible psychic life of a new hybrid entity (a 'terminal identity', to use Scott Bukatman's term[13]) is not explored.

In *Johnny Mnemonic*, the logic of incorporation hinges on the maternal voice as sonorous envelope, and jacks it into the cybernetic age. Kaja Silverman describes how

> the trope of the maternal voice as sonorous envelope grows out of a powerful cultural fantasy, a fantasy which recent psychoanalytic theory shares with classic cinema. The fantasy in question turns upon the image of infantile containment – upon the image of a child held within the environment or sphere of the mother's voice.[14]

Silverman goes on to argue that every enactment of this fantasy treats it as either immensely gratifying or as intolerable, revealing the profoundly ambivalent nature of the fantasy, 'an ambivalence which attests to the divided nature of subjectivity'.[15] *Johnny Mnemonic* turns the computer into a sonorous envelope, for it is in cyberspace that Johnny's virtual self is surrounded by his mother's voice calling, 'Johnny, Johnny.' Until his mother has been destroyed, he recoils in confusion and horror. Then he enters cyberspace and embraces her image without fear of her voice engulfing him: he is now in control and her voice exists only in his memory. For *Johnny Mnemonic*, saving the world from a plague unleashed by technology is identical to taking the mother out of the machine and turning it into a man's world where the male ego can swoop and soar at dazzling speeds without fear of containment by the mother's sonorous voice.

In *The Net*, Angela's slippery identity, like Johnny's, is entwined with her mother's. In this case, the mother has Alzheimer's disease and is living in a state of benign confusion in a retirement home. When she fails to recognize her own daughter, Angela is distraught. Angela has actually lost her identity before the cyber-terrorists even enter the scene, because her mother does not know her. Unlike Johnny, Angela returns to a relationship of maternal plenitude, albeit one in which she dominates her confused mother. When Angela has her identity restored, she is shown living in a cosy house with her mother. Her subjectivity is not dependent on her mother's death, whereas Johnny's conforms to the classic Lacanian masculine paradigm, which requires separation from the mother in order to enter the Symbolic order of the father.

The film *Hackers* is also explicitly preoccupied with mothers. Dade Murphy (Jonny Lee Miller), the eighteen-year-old hacker who goes by the moniker Zero Cool, also frees himself from his mother before he is able to defeat the villainous The Plague and find romance. The key to his success, to a release from years on probation for the hacking crimes of his youth, is to learn that his mother respects him and that he has the power to decide her fate. *Virtuosity* and *Strange Days* are less explicitly concerned with mothers, but they link their male protagonists with 'safe' maternal women (who are both mothers of young children) – Madison Carter in *Virtuosity* and Mace in *Strange Days* – who nurture them without threatening to engulf them.

Cyberspace in these films, then, plays out a series of psychological tropes: it signifies fractured, unstable subjectivity or amnesia and the Imaginary realm's uneasy maternal bond. It also holds the therapeutic power to solve the problems it is responsible for creating. Resolution consists of asserting the primacy of 'the real', of restoring or attaining an identity that exists 'outside' of the electronic arena. This is an essentialist resolution that hinges on the assumption that an individual is defined by a single true subjectivity. This closure is consistent with the films' overall essentialism, which emerges most obviously in their racial politics. In several of the films, race is a central presence and African-Americans are consistently associated with the 'real'. There is an implicit message that African-Americans have a fundamentally 'grounded' essence that resists electronically induced instability and can 'heal' white people who are careening out of control.

In *Johnny Mnemonic*, Johnny is only able to defeat the Yakuza, download the excess data from his head, and televise the cure for NAS with the assistance of the Loteks, a fringe group of dissidents in Newark led by J-Bone, played by the African-American rap artist Ice-T, who is well known for his staunch anti-racism. Throughout the film the Loteks are diametrically opposed to the elite Pharmakom corporation. While Pharmakom employs streamlined electronic technology to confuse and manipulate consumers, the Loteks use their cobbled-together technological detritus to tell people 'the truth'. J-Bone's face periodically appears on diegetic television screens with an urgent direct-address message when his Lotek hackers jam television broadcasts. The Loteks exemplify the slogan popularized by William Gibson in his fiction: 'the street finds its own uses for things'. To emphasize the point, the Loteks literally inhabit the streets in *Johnny Mnemonic*, while corporate executives live high above in their stratospheric skyscrapers. But as science-fiction author Samuel R. Delany points out, the slogan 'the street finds its own uses for things' is naive in the wake of the 1992 uprising in Los Angeles that followed the acquittal of the police officers who beat Rodney King. Interviewed by cultural critic Mark Dery, Delany states: 'To stand in the midst of the millions of dollars of devastation in Los Angeles and say, with an ironic smile, "The street finds its own uses for things" is beyond irony and into the lunatic.'[16]

The Loteks' role in the film is not only to challenge corporate control but also to help Johnny resolve his identity crisis. By placing J-Bone and his people at the service of Johnny, the film shows black people risking (and losing) their lives to save white people. J-Bone's devotion to Johnny repeats a familiar trope from the cyberpunk trilogy of William Gibson. In Gibson's *Neuromancer*, *Count Zero* and *Mona Lisa Overdrive*, white protagonists encounter helpful black people who figure as uncorrupted primitives. As Kathleen Biddick writes in her analysis of the trope of healing and its relationship to colonial rhetoric in Gibson's novels, 'The turn to the "native" for healing can repeat the colonialist desire for redemption from the other, the repetition of the dream to restore the Christian Paradise that failed in the Old New World through the New New World.'[17] When J-Bone, Johnny, and Johnny's bodyguard/love interest Jane share the screen in a vision of racial and gender harmony at *Johnny Mnemonic*'s end, the film asserts just such a 'paradise'.

Strange Days joins *Johnny Mnemonic* in turning to African-Americans for healing. Mace, who is black, devotes her energies to assisting and protecting Lenny, a white man. Mace is opposed to a white woman, Faith, with Faith representing the regressive seduction of playback and Mace representing the 'real'. It is Mace who destroys Lenny's playback tapes and angrily exhorts him to reject their hold on him, shouting, 'Lenny! This is your life, Right here, Right now! It's real-time, you hear me? Real-time. Time to get real, not playback. You understand me?' Lenny gets 'real' at the end of the film when he relinquishes Faith, who is handcuffed and led away by police, and passionately kisses Mace.

Strange Days reinforces its essentializing view of African-Americans with a parallel plot about the brutal killing of a famous black musician, Jeriko One, who, through his music and powerful speeches, had mobilized black inner-city youth in a massive protest movement against the Los Angeles Police Department and the white power structure. Lenny and Mace discover that Jeriko One was killed by white racist policemen, and the film indicates that the city will explode with violence when Jeriko's followers are informed. A huge brawl erupts among a crowd of New Year's Eve revellers when Mace, having got the better of the murderous cops, is attacked by a group of white policemen who take turns kicking and pounding her with batons in a scene reminiscent of the Rodney King beating. But the film defuses the crowd's angry response with a *deus ex machina* – the LA Deputy Commissioner of Police – who descends from the heavens in a helicopter, arrests the two cops who killed Jeriko, and demands medical attention for Mace. In a grotesque revision of the events surrounding the Rodney King beating, the police chief proves to be ethical and benevolent, and the police force benign except for the two bad racist cops. The crowd returns to its celebration of the New Year and Lenny kisses Mace. Black rage has been erased, or, rather, redirected to support confused white people, at the film's dawn of the twenty-first century.

In *Virtuosity*, Parker Barnes is an angry victimized black man. White psychopaths killed his wife and daughter, the white legal system imprisoned him for taking revenge, and in prison he is taunted with racist slurs, pitted by the white prison guards against a white supremacist hulk who spits obscene racist remarks at Barnes while trying to kill him. The film contains and redirects Barnes's rage by using his focused intensity against Sid 6.7, the out-of-control electronic psychokiller. Parker Barnes is the only one who has what it takes, according to the film, to defeat his loopy but formidable opponent. Like J-Bone, Mace and Jeriko One, Barnes represents 'authenticity'. And like the others, Barnes's rage against racism is defused by his support for white individuals. In *Virtuosity*, Barnes risks his life in order to save a white woman (Madison Carter) and her daughter, despite the fact that whites killed his own wife and daughter. Barnes's disavowal of his rage and race becomes painfully clear when he is trying to defuse the bomb. With just seconds to go before detonation, he has to choose between several switches. Staring at the switches, he mutters, 'eenie, meenie, miney, mo'. He does not continue, but by this point has already been caught by the toe.

The cyberthrillers of the mid 1990s endow the psycho-cybernetic realm with extraordinary powers to disrupt and simultaneously to heal. The films imply that travelling 'into the heart of the mind' (the title of a 1984 book[18]) can transform the self and the world. It is a vision of a dangerously destabilizing and yet miraculously therapeutic cyberspace. Diving into cyberspace in the cyberthrillers activates all of the pleasures and dangers of the unconscious mind, and facilitates essentialist fantasies. If science-fiction films have scrapped the cyborg man of steel, Hollywood still insists on enforcing his rigid, rule-bound essentialist categories.

NOTES

1. Chapter 4 of my book *Electronic Eros*, Austin: University of Texas Press, 1996, analyses the figure of the cybernetic man-of-steel in popular culture.
2. One critic who uses the term 'cyberthriller' is Ty Burr, in his article '"Mnemonic" Plague', *Entertainment Weekly*, 17 November 1995, pp. 86–7.
3. The present chapter reproduces parts of my previous analysis of the cyberthrillers of 1995, 'Born to be Mild', in *21.C Scanning the Future: The Magazine of Culture, Technology and Science*, no. 23, 1996, pp. 13–17.
4. Margaret Morse, *Virtualities: Television, Media Art, and Cyberculture*, Bloomington: Indiana University Press, 1998, p. 6.
5. An excellent analysis of how science-fiction films of the 1950s incorporate religion and science can be found in Vivian Sobchack, *Screening Space: The American Science Fiction Film*, New York: Ungar, 1987, pp. 55–63.
6. McKenzie Wark, 'D-Filing the American Dream', in *21.C Scanning the Future: The Magazine of Culture, Technology and Science*, no. 4, 1996, p. 23.
7. Morse, *Virtualities*, p.103
8. Sadie Plant, *Zeroes and Ones: The Matrix of Women and Machines*, New York: Doubleday, 1997, p. 177.
9. Morse, *Virtualities*, p. 125.
10. Ibid., p. 127.
11. Ibid., p. 136.
12. Ibid., p. 135.
13. Scott Bukatman introduced and analysed this term in *Terminal Identity: The Virtual Subject in Postmodern Science Fiction*, Durham, NC: Duke University Press, 1993.
14. Kaja Silverman, *The Acoustic Mirror*, Bloomington: Indiana University Press, 1988, p. 72.
15. Ibid.
16. Mark Dery, 'Black to the Future: Interviews with Samuel R. Delany, Greg Tate, and Tricia Rose', in Mark Dery, ed., *Flame Wars: The Discourse of Cyberculture*, Durham, NC: Duke University Press, 1994, p. 194.
17. Kathleen Biddick, 'Humanist History and the Haunting of Virtual Worlds: Problems of Memory and Rememoration', *Genders*, no. 18, 1993, p. 53.
18. Frank Rose, *Into the Heart of the Mind: An American Quest for Artificial Intelligence*, New York: Vintage Books, 1984.

PART IV

SENSUOUS SPACES

INTRODUCTION

If special effects are a defining generic feature of science-fiction cinema, they are rarely systematically addressed by film scholars, who have devoted rather greater attention to the themes and narratives of science-fiction films than to their deployments of image and spectacle. While this state of affairs is perhaps in some measure attributable to a scholarly denigration of 'fannish' investments in science-fiction – investments in which special effects are often fetishized – it has also, and perhaps more significantly, to do with the changing agendas of film theory and cultural theory. In film theory, for instance, questions concerning image and spectacle in cinema have been most centrally addressed through an apparatical metapsychology which posits spectatorship in terms of looking, modes of vision shaped by primary unconscious processes or regressive psychical states.[1] Such metapsychological arguments are readily applicable to different forms of film spectatorship, particularly those proposed by science-fiction cinema's special effects. For example, conventional deployments of special-effects-produced motifs – such as, say, the launch into clear space of a small shuttle from a mothership – arguably evoke primal fantasies of merging and separation.[2] It has also been suggested that special effects sequences play on spectatorial credulity, eliciting an oscillation between knowledge on the one hand (that this is an illusion – special effects sequences being always at some level self-referential) and willing suspension of disbelief on the other – an oscillation characteristic of fetishistic forms of looking.[3]

The shift within film theory towards attention to questions of space, diegetic and spectatorial, offers a means of extending the apparatical metapsychology of cinema and rethinking the conceptualizations of visibility and looking which underpin it. A metapsychology of cinema's spaces, for example, might look to phenomenologies of vision for insights into the ways in which these spaces are experienced by the spectator. A phenomenological metapsychology of cinema would certainly open up new ways of understanding cinema's, in particular science-fiction cinema's, singular capacity to offer the spectator all-encompassing visual, kinetic and affective experiences.

Today, film theory is being challenged by changes both in the ways films are delivered to consumers and in the contexts in which films are consumed. The cinema auditorium now constitutes only one among a range of potential venues for film viewing – though many would contend that science fiction is still best seen in the cinema theatre, if only because of the uniquely all-encompassing experience it offers. Nonetheless, these changes at the level of reception are accompanied by a certain blurring of boundaries between the different visual media in which science fiction is produced, delivered and consumed. In this situation science-fiction cinema in general, and its special effects in particular, are usefully considered not only as cinema – in terms, that is, of their place in the history of cinema and their deployment of cinematic conventions – but also in relation to their cultural intertexts and contexts, and for their place within wider histories of media and technologies of vision – photography, painting, popular entertainments which offer 'adventures of perception', and suchlike.[4]

In 'Body Snatching: Science Fiction's Photographic Trace', Garrett Stewart looks at some of science-fiction cinema's cultural intertexts with a view to exploring the interface between metapsychologies of cinema and special effects technologies. Arguing that special effects at once distinguish science-fiction cinema from other film genres and exceed the medium of cinema, he discovers the roots of cinema in photography, signalling the long-standing preoccupation with the human body and its imaging shared by the two media. In science-fiction cinema in particular, he suggests, the human body figures as a 'placeholder' for developments in imaging techniques. The body is fragmented, cloned, morphed: like, say, the soft, shapeshifting T-1000 cyborg in *Terminator II: Judgment Day*, which renders obsolescent the earlier, armoured T-800 model, played by the ultimate hard-bodied movie star, Arnold Schwarzenegger. At the same time, says Stewart, within science-fiction films, references to photography figure as a frail hedge against the vertigo of the hyperreal: he cites examples from *The Terminator* to illustrate his point. The 'family photograph' produced by the replicant Rachael in *Blade Runner* as 'proof' that she is human likewise appeals to the slender promise of real-world referentiality embodied in the photochemically produced image; and yet this promise also calls into question whatever confidence we might have in the truth of the memories that we read off our photographs.[5]

In Part I, Brooks Landon argued that science fiction's distinctiveness as a film genre lies in the fact that the modes of spectatorship it proposes are, unlike those of much mainstream cinema, similar in many respects to those of early cinema. And indeed, though pushed to the cultural margins by classical cinema's hegemonic narrative linearity and closure and its psychological motivation and verisimilitude of setting and narrative space, the kinesis, the shock, the corporeal quality of the 'cinema of attractions' has always been an important element in the engagements proposed by science-fiction cinema.[6] In 'The Artificial Infinite: On Special Effects and the Sublime', Scott Bukatman extends this point by situating science-fiction cinema's special effects within a history of popular entertainments which draw on technologies of vision to offer the consumer various 'adventures of perception': from panoramas and dioramas to simulator-cinemas, these technologies are all aimed at producing a sense of bodily immersion in a virtual space.[7] Behind the 'tamed awe' proposed by such adventures, says Bukatman, lies an appeal to a desire for scopic mastery.

More significantly, however, '[exceeding] the logics of narrative and [exaggerating] the poetics of spectacle', this mode of presentation bears a relation to the sublime. In the context of nature, poetry and painting, the sublime – a category named by nineteenth-century critics – refers to experiences calculated to inspire awe, deep reverence or lofty emotion by reason of beauty, vastness or grandeur. Bukatman's contention is that today the sensations characteristic of sublimity are typically evoked not by the natural world but by technological objects and environments, including those produced through special effects in science-fiction cinema. The mark of sublimity is its combination of affect and kinesis: in its immediacy and sensuousness, the sublime evokes bodily movement and emotional sensations while corporealizing cognition. In her ground-breaking essay on *2001: A Space Odyssey*, Annette Michelson pointed out that

> Navigation – of a vessel or human body – through a space in which gravitational pull is suspended, introduces heightened pleasures and problems, the intensification of erotic liberation and of the difficulty of purposeful activity.… The dialectic of pleasure and performance principles, projected through the camera's radical restructuring of environment, the creation of ranges of change in light, scale, pace, heighten, to the point of transformation, the very conditions of film experience. Viewing becomes, as always but as never before, the discovery, through the acknowledgment of disorientation, of what it is to see, to learn, to know, and of what it is to be, seeing.[8]

This was written thirty years ago. It has taken as long as this for screen theory at last to begin to acknowledge the cultural significance of the spaces of science-fiction cinema.

NOTES

1. As, for example, in the work of Jean-Louis Baudry, 'The Apparatus', *Camera Obscura*, no. 1, 1976; Christian Metz, *Psychoanalysis and Cinema: The Imaginary Signifier*, London: Macmillan, 1982.
2. Daniel Dervin, 'Primal Conditions and Conventions: The Genre of Science Fiction', in Annette Kuhn, ed., *Alien Zone: Cultural Theory and Contemporary Science Fiction Cinema*, London: Verso, 1999.

3. Barbara Creed, '"You've Got To Be Fucking Kidding": Knowledge, Belief and Judgement in Science Fiction', in Kuhn, ed., *Alien Zone*.

4. For examples of such histories, see Leo Charney and Vanessa R. Schwartz, eds, *Cinema and the Invention of Modern Life*, Berkeley: University of California Press, 1995.

5. See Giuliana Bruno, 'Ramble City: Postmodernism and *Blade Runner*', in Kuhn, ed., *Alien Zone*.

6. The view that early cinema and new technologies of vision propose similar modes of engagement is currently widely endorsed in screen studies. See, for example, Miriam Hansen, 'Early Cinema, Late Cinema: Permutations of the Public Sphere', *Screen*, vol. 34, no. 3, 1993.

7. See also Scott Bukatman, *Blade Runner*, London: British Film Institute, 1997; Paul Virilio, 'Cataract Surgery: Cinema in the Year 2000', in Kuhn, ed., *Alien Zone*.

8. Annette Michelson, 'Bodies in Space: Film as "Carnal Knowledge"', *Artforum*, vol. 7, no. 6, 1969, pp. 57–8.

BODY SNATCHING: SCIENCE FICTION'S PHOTOGRAPHIC TRACE

GARRETT STEWART

It is generally acknowledged that wide-screen cinema played out part of its mid-century contest with television in the public arena of film narrative. Where would we look for cinema's comparable struggle with other modes of imaging – from video itself through holography to virtual reality – as we enter the digital millennium? How might recent cinema contrive to figure its strategic capitulation, through so-called special effects, to a generalized computer technology that threatens to swamp wholesale, even while locally enhancing in the meantime, the motion picture's representational privilege?

Closing in on an answer serves to rehearse an abiding tendency of the genre. Science-fiction cinema, it can be shown, has always taken media as its subject.[1] In particular, the genre often takes such mediation to task for its violations of the real. This directs us to an equally long-standing tradition within film science fiction, exacerbated lately under the reign of the electron: the tendency to take cinema itself back to its roots in the science of photography.[2] Within broad genre parameters, we can delimit further the photographic object as subject. Wherever film science fiction has worked to identify as well as to secure its place in the history of transmitted images, the human body has typically served as placeholder for this science of imaging. Duped or mutated, ejected or projected, vaporized or remade, cloned, morphed, sloughed off, beamed up or otherwise digitally repossessed, the body as host of consciousness becomes, in science fiction, more like a phantom, a vestige, or at best a leaky vessel. Put that body on screen, where all bodies are figments anyway, and the medium is tasked with unusual thematic obligations. To meet them, it often turns to its own prehistory in photographic procedures, where bodies were first automatically captured in the precise *form* – if no longer the *duration* – of their being.

The time of being versus the time of image is in fact the subject of one of the earliest instances of the genre to conceive deviant science in terms of an explicitly cinematic manipulation. In *Paris Qui Dort* (*The Crazy Ray*, René Clair, 1923), Dr Crase is able to make the world stand still by the turn of a giant lever in his laboratory. What results in the ensuing montage are freeze-frames of Paris scenes, some obvious camera or lab tricks, some looking more like held (refilmed) photographs of deserted streets. A typical hypothesis of the whole conjectural genre is here on view. What if a perverse technology could do to the world what a director can do to its simulation on film: toy with and distort our spatio-temporal relation to a surrounding environment? The typical fictive scientist of the genre is not only the crazed *auteur* of real-world *trucage* (trick effects) but, more specifically, an evil genius who can metamorphose the world's being (ontology) the way a filmmaker does the material basis (celluloid photograms) of the strip: in other words, a photomechanical alchemist. The human body – stilled in progress, converted from lived duration into figuration – becomes a frequent laboratory specimen in this process, with photography the baseline for an untold array of proliferating virtualities.

When futurist science fiction projects the state of its own art into the visual technologies of some future state, the image of the future looms as the future of the image. At this point photography, with its own more primitive (if still cinematically primal) mechanics, tends to come forward as a picture of something more than ordinarily past, outmoded. If such photography takes the form of human images, as it often does, that lost thing may be not only the superannuated photochemical process in an electronic new world but the oldfashioned human body in its biological integrity and ontological stability. And so we are back with the constituents of the genre itself as a limit-testing investigation of the human. Here is where the famous photograph of mother and child in *Blade Runner* (1982), which cannot be used to prove the human existence of Rachael, its cyborg subject, is shocking in its fake memento: not just because, as Deckard says, it is a photo of 'any mother and daughter', nor even because it can be digitally engineered in the first place, but because *they* can be – the woman and child themselves. The photograph marks a nostalgia for the human body *per se*.

In its distance from the photochemical imprint, the refilmed computer monitor offers in this respect merely the digital update of the screens-within-the-screen that have always been the internal touchstones of the genre.[3] The more drastic encroachment upon the cinematic frame itself (rather than just within its internal monitors) by the *trucage* of digital technology is the genuinely new turn. But long before this, in the magic or machinated viewing panels of science fiction, the technical iconography of the mode has often been marked by what we might call a postcinematographic iconophobia: a fear of images either more or less dependent on mediated presence than are movies themselves, images mesmerizing in their artifice, delusory in their surrogate force, or coercive in their deployment. In Fritz Lang's *Metropolis* (1926), a mesh of diagonal wire crosshatching the overlord's internal monitor is faintly visible in a production still (Figure 1). A 'screen'-like bracing of the image plane thus emerges along with the suggestion that the workers' underground city, brought to view only across the safe distance of transmission (in a prophecy of closed-circuit television), is a space safely caged away from the control panels of power.

The inset film-like rectangle can operate in this way even when no image is engaged. The habit of the futuristic screens-within-the-screen was so generically ingrained by the time of Stanley Kubrick's *2001: A Space Odyssey* (1968) that one detects its ironic evocation in the film's most dramatically inert scene. This is where US scientist Heywood Floyd addresses the assembled top brass at the

Clavius moonbase about the mysterious appearance of the monolith, his lectern backed and flanked by the luminous walls of a blandly improbable set (Figure 2). The rectangular panels are cut to the measure of the CinemaScope ratio yet glow only with a dull, migraine-inducing intensity. Not credible as slide-projection screens, they look like nothing so much as latent, disengaged surfaces for the rear projection of some engulfing special effect – for, in other words, the potential disclosure foreclosed by Floyd's bland cover-up. They operate in this way almost as a visual pun for the glaring whitewash delivered from the podium. Moreover, each of the three panels, anticipating the often vertical dimensions of the black monolith in its own remaining three appearances in the film (in the following scene at the moon crater, in Jupiter space, and in the final cosmic bedroom), reads as the bleached negative image of the film's first

2

cause and prime mover: the midnight-black rectangle of galactic revelation, which coincides with the lateral reach of the screen frame in the film's penultimate dolly shot.

Kubrick's knowing allusions to the emblematic screen-within-the-screen send us back across the history of the genre once more. In the film version of H.G. Wells's *The Shape of Things to Come* (*Things to Come*, 1936), one of the most visible signs of the coming times is the proliferation of optical technology cast forward to 2036 from the film's date of production a century earlier. At its climax, the film concerns in good part the shape of screens to come. The future's image technology includes a massive state-wide network of visual transmission which somehow permits the simultaneous broadcast of the human image (Figure 3) – though neither projected (as in film) nor generated from an unseen apparatus behind the viewing panel (as in television). Rather, such images of the live body are materialized as translucent pictures from within

3

transparent plates or 'windows' that punctuate the air space of the gleaming metropolis, appearing even in milky three-dimensional forms within quasi-holographic cylinders. We in the audience know, of course, that we are watching film technology operating by *trucage* (mattes, rear projection, and so on) to simulate its own outmoding by electronic magic.

Nonetheless, the basis of the photochemical procedure remains oddly intact in the control room. Racing across an inset groove on the broadcast console is a chain of single images like an outsized film strip – filing by as if on a flat-bed editing machine (Figure 4). In 1936, the democratizing wonder of world-wide simultaneous broadcast can only be summoned up for us, it would seem, as a technology of analogous rather than electronic representation, frame by still frame. The moment bears dwelling upon. More is at stake than technology,

4

because more is at risk than the image. The human body is figuratively on the line in the channelling of oversized photograms. In its quaint anachronism, that is, this third-millennium projection booth houses nothing less than a vestigial feeling not just for the body's original presence to reproduction, microsecond by microsecond, but for its need to be taken down whole rather than by digitalized bits. For all the electronic mystification of the future viewing panels, the integral body remains even here the imprimatur, the foundational validation as optic imprint, of even the most advanced specular projection.

In *Things to Come*, the body has to have been there for the image to take, its ghostly multiplications notwithstanding. In a lower budget science-fiction film from the same year, *The Invisible Ray* (1936), the body provides both the aperture and the surface of the *retained* image – and does so as an almost redundant diversion from a loony pseudoscientific fantasy about the universe itself as both a virtual movie camera and an infinite scroll of exposed film stock. First things first. According to the film's mandatory mad scientist (Boris Karloff), the universe is one huge visual imprint, the post-Gutenberg equivalent of nature as God's book. Every ray of light that has ever fallen upon an object 'has left its mark on nature's film' – if only science could 'reproduce what is written' on this infinite text. The scientist's optical decoder has in fact captured a beam in the galaxy of Andromeda and is able to travel back along the trajectory of its single ray – emitted centuries ago from Earth – to reproduce the optic event at its source, an exploding meteor reseen as if in real time.

Once contaminated by radiation from the discovered meteor still buried in Africa, and become a lethal weapon in his own right, Karloff, like any screen actor, glows in the dark. No sooner has the protagonist become a living ray than his first victim becomes a camera for the recording of that ray. The film draws here on an overturned theory of nineteenth-century medical and forensic biology, explicit in the mouth of one of the characters, that the eyes of a murdered man may retain the image of his nemesis.[4] In *The Invisible Ray*, the unspoken and long since discredited concept of the *optogramme* is given an additional science-fiction twist, because the image from the retina of the corpse can actually be recovered by media technology. It can indeed be rephotographed from the material body of its first imprint. In one of the most deliciously absurd lines in all talking film, a scientist (Bela Lugosi) in the murdered man's bedroom asks the widow if 'there is an ultraviolet camera here'. Sure enough – and the result, when the open eye of the corpse has its carnal film transferred to celluloid for detection, is an image of the scene we have missed. In a somatic point-of-view shot seared upon the body in the very moment of its choked-off subjectivity, we look upon the crazed scientist strangling his victim in an irradiated death grip (Figure 5). In both the Andromeda prologue and in this later plot twist, *The Invisible Ray* envisions a universe all of whose conditions are radiant, specular, photogenetic, all of whose motions are optically captured and indefinitely retained: in short, and by any other name, a film world, however fleeting its image may seem in the moment.

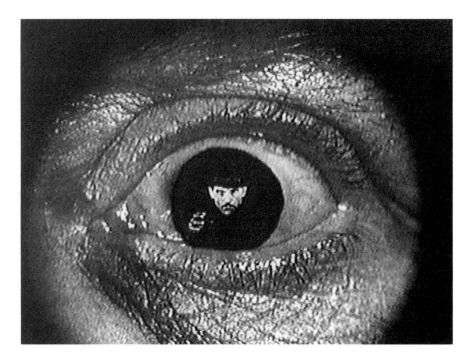

5

In *Things to Come*, the imaged body, stilled in the instant of its captured motion and resynthesized for transmission, is the ground zero of image production, the carnal given of all simulation. In *The Invisible Ray*, the body is so entirely the measure of all imaging that it is both beam and plate at once, source and trace of ocular energy. Between them, these films offer a bioptic conflation that forms the seedbed of an entire science-fiction motif. Film after film in the subsequent decades of the genre, reflexively prefiguring whatever variety of future image system its plot may concoct, will come round once more to the body not only as mutable ingredient in the narrative but as the primal (if often forsworn) organic benchmark for the artificial projections of the so-called *biograph* itself (one of the early names for cinema). This is the body, the photographable envelope of self, as point of departure (in both senses: historical and mortal) for films of a depicted future where the lived body no longer grounds the simulated corporeality of its own electronically mediated or downright illusory presence. In such films, the functional absence of the body outmodes its own death. In them, photography stages a double mourning, including a retroactive lament for the brute fact of the human corpse itself.

Our remaining exhibits come from the first and second wave of 1970s and 1980s digitophobia, to be brought up to date by two further examples, from the late 1990s, of all they feared: a future not just of genetic tampering but of digital co-optation that may at any moment threaten to eviscerate further the already disembodied medium that envisages it. Like many other films of its period, Michael Crichton's *Looker* (1981), a motion picture concerned with the image technologies that will supersede cinema, focuses this concern upon a violence already associated with the precedent technology of photographic capture. Its plot works to allegorize this memorial effect in an explicit play between the technical rudiments of both photography and film, overridden together by digital simulation. In the process, such scopic ironies divert an ongoing melodrama away from its main theme into an extraneous bit of technological business (involving a tool accessory to murder: a kind of photo-flash stun gun) that ends up as emblem of the film's whole plot of lethal electronic co-optation.

Looker names by perfect title both the object and the subject of the mediated and fetishistic gaze, the so-called photomodel and her transfixed audience. Star models are being killed off as soon as their computerized holographic images have been fully synthesized for television transmission. This scheme is discovered by none other than a Beverly Hills cosmetic surgeon (Albert Finney), as if the whole phobic fantasy were an extended pun on a reconstructive surgery so complete that it ends up deplasticizing the body altogether: converting the female model into a sheer and perfect computer graphic. But the photomodels are not, as it happens, just murdered. They are, as it were, shot to death first. In order to confiscate their bodies so as to perfect their images, they are frozen by a sophisticated electronic weapon that operates like a blinding photographic flash. But this is a device that actually arrests their persons, not their images, rendering the women unconscious (suspending their subjectivity) long enough so that, lest they compete with their own surrogate images, they can be brutally removed from all further public sight. To demarcate the very instant of that removal, that photographic exclusion, the medium close-ups of the victims, already 'sized up' for holographic replication, are seized up as photogrammatic reductions of their own filmic presence in a strictly photochemical reversion. This is brought about by having a brief freeze-frame on one of their stunned faces immediately dissolve to negative image (Figure 6) and then instantly cut away to the next scene, while the 'model' for all subsequent commercial images is being done in offscreen. Form infiltrates content yet again, as the elliptical becomes lethal. The inference all but spells itself out: where there might have been a new photograph developed from its own full-screen negative imprint, there is instead a death.

In this way, the aggravated vestige of the photographic apparatus clinches the film's satire of the hollow feminine image. The principle of *corpus delicti* requires the presence of a demonstrably dead body for the charge of murder. But the stun gun allows the removal of the body from the scene of consciousness, the 'models' remade as replicas of themselves on the trace of their own annihilation. It is only necessary to press this extrapolation from our present image culture one notch further to foresee a time when the bodies of such murder victims would be submitted to biosynthetic rather than merely digital duplication: 'morphed' in person, as it were, rather than just on screen. Science-fiction films of the period were quick to do so.

The specifically photographic measure of this outdistanced real emerges in the sequel to Crichton's *Westworld* (1973), the bluntly titled *Futureworld* (1976). Both titles designate, in fact, the trademark locales of high-priced, high-tech theme parks featuring the lifelike thrills of robotic interaction. In *Futureworld*, the managers and operatives of the corporation are no longer in danger of being sabotaged from below, as in *Westworld*, by their cybernetic underlings.

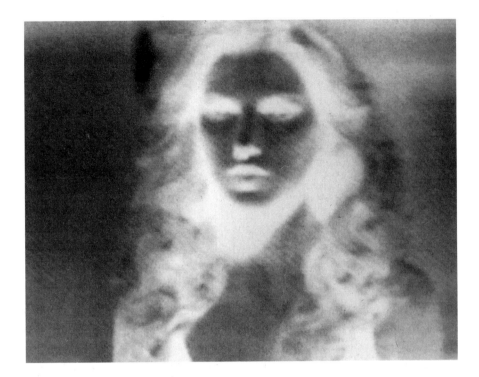

6

Rather, it is the customers of the theme park, in this case the world's political elite themselves, who are at peril of death and replication. One detects a shadowy parable arching across both films: to the effect that the indulging of such electronically aided fantasies as virtual-reality vacation centres will eventually, like the primitive rituals of television before them, robotize your imagination. At the level of plot, the idea in *Futureworld* is to turn these moguls and power players into mere images of themselves, so that the corporate figurehead is literalized in the corporeal simulation. Video cameras record the images of these dignitaries upon arrival at the adventure park from every possible angle and distance. The recorded images are then submitted to three-dimensional computer analysis in order to produce electronic replicas of these so-called world-stage figures, dummies indistinguishable from their originals except in their hard-wired determination to keep an economically serviceable peace. The first programmed action of each of the electronic replicants is, we soon find, to assassinate its prototype. Thus does the image, the simulation, come into presence as the violent absentation of reality, the very death of its referent.

The logic seems irresistible. Electronic surveillance leads to the electronic contrivance of the scanned subject. Devious representation comes of age in total substitution. The film has opened with the murder of an informant from Futureworld who has tried to tell the investigative-journalist hero (Peter Fonda) the inside story of the transnational corporate complot. A close-up photograph of the dead man – discernible only as open-eyed subject rather than corpse – is later shown, by the journalist seeking information, to one of the robots on duty at the theme park, as if it were a perfectly normal portrait. No recognition is forthcoming. Indeed, the photo is immediately stolen from him, its very existence subsequently denied. But there before us for a moment, miniaturized as a photographic print, is the once lived rather than wholly simulated body fixated in a double last rite: funerary icon for the death of animate presence and of organic basis alike.

Turning almost unnoticeably on this photographic pivot point and its denied recognition, film technology is now mobilized to narrate its own overthrow by less candid representations of reality. In the 'theatre' of international intrigue enacted by this one cinematic plot, actors no longer present but replaced by optical illusion on film (the cinematic given) are seen playing first characters and then indistinguishably (by the trick photography of the double image) their replicants. Nonetheless, as marked by the photographic moment of the body as corpse, the film participates in a certain entrenched defence of cinema (in its photographic, hence human, basis). It is a line of defence hardly foreign to the science-fiction genre. The line is held not only against video (in its capacity for secret surveillance and transmission) but also against other

7

8

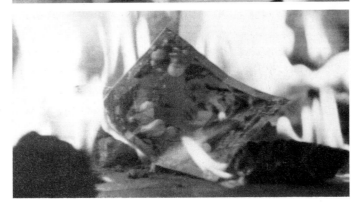

9

electronically derived and fiendishly sophisticated technologies of deceptive simulation. By the next decade this line will be harder to draw. By then, films have begun to incorporate in their own method the very threat of the digital they still seem rhetorically bent on staving off.

Film science fiction, we are seeing, asks us to contend with mortality in a double sense: the body born to die and the very death, through simulation, of that rooting human condition. Photography is the recurrent trace, evidence or residue of just that body. As we carry the genre's preoccupation with mortal embodiment into the second wave of cyberphobic science fiction, the computerized doppelganger stands as a negative apotheosis of 1980s fitness culture. Enter Schwarzenegger, not as body builder but as built body. When the paradoxes of photographic temporality (the 'then' that is always 'now' and always gone at once) – paradoxes which appear as such only because of the irreversible temporal constitution of human mortality – collide with a time-loop science-fiction narrative like *The Terminator* (1984), the inferences for the reanimation machine of cinema may be pressed to new emphasis. When these elements collide at the same time with a computerized cyborg plot, the cinematic and the postorganic come into unusually stark confrontation. The photograph as antithesis of an electronic virtuality works overtime to situate cinema along the very spectrum of similitudes that the film itself is busily narrating.

Four times over, a portable photograph of the heroine, Sarah Connor, appears in *The Terminator*, with the first in every sense an evidentiary setup. It is because of her college ID photo (Figure 7) that the newly arrived Terminator can match her face with her name in his quest to assassinate her. The second photograph of Sarah is recalled in flashback (flashforward in the time-loop narrative) by the character Reese, who has tracked her back into the present in order to head off the cybernetic nemesis. Reese has been impassioned to do so by the hero of a postnuclear resistance movement, John Connor, who was in fact conceived by the time-traveller himself to make possible Connor's own future and the liberation movement he (will have) galvanized. That wrinkled, time-worn photograph, which has stirred Reese's future desire as well as

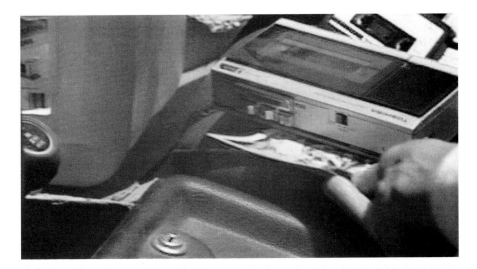

his admiration (Figure 8), is next seen when it is blasted from him by a Terminator assault (still remembered from the future) and is framed by the camera shrivelling in flames (Figure 9) – its 'skin' buckling and peeling like that of the cyborg in the tanker-truck explosion at the end.[5] After the later (former) night of love with his hero's mother, and Reese's subsequent sacrificial death in the destruction of the Terminator, whose own human surface has now been burnt away by flame to reveal merely an ambulatory metallic skeleton, we see that same photograph actually being taken by a Mexican boy near the Arizona border. Just before the film's last shot of her receding Jeep, Sarah inserts the rapidly developed Polaroid print under the taperecorder on which she has just left a funerary message to the future (Figure 10), promising the unborn son with whom she is pregnant to tell him about his father in order that he will one day permit his compatriot's return through time – and hence allow for his own possibility. Together with the sound of her voice (which we know from an earlier scene that the Terminator could readily duplicate, like any aural data), the still image completes this double and mediated prosthesis of the human at its point of transmission – and this in contrast to the Terminator's originally simulated body and its illusory apparatuses: the cyborg a prosthesis of himself at point of manufacture.

A photomechanical parable once more glimmers into view. A single photograph in frame, then seen vanishing in a liquidating brightness (fire, lamp), but yet (again) imprinted and rapidly materializing into view, while accompanied (without being fully conjoined) to the voice of the subject: this is all the future will have of its mythic heroine, just as in another sense it is all the film audience has of our own in the narrative's machinated progress. But we know this underlying filmic materiality to guarantee the body, know that the present of film always photographically testifies to the past of its actors. Not just the plot's first, but all subsequent photos – and precisely in their disappearance and reappearance within an unstable temporality of the foregone and the oncoming – are in this sense ID photos: witness to the surviving fact of human identity even under the electronic stare of its cyborgian double.

The Terminator is no doubt the paradigmatic film for the subsequent decade of biotech action picture and the mayhem of electronic predation. We find continued – if divergent – signs of this cautionary strain in two films of 1997. One of them, *Gattaca*, tactically eschews the *trucage* in which the other more predictably wallows. This is because *Gattaca* concentrates on the genetic engineering rather than computer simulation of the organic body, with the usual digitalized decor of science fiction – and its multiplied screens-within-the-screen – thus held to a minimum. The visible surface of the human organism is, therefore, not at immediate peril, only the 'faith-born' body willing to take genetic risks.

True to genre form, however, photography remains the yardstick of its own outdating. To measure the future's distance from an image culture that once valued the *undecidedness* – hence mystery – of the human body and its fate, *Gattaca* portrays a world in which 'no one looks at photographs any more', only at the indexicality of the genetic code – as 'read out' by portable blood scanners able to download in the process, almost incidentally, a video image of the identified subject.[6] By contrast, the 'de-gene-erate' or 'non-valid' hero, born without genetic intercession, is seen leaving his family after ripping off his own corner of the family portrait. It is the photographic image of a self more authentic, less constructed, than his genetically programmed younger brother, an image of himself he takes with him into the unforeseen.

Where the human individuations associated with photography are marginalized by a culture of perfection in *Gattaca*, they are even more violently overmastered by digital technology in the same year's dreary *Event Horizon*, in which morphing technology as *trucage* has entered the diegesis in the ambiguous form of hallucination or premonition. Characters thus bear the burden of the technology that materializes for us the brutal disfigurement of themselves and others. When, for instance, a crew member sees the deformed and bleeding body of her son (whom we know to be back on Earth) floating in the onboard laboratory before her, the film's trick effect has become her traumatic vision, so real no one could tell the difference. In the bludgeoning home of such epistemological ironies, this overwrought narrative pounds the whole logic of *trucage* into the psychic chinks and crannies of the unconscious. The subjective flashback is indistinguishable from the apocalyptic blitz, so that volcanic memory bursts and the onset of destined terrors exist on the same time-warped plane.

The nominal 'event horizon' (technical term for the liminal zone that rims a black hole) names the limbo and holding action of the plot. A gravity-warp supership was lost in Neptune space in 2040 when attempting its first effort at 'bending timespace' and transmitting itself to a distant galaxy. A rescue mission seven years later, led by the ship's inventor, Dr Weir, slowly uncovers the grotesque results of that experiment. The electromagnetically self-generated black hole through which the ship is designed to plummet, via a fold in time itself, has spat it out again from the unspeakable (but gradually all too visible) abyss of hell itself, the ship's mechanisms now transformed into the living being of evil incarnate. Such developments cannot be taken in all at once, by us or the crew, even as a previously recorded revelation. So narration needs the digital update of the evidentiary film-within-the-film or the stash of verifying photographs. As it happens, disclosure occurs in stages as the ship's log is downloaded from its CD-ROM storage in order to monitor (to screen) in retrospect the moment of the ship's first disappearance. Just as it took the plunge, the roar of the underworld has intervened and blocked digital transmission – after a few words of warning in Latin, apparently the devil's own tongue. Only much further along in the present-day reconnaissance plot does the rest of the videodisk become suddenly readable as the mayhem of the pit: electronic equivalent of an old-fangled internal film screening (or video playback) of previously sighted visitations. Though in a difference sense than intended, from here onwards this movie is hell to watch.

Since so much of what we now see on the genre screen of this or any science-fiction film – just over the far horizon of any real staged event – is digitally induced rather than photographically reproduced, the narrative convergence marked by CD-ROM retrieval constitutes a textual disclosure as well as a plot revelation. And against its onslaught, ordinary photography – as so often in the genre – is only a frail stopgap, dated, temporary, atavistic, and ultimately ineffectual. Once again, as in *Futureworld*, *The Terminator* and *Gattaca*, photography offers a frail hedge against the hyperreal – until the photographic image itself is bent to the will, in this case of the electronic counter-sublime. This contortion of the photographic role takes place in two cumulative stages. After the first scene of violent shock, in which Dr Weir is accosted by his wife with bloody sockets where her eyes should be, he turns out to be awakening from a 'mere' nightmare. Hell, we later find, will be no more than the bringing true of these and other fears. Lurching to consciousness, he reaches out for one of many photographs of his wife, eyes intact, on the wall next to him, stares mournfully at it (we later learn she has committed suicide in the face of his scientific obsessions), and deposits it on a dresser full of many more such snapshots. The camera eye of photographic registration assures us of the former autonomous presence of the sighted body (both senses) before its duping and desecration. This is the first stage in the counterpoint between technogothic conjurings and photographic documentation. The next takes a turn from funerary fetish into locker-room sex comedy.

At the point of no return where Dr Weir is forced by the rescue team to explain the scientific basis for the ship's electromagnetically manufactured black hole, he returns to the erotic and ontological consolations of photography, while warping them to his own purpose. When all the gobbledygook of standard Hollywood astrophysics is rejected by the crew as impenetrable, Weir grabs a *Playboy*-like centrefold from the cubicle of an irate crewman – 'Hey, leave that alone, that's my Vanessa' – which he stabs at two points (the pinup pierced again) and loops together as a band. He wants to illustrate that the shortest distance between two points is not a line but a reduction of the distance to zero: a veritable fold in time. His need to deface and render illegible the two-dimensionality of a photographic image in order to suggest that the fourth-dimensionality of infernal metaspace (and its coming digital simulations) is the film's fullest measure of its own prognosticated (and soon paraded) technology. For the viewer of *Event Horizon*, the bodiless scopic spectacle to come is meant, of course, to be no less of a turn-on than the former photographic centrefold sacrificed to explain it. But this is only to say that science-fiction spectacle, no longer entirely generated but only transcribed by the photographically based medium of cinema, continues to indicate vestigially, if no longer to mourn, the photo-ontology of its original magic.

The evidentiary use of such photo portraiture is rendered obsolete in an even more recent dystopian science-fiction film, *Dark City* (1998), eclipsed by the digital manipulations of a panoptic Master Race. In an updating of the stop-the-world premiss from René Clair's *Paris Qui Dort* (1923), the plot concerns a future metropolis in which each midnight all motion, both organic and mechanical, is suspended so that certain wholesale adjustments to the spatial arrangement of the urban space can be carried out in order to test the cognitive resilience of the human mind. What results is a melange of architectural transformations whose logic is only that of postmodernism itself, its spatial distortions offering the objective correlative of 'stolen memories, different eras, all rolled into one'. The computer visuals that facilitate such metamorphoses are then placed in direct opposition to an older photomechanical technology. With their obvious evocation of the cyborg's faked photographic prehistory in *Blade Runner*, the several scenes of family photos and slides that punctuate the hero's slow realization of his own concocted subjectivity in *Dark City* diagnose more than the rewiring of human consciousness by the invasive mediation of the Strangers. They mark further, by a double technical estrangement, the outmoding not just of photography by the simulacral mock-up but of cinema, from within itself, by computerized encroachments of every description.

As the most durable of screen genres in the second half of this century, science fiction has continued, more and more vividly, to imagine the technologies that would outdo it, do it in. In the digital era, however, futurist cinema has for the first time mobilized rather than merely evoked its own self-anachronizing upgrades. Engineered by computer enhancements, the superannuation of a suddenly hybrid medium has become a manifestly planned obsolescence, performed from within rather than simply foreseen. The technological overkill has spilled back into plot as an ontological dead end.

Building on the tradition of reflexive parable in science-fiction narrative, screen plots still find ways to refigure as a crisis (rather than just to deploy) what we can only call this invasive present eventuality, this haunting of projected photomechanical space by the spectre(s) of the digital. As evidence has shown, the incorporated foreign body of electronic simulation, infecting the filmic system by design, takes its greatest toll on the corporeal integrity of the represented human body. In everyday social space, environments can often be artificial – but not as a rule the agents that 'people' them and receive their stimuli. It is one thing to say that science-fiction film always glimpsed the dystopian shadow of its medium's eclipse as a privileged representational system. It is another to suggest that the genre contemplates the metamorphosis of its own viewing subject to mere simulated being, a receptor without presence.

In response to the technological proliferation it has always thematized, science-fiction cinema has devolved to the point where so-called human representation is not necessarily derivative but often original. As *simulacrum*, the mobile body offers merely the sign of itself at its source, so that absent presence passes from a fact of photographic representation to a condition of being itself. As before, only more so, the photomechanical medium of science-fiction cinema keeps pace by putting into marked narrative recess the signs of its own ontological as well as technological supersession. In the future that is now, the photographic image is held hostage to a pervasive cultural nostalgia for the very bodies its chemistry used to embalm.

NOTES

1. See Garrett Stewart, 'The "Videology" of Science Fiction Film', in George Slusser and Eric S. Rabkin, eds, *Shadows of the Magic Lamp*, Carbondale: Southern Illinois University Press, 1985, pp. 159–207. The present chapter is a shortened version of my article, 'The Photographic Ontology of Science Fiction Film', *Iris*, no. 25, 1998, pp. 99–132.

2. On the photographic basis of the cinematic animation effect, see Garrett Stewart, 'Photo-gravure: Death, Photography, and Film Narrative', *Wide Angle*, vol. 9, no. 1, 1987, pp. 11–31; and Garrett Stewart, 'Negative Imprint: Film, Photogram, and the Apocalyptic Moment', *Genre*, vol. 29, nos 1–2, 1996, pp. 193–241. In this last essay, the relation of photogrammatic disclosure to the genre of science fiction is touched upon in connection with three science-fiction films, *La Jetée, 2001: A Space Odyssey*, and *Man Facing Southeast* (pp. 222–32).

3. In the revised version of Vivian Sobchack's *The Limits of Infinity: The American Science Fiction Film, 1950–1975*, New York: Ungar, 1980 (pointedly retitled *Screening Space: The American Science Fiction Film*, New York: Ungar, 1988), her new material stresses the internally reframed zones of monitored cyberspace without connecting these bracketed manifestations of the chip with the science-fiction tradition of embedded mediations from which they derive. On the tacit phenomenological assumptions of this emphasis in connection with her more theoretical work on cinema, see Stewart, 'The Photographic Ontology of Science Fiction Film'.

4. In 'Tracing the Individual Body: Photography, Detectives, and Early Cinema' (in Leo Charney and Vanessa R. Schwartz, eds, *Cinema and the Invention of Modern Life*, Berkeley: University of California Press, 1995), Tom Gunning pursues Philippe Dubois' interest in the once reputable science of the *optogramme*. Under the auspices of the Paris Society

for Legal Medicine, a belief in this hypothetical image trace led to experimental procedures whereby murder victims had their retinas surgically removed to produce 'an
imprint of the victims' last sight – an image of their murderers' (p. 37).

5. This incineration of the human image has been figured just before when, in the underground resistance shelter, we first see two ragged children staring into a television set,
which, when viewed from the front, turns out to have been gutted of its electronic
works and used instead as a makeshift fireplace.

6. The film's vision of altered biological status thus approaches the double valence of
Scott Bukatman's title *Terminal Identity: The Virtual Subject in Postmodern Science Fiction*
(Durham, NC: Duke University Press, 1993).

11

THE ARTIFICIAL INFINITE:
ON SPECIAL EFFECTS AND THE SUBLIME

SCOTT BUKATMAN

In the eighteenth and nineteenth centuries, as new technologies and social formations displaced the haptic in favour of the visual as a source of knowledge about an increasingly complicated set of lived realities, popular culture offered a surfeit of spectacular forms that compensated for the lack of touch with what might be termed a hyperbole of the visible. An apparently direct address towards the spectator depended upon techniques of perspectival composition, *trompe l'oeil*, a hiding or de-emphasis of the frame, an often overwhelming scale, and a mimesis of the natural. Historians tend to agree that underlying the fascination with these displays were anxieties regarding urban growth, technological development and social change. The spectacle was a simulacrum of reality, but spectators were not duped by these illusions – by paying an admission fee the customer indicated at least some understanding of the rules of the game. Some pleasure, however, clearly derived from responding to these entertainments *as if they were real*. Visual spectacle provided a reassurance in the form of a panoptic power (minus the inscribed and very real power relations described by Foucault) – the human subject was, after all, capable of perceiving and comprehending these new conditions through the projection of an almost omnipotent gaze out into the represented world.[1]

The overwhelming perceptual power granted by these panoramic displays addressed the perceived loss of cognitive power experienced by the subject in an increasingly technologized world. In acknowledging anxiety while ultimately producing a sense of cognitive mastery, these entertainments frequently evoked the rhetorical figures of the sublime. The nature of popular, commercial entertainment suggests that this was actually a *tamed* sublime rather than truly awe-inspiring, transcendent visions: nevertheless, the sublime became an important mode for these mareoramas, landscape paintings, stereoscopic views and science-fiction films.

The cosmic displays of science-fiction cinema produced by technologically advanced optical effects surely derive from a similar drive for scopic mastery. The stock scripts and relatively wooden performances of science-fiction cinema should not distract from the articulations of meaning located in the mise-en-scene as well as in the state-of-the-art technological spectacle on display. While there are relatively few director-*auteurs* in science-fiction film, cinematic style (as well as authorial consistency) can be located in the fields of art and effects direction. The special effects work of Douglas Trumbull is particularly distinctive and sustained in its evocation of the sublime. Trumbull supervised the Stargate sequence of *2001: A Space Odyssey* and produced the luminous alien spacecraft for *Close Encounters of the Third Kind*. He worked in conjunction with 'visual futurist' Syd Mead on *Star Trek: The Motion Picture* and *Blade Runner*. Beyond his work as an effects designer, Trumbull directed two features, *Silent Running* and *Brainstorm* – both interesting in themselves – while developing his 65 mm, 60 fps Showscan exhibition system. Leaving behind Hollywood and a system that was 'multiplexing itself to death', Trumbull turned to 'special venue' productions, developing multimedia technologies for theme parks or World's Fair exhibitions. The popularity of simulation rides in a surprising range of settings has provided new opportunities for Trumbull to experiment with the kind of experiential cinema that has been his forte since the 1960s. The attention to spectacle and the conditions of exhibition reconnects Trumbull's work to the early history of the cinema as well as to that of precinematic phantasmagoria.

In Trumbull's effects sequences, the sublime is elicited around a massive technological object or environment: the Stargate (*2001*), the mothership (*Close Encounters*), V'ger (*Star Trek*), and the city (*Blade Runner*). It is technology that inspires the sensations characteristic of sublimity; therefore it is technology that alludes to the limits of human definition and comprehension.[2] The special effect unfolds before the human gaze and becomes susceptible to an encompassing control that inheres in the very act of seeing. Trumbull's sequences, however, are different from other effects work in their ambivalence: they are neither unabashedly celebratory (*Star Wars*) nor darkly condemning (*Alien*). As with the panoramas and other displays of the last two hundred years, then, Trumbull's effects are rooted in an ambivalent relation to new technologies; and, like those other forms, they depend upon new technologies for their very effect(s).

The displacement or disorientation produced by the environment of the industrial city gave rise to new entertainments that produced a cognitive and *corporeal* mapping of the subject into a previously overwhelming and intolerable space. Panoramic perception became a fundament of the Machine Age, a function of new architectures of steel and glass: it defined the arcades and department stores of consumerist abundance as well as a set of spectacular forms which reinforced the new dominance of an epistemology of vision. Telescopes, microscopes, maps of contintents, geological periods and human anatomy further extended the reach of human perception, as Barbara Stafford notes:

> The extension of vision permitted a new form of travel. Opaque depths were opened up, becoming transparent without the infliction of violence. The veil of the invisible was gently and noninvasively lifted. The eye could easily voyage through and beyond the densities of a plane, or silently journey beneath the stratified level.[3]

Travel provided the metaphor for a broad evocation of a spatiotemporal continuity wedded to a utopian dedication to 'progress': Susan Buck-Morss writes that 'Railroads were the referent, and progress the sign, as spatial movement became so wedded to the concept of historical movement that these could no longer be distinguished.'[4] Journeys to new heights, new perspectives and new worlds became the substance of such recreations as the package tour, the panorama, the scenic garden, and the World's Fair. In popular literature, Jules Verne took his readers up in a hot-air balloon to go *Around the World in Eighty Days* and fired them from a cannon to bring them *From the Earth to the Moon*. As Buck-Morss notes, new modes of conveyance became linked to new fields of knowledge and new possibilities for human advancement.

Here, then, is the start of at least one thread of what we have come to refer to as the information age, as an abundance of physical data was fitted to the epistemological desires and requirements of the public consciousness. Spectacular displays depended upon a new mode of spectatorial address – essentially, you are there (even though you are not) – linked to new technologies of visual representation. Of course, these presentations can, in their turn, be traced to the geometric specificities of perspectival composition, which situated the observer in an illusory relation to the scene observed: now the spectator was granted vivid revelations of the insides of the human body, astronomical phenomena and newsworthy events. Panoramas of exotic ports evoked an immersion in faraway places:

> The panorama struck a responsive chord in the nineteenth century. It satisfied, or at least helped to satisfy, an increasing appetite for visual information. A revolution in travel had made the world seem smaller. The growth of a literate middle class and the burgeoning newspaper industry meant that many more people were aware of a greater number of happenings over a larger area of the globe. It is not surprising that people should desire visual images of a world of which they were becoming increasingly aware through the printed word. The panorama supplied a substitute for travel and a supplement to the newspaper.[5]

Bodily experience and cognitive understanding were thus both supplemented and largely replaced by a reliance on vision within a simulacrum of the real.

If the visual was now largely removed from the confirmation of haptic experience (a fundament of the information age), then, first the visual would become a hyperbolically self-sufficient source of knowledge and information for the general public as well as for the scientist, and, second, a significant set of entertainments would re-call the body into a pleasurable ersatz existence. The panorama and its successor, the diorama, would eventually incorporate simulated motion, lighting and sound effects; platforms to rock or even move the audience; photography; and even, in the case of Hale's Tours, cinema. Such attractions have made an important return: Trumbull has developed the 'Ridefilm Theater', a simulator-theatre system which features a fifteen-passenger motion base encompassed by a 180-degree spherically curved screen. High-resolution images are projected with synchronized movement to produce a striking sense of kinaesthetic immersion in a complex technological space.

A too-easy historicism has tended to divide cinematic representations into naturalist and anti-naturalist categories (Kracauer's realist vs formalist debate). Within this dichotomous schema, special effects hark back to the imagistic manipulations of Méliès; but it should be clear that even the supposedly naturalistic Lumière brothers were purveyors of spectacle and novelty. Cinema is, of course, a special effect, and that is how it was regarded by its initial audiences. The illusion of motion, with its consequent sensations of temporal flow and spatial volume, provided enough innovation for spectators already familiar with a range of spectacular visual novelties. If cinema's unique blend of spatiotemporal solidity and metamorphic fluidity was largely assigned to the representation of narrative, the effect(s) of the medium nevertheless remained central to the spectatorial experience.

Writings on early cinema by both Tom Gunning and Miriam Hansen describe a 'cinema of attractions': an 'unabashed eclecticism' that was figured in a direct address to the viewer. '[T]his is an exhibitionistic cinema' Gunning claims; while Hansen, following Jean Mitry, writes that 'The frontality and uniformity of viewpoint is clearly the mark of a *presentational* – as opposed to *representational* – conception of space and address.'[6] The presentational mode ultimately yielded to a more univocal narrational system that stabilized space, and introduced 'the segregation of the fictional space–time on the screen from the actual one of the theater or, rather, the subordination of the latter under the spell of the former'.[7]

Nevertheless, Gunning argues that the fascination of the attraction 'does not disappear with the dominance of narrative, but rather goes underground, both into certain avant-garde practices and as a component of narrative films, more evident in some genres (e.g. the musical) than in others'.[8] The genre of science fiction often exhibits its spectatorial excess in the form of the *special effect*, which is especially effective at bringing the narrative to a spectacular halt. Science fiction participates in the presentational mode through the prevalence of optical effects that in fact *re*-integrate the virtual space of the spectacle with the physical space of the cinema.

Special effects redirect the spectator to the visual (and auditory and even kinaesthetic) conditions of the cinema, and thus bring the principles of perception to the foreground of consciousness. This idea is at the centre of Annette Michelson's superb analysis of *2001: A Space Odyssey*. The expansion of the visible field to Cineramic proportions, the removal of perceptual clues to verticality and other conditions of physical orientation, the sustained evocation of bodily weightlessness, the imposition of the rhythms of respiration and circulation on the soundtrack – all contributed to the profound redefinition of haptic experience undergone by the voyagers in the audience.[9] If *2001* is more radical in its affect than other works of narrative cinema, visual effects remain central to science fiction for closely related reasons. 'If we think of what it is that science fiction "does"', writes Brooks Landon, 'surely we must acknowledge that its frequently mentioned "sense of wonder" derives from "a new way of seeing"'.[10]

The special effects of contemporary cinema are thus only a more recent manifestation of optical, spectacular technologies that created immersive, overwhelming and apparently immediate sensory experiences, such as 'Renaissance' and elevated perspectives, panoramas, landscape paintings, kaleidoscopes, dioramas and cinema – a cinema, to borrow Eisenstein's phrase, of *attractions*.

The presentational mode described by Gunning or Hansen exceeds the logics of narrative and exaggerates the poetics of spectacle, and thus bears a relation to certain conceptions, in poetry and painting, of the sublime – especially the sublime as figured in American art of the nineteenth century.[11] The classical conception of the sublime, as described by Longinus in relation to spoken rhetoric, emphasizes its power to enthral and elevate the mind of man: in a famous passage, Longinus celebrated its unambiguous glory through his own little special effects sequence, writing that 'our soul is uplifted by the true sublime; it takes a proud flight, and is filled with joy and vaunting, as though it had itself produced what it has heard.'[12]

Joseph Addison and Edmund Burke were largely responsible for transforming the sublime from Kantian doctrine to aesthetic strategy. The field of the sublime comprised the majestic, the awe-inspiring, and the literally overpowering: it spoke the languages of excess and hyperbole to suggest realms beyond human articulation and comprehension. The sublime was constituted through the combined sensations of astonishment, terror and awe that occur through the revelation of a power greater by far than the human. Those commingled sensations result from the rhetorical construction of grandeur (either grandly large or small) and the infinite. The object of sublime rhetoric is often not fully available to vision or description: uniformity (the similarity of all parts) and succession (a sense that the object extends on and on) characterize this 'obscurity'. The sublime initiates a crisis in the subject by disrupting the customary cognized relationship between subject and external reality. It threatens human thought, habitual signifying systems and, finally, human prowess: 'the mind is hurried out of itself, by a crowd of great and confused images; which affect because they are crowded and confused'.[13] The final effect is not a negative experience of anxious confusion, however, because it is almost immediately accompanied by a process of appropriation of, and identification with, the infinite powers on display. The phenomenal world is transcended as the mind moves to encompass what cannot be contained. And so the sublime is grounded in a pervasive ambivalence – the tension between diminution and exaltation is evident in the oxymoron of Burke's 'delightful horror' and in Kant's description of 'a quickly alternating attraction toward, and repulsion from, the same object'.[14]

As telescopes provided tantalizing glimpses of worlds beyond our own, astronomy provided a new and exalted ground for the rhetoric of the sublime. In 1712, Joseph Addison wrote of the infinitude of the heavens in language typical of the mode:

> When we survey the whole earth at once, and the several planets that lie within its neighbourhood we are filled with a pleasing astonishment, to see so many worlds, hanging one above another, and sliding round their axles in such an amazing pomp and solemnity. If, after this, we contemplate those wild fields of ether, that reach in height as far as from Saturn to the fixed stars, and run abroad almost to an infinitude, our imagination finds its capacity filled with so immense a prospect, and puts itself upon the stretch to comprehend it. But if we rise yet higher, and consider the fixed stars as so many vast oceans of flame, that are each of them attended with a different set of planets, and still discover new firmaments and new lights that are sunk further into those unfathomable depths of ether, so as not to be seen by the strongest of our telescopes, we are lost in such a labyrinth of suns and worlds, and confounded with the immensity and magnificence of nature.[15]

Here, in a sense, the cosmic trajectories of *2001* are prefigured not only in the evocation of astronomical scale, but in the description of successive levels of macrocosmic order that ultimately yield to a chaos that signals the very limits of our ability to comprehend the vastness of the universe. The universe is without end – it confounds us; but the rhetoric of the sublime paradoxically permits an understanding of these sensory and conceptual limits. The rhetorical threat posed by the sublime is finally, then, not really much of a threat.

The precise function of science fiction, in many ways, is to *create* the boundless and infinite stuff of sublime experience, and thus to produce a sense of transcendence beyond human finitudes (true to the form of the sublime, most works produce transcendence of, and acknowledgement of, human limits). Indeed, the objects of science fiction are characterized by a spatiotemporal grandeur revealed by the titles alone: *A Space Odyssey*, *Last and First Men*, *When*

Worlds Collide, *The Star Maker* (and consider the titles of early science-fiction magazines: *Astounding, Amazing, Thrilling Wonder Stories, Weird Tales*). Science-fictional objects are sublimely obscure: the city of Trantor in Isaac Asimov's Foundation series covers an entire planet – one of the boundless cities of science fiction – and there is the spaceship with which *Star Wars* opens: too large for the screen – or our consciousness – to hold. Science fiction is immediately and deeply bound to the tropologies of the sublime. Burke's 'artificial infinite' is echoed in *2001*'s 'Jupiter and Beyond the Infinite': rhetorical allusions to the unrepresentable forms of infinity.

The figures of sublime rhetoric were developed and understood primarily with reference to poetic language, and were first related to the register of the visual arts only with suspicion. With the unintentional influence of Burke in the nineteenth century, however, painting became a new site for the instantiation of the sublime. While the concrete and exteriorized representations common to painting had long been regarded as deficient when compared with poetry's grand abstractions, Burke's categorization of sublime effects ('obscurity, privation, vastness, succession, uniformity, magnificence, loudness, suddenness and so on') proved easily applicable to the painter's depiction of the natural order.[16] Painting's concreteness, once regarded as its very limitation, now became its great strength: 'The vast, the remote, the obscure, qualities that give rein to the imagination, can be enumerated in respect to landscape more easily and precisely than in connection with religious, mental or abstract ideas.'[17]

The landscape sublime is rooted in an activity of contemplation, in the attempt to grasp what, fundamentally, cannot be grasped. The breadth of Nature proves ideal in stimulating the dynamic cognitive processes that exalt the mind that engages with it. The artworks most closely associated with the sublime are therefore often detailed and scrupulous revelations of nature's grandeur – but less from an impulse towards mimesis than from the encouragement of specific spectatorial behaviours. For landscape painting to inspire dynamic contemplation, however, it is not enough to duplicate external form.

Many artists, Turner and Church among them, provide a kind of viewing instruction in the depiction of a frequently tiny figure fixed in contemplation of the very wonders that the painter has chosen to embellish.[18]

Spectacular and monumental elements, all encompassed by a dynamic spectatorial gaze, are easily found among the plethora of special effects sequences in the history of cinema. If the poetics of the sublime anticipated the thematics of science fiction, then the visual sublime elaborated through painting just as surely prefigures the visible excesses of science-fiction film, and they are particularly pronounced in the film work of Douglas Trumbull.

An examination of Trumbull's work reveals a surprisingly coherent aesthetics. A Trumbull sequence is less the description of an object than the construction of an environment. He has expressed dissatisfaction with the flatness of most special effects sequences, which require rapid cutaways to distract the audience: 'I like the idea of creating some crazy illusion that looks so great that you can really hang on it like a big master shot of an epic landscape'[19] ('epic landscape' suggests the affinity between Trumbull's effects and the majestic paintings of Turner, Church, Bierstadt, et al.). The work privileges a sense of environmental grandeur: the wide-screen effect becomes an enveloping *thing,* such as the roiling cloudscapes which presage the appearance of the mothership in *Close Encounters,* the gorgeous and monstrous Los Angeles of *Blade Runner,* or the amorphous, infinite interiority of V'ger in *Star Trek.* The Stargate sequence in *2001* features scarcely any objects: it emphasizes instead a continuum of spatiotemporal transmutations.

Citing the moments of turbulence in Turner's painting, Andrew Wilton evokes a powerful spectatorial kinesis:

> Views through arcades, avenues of trees, tunnels of rock, even vortices of dust or storm, create an arrow-like retreat through the picture-space that is often at odds with the calmer perspective of the principal view. These distortions ... impose a *dramatic mode of vision* upon the viewer, who is compelled to enact with the eye leaps and plunges, ascents, *penetrations* and progressions that plot for him the three-dimensional presence of the perceived landscape.[20]

Such turbulent moments are usually grounded within the calmer description of a larger landscape, just as Trumbull's kinetic effects are rooted in the narrative progression of a feature film. In American landscape painting, the work of Martin Johnson Heade also puts the spectator in motion, this time in an act of spatial penetration of the picture plane:

> The lines of the juncture between the higher ground on the perimeter of the marsh and the edge of the marsh itself also expand to exaggerate and reinforce the visual experience of rushing into deep space. In no other American landscapes does spatial recession play such an important role or is it developed with such careful geometric precision.[21]

Trumbull's effects are also grounded in a phenomenologically powerful spatial probing.[22]

Trumbull emphasizes the spectatorial relation to the effect/environment. To some degree, all special effects are so inscribed: the effect is designed to be seen, and frequently the narrative will pause to permit the audience to appreciate the technologies on display (what, in a different context, Laura Mulvey has referred to as 'erotic contemplation'). However, Trumbull's sequences are different. Where John Dykstra's work in *Star Wars* or *Firefox* (1982) is all hyperkinesis and participatory action, Trumbull's work is especially contemplative. If he desires to create effects 'good enough to look at for a long period of time', then his sequences have encouraged precisely this kind of activity.

Further, and regardless of the director involved, these scenes frequently include an explicit and pronounced spectatorial position within the diegesis: witness the cutaways to an astronaut's frozen features, Spielberg's typically slack-jawed observers, the crew of the starship *Enterprise*, or the disembodied eye that holds the infernal city reflected in its gaze. Much of this is typical of cinematic science fiction, a genre that is almost defined by its incorporation of new technologies of vision. But again, Dykstra's work on *Star Wars* is not so inscribed: the passage of the first, impossibly enormous, spaceship is witnessed by the audience, but there is no spectator *within* the diegesis (the same holds for the climactic explosion of the Death Star). The presence of the diegetic spectator stages an extended encounter with the sublime, rehearsing (and hyperbolizing) the filmic spectator's own response.

In *Star Trek: The Motion Picture*, to take the most obvious example, the spectatorial function is taken by the crew of the USS *Enterprise*, who have been brought out of retirement to confront an immensely powerful techno-organic entity that is heading (as usual) for Earth. The visual centrepiece of the film (aside from the hilariously fetishized *Enterprise* itself) was the mysterious V'ger entity: essentially an old Voyager spacecraft with some loose screws. The V'ger model, as designed by Syd Mead (who would later work with Trumbull on *Blade Runner*) was sixty-eight foot in length, peppered with lamps, fibre optics, fluorescent tubing and laser lights, all augmented by additional animation effects and Dykstra's computerized camera. V'ger is perhaps exemplary of the sublime object in its boundlessness. Trumbull's unit developed a Computerized Multiplane System (Compsy) that provided complex movements through the ethereal, multi-layered space within V'ger, as well as some beautiful streaked footage of the *Enterprise* flying through a 'wormhole' in space.[23] Although the film is poorly paced, and plays like a high-school version of *2001*, the effects work is not without interest. The extended penetration of V'ger places the human within and against the alien landscape. In these shots of a touchingly diminutive *Enterprise*, the human is nearly lost, barely visible against V'ger's dark monumentalism. There is, perhaps, a similarity here to the tiny figures that occupy the lower foreground of Church's South American paintings – 'insertions of culture into nature', as Barbara Novak calls them.[24] Of course, V'ger is not natural, but rather is possessed of the brutal force that one associates with nature: this is a distinction to which I shall return.

Through the prevalence of such temporally distended special effects sequences, science fiction clearly participates in the presentational mode of cinematic discourse. Audiences may use a diegetic human figure as a provisional guide through the immensities of alien space, but this character does not serve to defuse or anchor the spectator's own phenomenological experience. The passage into the kinetic lights and amorphous shapes of the Stargate sequence

in *2001*, to take another example, is explicitly directed right at the viewer. Close-ups of David Poole, the astronaut, do not reintegrate us into a fictional (*re-presentational*) space; and neither do they situate Dave as a psychologized subject meant to focus audience identification. Cutaways to human observers in Trumbull's sequences re-establish scale and re-emphasize the 'otherness' of the sublime environment; but they do not mediate the experience through the psychology of characters who are, uniformly, stunned into a profound passivity. In their increasing magnification they suggest something of the 'extraordinary intensity' of the close-up as celebrated by Jean Epstein. Fictive and theatrical spaces are collapsed, as diegetic and cinematic spectators are, in a metaphorical sense, united. (Michelson argues that *2001* is predicated upon just such a confusion between astronaut and spectator. In other science-fiction films, these tropes are often present, but in less overt form.) The presence of diegetic spectators, then, here actually enhances the presentational aspect of the cinema, while also evoking the sublime.

In the nineteenth century, America revealed its obsession with the relation between nature and human power and human destiny in prose, paint and politics. A rhetoric of progress mingled with the sense of a people chosen by God and history, privileged to engage with and to tame a New World that still seemed to bear the fresh touch of its Creator. The vast reaches of the American West seemed to test the will of the nation's new citizens, and the emerging technologies of industrial capitalism were extraordinarily suited to the colonization and economic exploitation of these territories. Alan Trachtenberg has written that 'the American railroad seemed to create new spaces, new regions of comprehension and economic value, and finally to incorporate a prehistoric geological terrain into historical time'[25] (this powerful spatiotemporal collapse echoes Buck-Morss's contention that spatial movement analogized historical progress).

In an oft-quoted section of *Nature* (1836), Emerson – who also could be somewhat delirious about train travel – narrates a state of mind characteristic of the transcendental sublime:

> Standing on the bare ground, – my head bathed by the blithe air and uplifted into infi-
> nite space – all mean egotism vanishes. I become a transparent eyeball; I am nothing; I
> see all; the currents of the Universal Being circulate through me; I am part or parcel of
> God.... In the wilderness, I find something more dear and connate than in streets or
> villages. In the tranquil landscape, and especially in the distant line of the horizon, man
> beholds somewhat as beautiful as his own nature.

Emerson's debt to Kant is evident in his version of the sublime as exaltation,
and in his description of the ego's dissolution which is ultimately recuperated
in the beauty of human nature. His 'transparent eyeball' anticipates those
infradiegetic, but impossibly positioned, spectators that populate Trumbull's
effects sequences, and provides a strikingly direct gloss on Trumbull's evident
transcendentalist bias.

American painting became 'immersed in nature'.[26] In the union of sublime
aesthetics and transcendental philosophy, one critic has written that 'the sublime
experience was transformed into a new mode of landscape expression; the
traditional sublime setting was augmented by the transcendental sublime
sensibility, a sensibility that found its roots in man's internal perception of time
and space.'[27] This sensibility found its clearest expression in the genre of
luminist painting. Barbara Novak has defined luminism in relation to transcendentalist philosophy as an aesthetic that emphasized impersonal expression, horizontality, minute tonal gradations, intimate size, immobility and
silence. The luminist work is marked by a 'calculated control': an order is
imposed on visible reality. Stroke is de-emphasized, because stroke implies the
artist, paint as a medium rather than a transparent representation, and an
ongoing temporality. And, above all, luminist work is defined by its representation of light: a cool, hard, palpable light, spread across a glassy surface. 'The
linear edges of reality are pulled taut', Novak writes, 'strained almost to the
point of breaking'.[28]

Luminism was not the only means of evoking the sublimity of the American
landscape. The monumental paintings of such nineteenth-century figures as
Copley, Cole, Church, Bierstadt and others constructed a visual rhetoric of the
sublime far removed from the solitude and silence of the luminists, although

there were numerous shared concerns.[29] 'The landscape painter must astonish his audience by the immediacy of his *effects*', Wilton writes.[30] While much of this immediacy was achieved through the hyperbolized detail of the rendering, the scale of the works was also meant to overwhelm the sensibility of the spectator. These representations of exotic landscapes in the American West or South America were too large and too detailed to be 'taken in' with a single glance: the spectator's gaze had to be put into motion in order to assimilate the work. Furthermore, this especially exhibitionistic mode of representation was often put on show like a fairground attraction. In its construction of a dynamic, kinetic gaze, as well as in its mode of exhibition, the monumental landscape painting takes its place alongside such contemporaneous 'phantasmagoria of progress' as the diorama and the magic lantern show.

The paintings of Frederick Church are particularly appropriately considered alongside Trumbull's effects. The astonishing, bold colour experiments (special effects) that Church unleashed in depicting his twilight skies and volcanic eruptions were the result of new technologies in cadmium-based pigment production. These effects were placed at the service of atmospheric and cosmological phenomena: not just the sky, but also the sun and moon, a meteor, and the aurora borealis. One critic has pointed to the promise of *revelation* that underlies the dramatic scenography and monumental scale of Church's later paintings.[31] Another writes of 'Twilight in the Wilderness' (1860) that

> The painting defies simple categorization as a 'luminist' work of art, but there can be no doubt that the subject of the picture is, literally, American light, symbolic of the new world Apocalypse. It is a compelling work of art which combines two aspects of the sublime, the traditional interest in nature as object and the transcendental concern for nature as experience, through color, space, and silence.[32]

The dual contexts of luminism and 'great pictures' provide a further context for the Stargate sequence. The passage through the Stargate is a voyage 'beyond the infinite': a movement beyond anthropocentric experience and understanding. Through slitscan technologies, Trumbull created a set of images that were little more than organized patterns of light – the very stuff of cinema. Light, with its implications of revelation and blinding power, is also the very stuff of the sublime:

> Light is … the alchemistic medium by which the landscape artist turns matter into spirit.… In American art especially, light has often been used in conjunction with water to assist spiritual transformation, either dissolving form, as in some of Church's large South American pieces, or rendering it crystalline, as in the works of Lane. In the former, light is more closely attached to what we generally call atmosphere, and has a diffusive, vaporous quality. In the latter, light itself partakes of the hard shiny substance of glass.[33]

'In the large paintings by Church and Bierstadt', Novak concludes, 'light moves, consumes, agitates and drowns. Its ecstasy approaches transcendence, but its activity is an impediment to consummating a complete unity with Godhead.' In *2001*, light's transformative power illustrates, embodies and enacts precisely the supersession of the human (and the human's rebirth as a super-human, a Star Child).

The *Sturm und Drang* of the Stargate sequence is clearly different from the luminism of Fitz Hugh Lane; but I would argue that the sequence participates in both of these tropologies of light, moving from the diffusion and mutability of the first section to the colour-tinted, crystalline silence of the landscapes at the end. Light 'moves, consumes, agitates and drowns', but there is nevertheless a stillness that subtends the sequence's last minutes. Here the landscape becomes more concrete, but commensurately more barren; and sky and sea blend as the horizon disappears. The penetrating camera movements persist, but are now overwhelmed by the quietude of these enormous and empty worlds.[34]

John Wilmerding has written about Church in terms that seem equally applicable to the Stargate sequence: 'while Church's handling of composition and paint only peripherally borders on luminism', he nevertheless notes 'the sense of vast stillness verging on an imminent crescendo of light and sound'.[35] The 'imminent crescendo' directs us to the function of sound here and in other sequences in the film. While most are accompanied by tumultuously loud sound effects or scoring, language is, in every instance, absent. Again, there is a conflation of two tropes found in the American landscape sublime: the evocation of Apocalypse ('sublimity overwhelms with a deafening roar') and the quietude of luminism ('the spectator is brought into a wordless dialogue with nature').[36]

Mark Seltzer has astutely proposed that 'Nothing typifies the American sense of identity more than the love of nature (nature's nation) except perhaps the love of technology (made in America).'[37] To the American paradigm that opposed nature's might and human will, American painters, poets, essayists and novelists added the newly unleashed forces of technology to produce what Leo Marx has labelled 'the rhetoric of the technological sublime'.[38] The anxiety surrounding the new prominence of technology has received much attention since the Industrial Revolution, and the representation of technology has hardly been limited to science fiction.

In nineteenth-century America, technological anxiety was transformed by a sense of destiny. 'Above all, the rhetoric conveys that sense of unlimited possibility which seizes the American imagination at this remarkable juncture.'[39] This rhetoric of unlimited possibility does not, however, mask some residual anxieties, as a surfeit of landscapes featuring decimated woodlands and smoke-obscured vistas demonstrates: 'The new significance of nature and the development of landscape painting coincided paradoxically with the relentless destruction of the wilderness in the early nineteenth century.'[40] As Rosalind Williams notes in her study of subterranean environments in the nineteenth century, 'Technological blight promotes technological fantasy.'[41] The presence of the sublime in the deeply American genre of science fiction implies that our fantasies of superiority emerge from our ambivalence regarding technological power, rather than nature's might. The might of technology, supposedly our own creation, is mastered through a powerful display that acknowledges anxiety but recontains it within the field of spectatorial power.

What Buck-Morss refers to as the 'phantasmagoria of progress' (panoramas,

World's Fairs and the like) are visual displays that concretized metaphors of progress to provide some means of contending with the complexity of what Walter Benjamin called a 'new nature'. By this, she contends that Benjamin meant 'not just industrial technology but the entire world of matter (including human beings) as it has been transformed by that technology'. For Benjamin, then, there were two epochs of nature: one static and evolutionary; the other industrial and rapidly shifting.[42] The sublime is, in these spectacles, an idealist response to significant and continuing alterations in lived experience. Hence the sustained reappearance of the sublime in popular technologically based entertainments. Then and now, the language of consumption and the display of spectacle grounds the spectator/visitor and hides the awful truth: that an environment that we made has moved beyond our ability to control and cognize it. Hence, too, the experience of technology as both alien and enveloping in Trumbull's effects sequences. The fascination with, and fear of, technology's beauty, majesty and power reveal an ambivalence through which the sublime becomes a crucial tool of cognitive mapping.

Technology has come to comprise an environment, a second nature 'with its own attendant pleasures and hazards'.[43] Nature is displaced by technology in *2001*, *Close Encounters* and *Silent Running*, and this displacement is complete in *Star Trek* and *Blade Runner*. Buck-Morss notes that the new space of the Crystal Palace, a space permitted by new technologies of glass and steel architecture, 'blended together old nature and new nature – palms as well as pumps and pistons'.[44] Technology permits a containment of nature in the Crystal Palace and in the crystalline domes of *Silent Running* (the garden in the machine, perhaps). But the appearance of nature has become little more than nostalgia for a pastoral ideal (the machine is the garden).[45]

The ambivalent relation between technology and human definition is evident in the mothership sequence in *Close Encounters*. First, one must note the sky in the film's night scenes – abundant stars allude to the infinite reaches of space: as we know, 'theorists of the sublime attached much importance to the associational significance of the sky, and usually placed the night sky full of stars at the head of their list of its sublimities'.[46] For landscape painters, clouds also afford the opportunity to depict 'the storm cloud, with its obvious propensities for sublimity',[47] and *Close Encounters* provides strikingly exaggerated clouds – substantial yet strangely liquid, and far more animated than the dumbfounded characters themselves.

The star-filled skies presage the appearance of the mothership. The ship's design was inspired, according to Spielberg, by the sight of an oil refinery – the sublime is thus constituted around an anxious technological object. We might additionally note how nature, in the form of Devil's Tower, dwarfs the humans who nestle against it until the mothership, in its turn, dwarfs nature. The complex relationship between nature and technology is also manifested in the first appearance of the mothership, which emerges from behind the mountain: that is, from the Earth rather than from the improbably starry sky. The scale of the ship further indicates the subjugation of nature by the power of technology: Spielberg wanted it to be 'so big it would blot out the stars'. Finally, while the ship is defined by brilliant and beautiful light, it is also distinguished by the black shadows that swallow the observers: for all its beauty, the mothership is something of a dark, visually negative, force. Burke noted the same dialectic between light and its absence in Milton's descriptions of God: 'Dark with excessive light thy skirts appear.' The subsequent communication between human and alien happens via music and colour, continuing the avoidance of linguistic rationalism and so remaining firmly within the experience of the sublime. In Trumbull's films, as a rule, the effects sequences unfold, if not in a reflective silence, then at least in the absence of language. ('The eye is not the only organ of sensation by which a sublime passion may be produced', Burke wrote. 'Sounds have a great power in these as in most other passions. I do not mean words.'[48]) The tension that obtains between visibility and obscurity; the explosions of vivid chromatics and sound; the evacuation of language and narrative – all this speaks to the powers of the human sensorium, even as it also seems to diminish and displace the human.

Artificial infinities abound in science fiction: generation ships, outer space, cyberspace, boundless cities, cosmic time, galactic empires, *2001*'s mysterious monolith, the endless underground cities of the Krel in *Forbidden Planet*. Rosalind Williams has written about the craze for artificial environments that punctuated the fancies of the nineteenth century, and notes that these industrial fantasies have continued unabated into the present era 'in the form of retreats into personal or collective environments of consumption – the artificial paradises of the shopping mall or of the media room, for example. This is a journey further inward, a retreat from technology into technology'.[49]

Trumbull's accomplishment is the articulation of the tension between anxiety and identification as we strain to assimilate the imagined infinities of technological power. Such tension is exemplified in the opening sequences of *Silent Running*, as a lush, natural forest is slowly revealed to exist within the hyper-technologized spaces of a vast spacecraft: nature is now enclosed and redefined by the experience of the technological, as 'man's traces' become increasingly more evident until they finally overwhelm.[50] The ending is even more complex: the drones are left to care forever for the forests as they drift through deep space. The spaceship explodes in a, well, *sublime* pyrotechnic display (a new sun). The drones tend to the forest in a series of interior shots. Then the drifting domed biosphere is seen in its entirety, slowly receding in the visual field. Culture (the ship) is superseded by nature (the pure light of the explosion); then the natural (forest) is contained by the technological (dome), which in its turn is contained by the cosmological (space).

The archetype of the artificial environment is, of course, the industrial city, revisited and hyperbolized in *Blade Runner*. The oil refinery motif of *Close Encounters* has become more pronounced as an entire city is now explicitly figured as an anxious technological object. There is no more nature, only its simulacra in the form of synthetic animals and humans, and no escape from the encompassing technological landscape. Williams argues that 'in the late twentieth century, our technologies less and less resemble tools – discrete objects that can be considered separately from their surroundings – and more and more resemble systems that are intertwined with global systems, some-times on a global scale.'[51] In *Blade Runner*, as the hover car glides above and through the city, we indeed 'take a proud flight' and attain a position of conceptual mastery over the complex and superbly synchronized urban scene. The film provides two fields of vision – there is the physical reality beyond the windscreen and a graphic display of what must be an electronic traffic corridor along which the car glides. Each view explains the other, as urban space and information space map each other to produce an intertwined global system.

The phantasmagoria of progress involves a sustained immersion within an artificial, technological environment that suggests technology's own ability to incorporate what it has generally excluded. If the disappearance of nature is seen as a consequence of a burgeoning technosphere, then utopian technologies will incorporate Arcadia (Crystal Palace, Futurama, *Silent Running*). If technology is seen as a dehumanizing force that leads to an impoverishment of spirit, then utopian technologies will permit a new emergence of spirituality and cosmic connectedness (V'ger, virtual reality). It might even be argued that cinema is the very paradigm of an artificial, technological environment that has incorporated utopian fantasies of nature, kinetic power, spiritual truth and human connection.

Trumbull's effects are not the sole staging ground for sublime experience in electronic technoculture, and the reasons for its return are not difficult to fathom. The sublime came to prominence in response to the increasing secular rationalization of modern life,[52] and was later co-opted as a mode of accommodation to the power of industrial technology. The late twentieth century presents a historically analogous time of technological development and expansion, and so it is not at all surprising that this rhetoric should recur to ground an understanding of an ostensibly new phenomenon. Just as Gibson's cyberspace recasts the new 'terrain' of digital information processing in the familiar terms of a sprawling yet concentrated American urbanism, the sublime becomes a means of looking back in order to recognize what lies ahead.

But something else is going on. The sublime not only points back towards an historical past; it also holds out the promise of self-fulfilment and technological transcendence in an imaginable near future. Under the terms of the sublime, technology is divorced from its sociological, rationalist underpinnings to become a technology without technocracy, a technology beyond the scope of human control. There is thus an inevitability to the fact of technological progress, and thus accommodation becomes the one valid response.

The sublime's rhetoric of confrontation and mastery smacks of phallocentrist bias, while the landscape sublime's predilection for the 'virgin landscapes' of South America and the North American West aligns it all too neatly with the colonialist usurpation that called itself manifest destiny. Its mystical overtones no longer resonate with a secularist culture that remains deeply suspicious of spiritual value. Despite these condemnations, however, any number of theorists and artists have attempted to 'rescue' the sublime, finding in its confrontational power an ethos of exploration and self-discovery that meshes with my own sense of Trumbull's effects work.

Patricia Yaeger has specifically challenged the masculinist modalities of sublime rhetoric. 'Subject and object have entered into an intersubjective dialectic of grandeur in which the poet refuses to annex what is alien, but revels, for a brief poetic moment, in a pre-oedipal longing for otherness and ecstasy.'[53] What she terms the 'feminine sublime' thus addresses the crucial problem of how to produce 'a model of the self that permits both a saving maintenance of ego-boundaries and an exploration of the pleasures of intersubjectivity'.[54] In *Agon*, Harold Bloom connects sublimity to the questioning traditions of gnostic thought, a 'performative knowledge' that can only emerge via experience. The sublime thus depends upon a disruption followed by a performative adaptation that yields a dynamic knowledge of a dialectically constituted self. Yaeger and Bloom might be approaching the sublime from very different directions, but for both the trope offers something more than phallocentric reassurance.

If a positive value can be assigned to the return of the sublime in science-fiction cinema, then it lies in a rhetoric of scopic destabilization that yields a new subject position with regard to the source of technological anxiety. Unlike *Star Trek*, *2001* does not 'explain' its ultimate trip, and so denies its viewers the firm ground provided by cognitive comprehensibility. I would argue that in *2001* Kubrick and Trumbull have emphasized and foregrounded the phenomenological instability that has always been more or less present in science-fiction cinema. If science fiction too often seems anchored (or mired) in rationalist cant, then the 'performative knowledge' provided by inventive special effects moves the spectator beyond the rational, and to a space beyond the infinite. Despite the recontainments and reassurances which are the function of these films' narratives, scopic instability and cognitive accommodation remain fundamental to, and implicit in, our experience of the works.

There were other moments when advanced technology was employed to (re)present advanced technology: 'The most exciting visual encounters with the railroad', writes Barbara Novak, 'were those that took place through the mediation of yet another machine – the camera. The photographer, having already accommodated one machine within his artistic perspective, had much less difficulty than painters in accommodating still another.'[55] Through the 'magic' of special effects, a contemporary rhetoric of technological sublimity is produced by technological means. Cinematic *affect* is rooted in cinematic technology, but *effects* emphasize those underpinnings: if cinema is rooted in illusions of light, for example, then optical effects endow light with an overwhelming physicality. Science-fiction cinema uses state-of-the-art effects to 'accommodate still another' realm of machinery. The effects put machinery in motion, offering technology up to dynamic contemplation (and in the Ridefilm theatres, machinery in motion puts the spectator in motion, as perception is now supplemented by bodily experience).

One must acknowledge the recurrent fantasies of sexuality and power at work within many of these texts. But their overdetermined phallocentric, um, *thrust* should not blind us to the real need to map ourselves into the anxious spaces of, first, industrial and, now, electronic, culture. Cognition, one hopes, does not necessarily automatically imply domination; and while science-fiction narrative often speaks to militaristic male fantasies, the spectator's immersion in the technologized environment of a wide-screen special effects sequence can retain its own phenomenological validity and importance. Relations between perception, cognition, knowledge and power are neither simple nor, I suspect, absolute; and the phenomenological status of these phantasmagoria of progress merits an attention that moves beyond simply classifying such spectacles as masculinist, colonialist or consumerist.

Special effects, in the cinema and in their extension to virtual reality systems, are but the latest in a series of popular cultural entertainments that emphasize what Stan Brakhage has referred to as the 'adventure of perception'. Despite their emphasis on perceptual mastery and the magisterial gaze, these recreations significantly balance sensory pleasure and cognitive play. The effects sequences of science-fiction cinema are significant for what they say, as well as for what they do not say, about our complicated relationship with complex technologies at this precarious historical moment. This ambivalence permeates the culture of visuality. As Miriam Hansen writes with regard to the development of cinema's moving camera: 'The mobilization of the gaze promises nothing less than the mobilization of the self, the transformation of seemingly fixed positions of social identity. This mobilization, however, is promise and delusion in one.'[56]

NOTES

1. A longer version of this chapter appeared in Linda Cooke and Peter Wollen, eds, *Visual Display: Culture Beyond Appearances*, Seattle, WA: Bay Press, 1995, pp. 255–89.
2. Such ontological questions are further emphasized when the technologies are *alien* in origin.
3. Barbara Maria Stafford, *Body Criticism: Imaging the Unseen in Enlightenment Art and Medicine*, Cambridge, MA: MIT Press, 1991, p. 343.
4. Susan Buck-Morss, *The Dialectics of Seeing: Walter Benjamin and the Arcades Project*, Cambridge, MA: MIT Press, 1989, p. 91.
5. Ralph Hyde, *Panoramania: The Art and Entertainment of the 'All-Embracing' View*, London: Trefoil Publications, 1988, p. 37.

6. Tom Gunning, 'The Cinema of Attractions: Early Film, Its Spectator and the Avant-Garde', in Thomas Elsaesser, ed., *Early Cinema: Space, Frame, Narrative*, London: British Film Institute, 1990, p. 57; Miriam Hansen, *Babel and Babylon: Spectatorship in American Silent Film,* Cambridge, MA: Harvard University Press, 1991, p. 34.

7. Hansen, *Babel and Babylon*, p. 83.

8. Gunning, 'Cinema of Attractions', p. 57.

9. Annette Michelson, 'Bodies in Space: Film as "Carnal Knowledge"', *Artforum*, vol. 7, no. 6, 1969: pp. 54–63.

10. Brooks Landon, *The Aesthetics of Ambivalence: Rethinking Science Fiction Film in the Age of Electronic (Re)Production,* Westport, CT: Greenwood Press, 1992, p. 94.

11. This is not the place to review the entire, complex history of the sublime. A very useful review is provided by Raimonda Modiano in *Coleridge and the Concept of Nature,* Tallahassee: Florida State University Press, 1985, pp. 101–14.

12. *Longinus on the Sublime*, trans. W.R. Roberts, 1935, p. 65.

13. Edmund Burke, *On the Sublime and the Beautiful*, Charlottesville, VA: Ibis Publishing, facsimile of 1812 edition, p. 106.

14. Ibid., p. 120.

15. Joseph Addison, *The Spectator*, no. 420, 2 July 1712 (cited in Andrew Wilton, *Turner and the Sublime*, Chicago: University of Chicago Press, 1980, p. 11).

16. Wilton, *Turner and the Sublime*, p. 30.

17. Ibid.

18. Wilton argues that this was a careful strategy of Turner's, and finds that a significant progression in his series of marine paintings (1801–10) 'is one of gradually increasing involvement of the spectator in the scenes depicted', ibid., p. 46.

19. This remark is made in an interview with Don Shay presented on the Criterion laser disk of *Close Encounters*.

20. Wilton, *Turner and the Sublime*, p. 79, my emphasis.

21. Earl A. Powell, 'Luminism and the American Sublime', in John Wilmerding, ed., *American Light: The Luminist Movement*, Washington DC: National Gallery of Art, 1980, p. 83.

22. To concentrate solely upon the phallic implications of this movement of penetration seems to me unfairly and uninterestingly reductive (except, I admit, in the case of *Star Trek*): Annette Michelson, for example, has linked this cinematic trope to the epistemological project of works by Kubrick, Michael Snow and Claude Lanzmann, among others.

23. Christopher Finch, *Special Effects: Creating Movie Magic*, New York: Abbeville Press, 1984, pp. 180–81.

24. Barbara Novak, *Nature and Culture: American Landscape and Painting, 1825–1875,* revised edn, New York: Oxford University Press, 1995, p. 198.

25. Alan Trachtenberg, *The Incorporation of America: Culture and Society in the Gilded Age,* New York: Hill & Wang, 1982, p. 59.

26. Wilmerding, ed., *American Light*, p. 98.

27. Powell, 'Luminism and the American Sublime', p. 72.

28. Novak, *Nature and Culture*, pp. 23 and 27.

29. These canvasses were indeed large-scale works (Church's 'The Heart of the Andes' [1859] measured about 66" × 120"), and Novak has noted that a consideration of these works must involve 'a consideration of art as spectacle'. She further notes that 'this art had a clear twentieth-century heir in the film, which rehearsed many of the nineteenth century's concerns' (ibid., p. 19).

30. Wilton, *Turner and the Sublime*, p. 39, my emphasis.

31. See David C. Huntington, 'Church and Luminism: Light for America's Elect', in Wilmerding, ed., *American Light*, pp. 155–92.

32. Powell, 'Luminism and the American Sublime', p. 90.

33. Novak, *Nature and Culture*, pp. 41–2.

34. It is also true that luminism produces a sense of distance from the carefully aestheticized landscape which differs from the immersion I am describing; nevertheless, the similarity abides in their suspended temporalities.

35. John Wilmerding, 'The Luminist Movement: Some Reflections', in Wilmerding, ed., *American Light*, p. 121.

36. Novak, *Nature and Culture*, pp. 37 and 29.

37. Mark Seltzer, *Bodies and Machines*, New York: Routledge, 1992, p. 3.

38. Leo Marx, *The Machine in the Garden: Technology and the Pastoral Ideal in America*, New York: Oxford University Press, 1964.

39. Ibid., p. 206.

40. Novak, *Nature and Culture*, p. 4.

41. Rosalind Williams, *Notes on the Underground: An Essay on Technology, Society and the Imagination*, Cambridge, MA: MIT Press, 1990, p. 114.

42. Buck-Morss, *Dialectics of Seeing*, p. 70, my emphasis.

43. Williams, *Notes on the Underground*, p. 140.

44. Buck-Morss, *Dialectics of Seeing*, pp. 83–5.

45. A trajectory completed in the cyberspace of William Gibson's novel *Neuromancer*.

46. Wilton, *Turner and the Sublime*, p. 101.

47. Novak, *Nature and Culture*, p. 97.

48. Burke, *On the Sublime and the Beautiful*, pp. 149–50.

49. Williams, *Notes on the Underground*, p. 185.

50. Novak, *Nature and Culture*, p. 157.

51. Williams, *Notes on the Underground*, p. 1.

52. On the resistance to progressivism, see T.J. Jackson Lears, *No Place of Grace: Antimodernism and the Transformation of American Culture, 1880–1920*, Chicago: University of Chicago Press, 1994.

53. Patricia Yaeger, 'Toward a Female Sublime', in Linda Kauffman, ed., *Gender and Theory: Dialogues on Feminist Criticism,* Oxford: Basil Blackwell, 1989, p. 209.
54. Ibid., p. 205.
55. Novak, *Nature and Culture*, p. 176.
56. Hansen, *Babel and Babylon*, p. 112.

FILMOGRAPHY

Alien
1979, USA/GB
director   Ridley Scott
production   Twentieth Century-Fox/Brandywine Productions
screenplay   Walter Hill, David Giler
original story   Dan O'Bannon, Ronald Shusett
cast   Sigourney Weaver, Harry Dean Stanton, John Hurt,
                    Ian Holm

Aliens
1986, USA
director   James Cameron
production   Twentieth Century-Fox/Brandywine Productions
screenplay   James Cameron
cast   Sigourney Weaver, Carrie Henn, Michael Biehn

Alien3
1992, USA
director   David Fincher
production   Brandywine Productions
screenplay   William Gibson, John Fasano, David Giler, Walter Hill, Larry
                    Ferguson
cast   Sigourney Weaver, Charles Dutton, Charles Dance

Alien Resurrection

1997, USA
director   Jean-Pierre Jeunet
production   Twentieth Century-Fox, Brandywine Productions
screenplay   Joss Whedon
cast   Sigourney Weaver, Winona Ryder, Dominique Pinon

Beast from 20,000 Fathoms

1953, USA
director   Eugène Lourié
production   Warner Bros
screenplay   Fred Freiberger
cast   Tom Nesbitt, Paula Raymond, Cecil Kellaway

Blade Runner

1982, USA
director   Ridley Scott
production   Ladd Company/Run Run Shaw
screenplay   Hampton Fancher, David Peoples
original novel   Philip K. Dick
cast   Harrison Ford, Rutger Hauer, Sean Young, Daryl Hannah

Blade Runner: The Director's Cut

1992, USA
director   Ridley Scott

Brainstorm

1983, USA
director   Douglas Trumbull
production   MGM/UA Entertainment/JF Productions
screenplay   Robert Stitzel, Philip Messina
original story   Bruce Joel Rubin
cast   Christopher Walken, Natalie Wood, Louise Fletcher

Brazil

1985, GB
director   Terry Gilliam
production   Embassy International Pictures
screenplay   Terry Gilliam, Tom Stoppard, Charles Mckeown
cast   Jonathan Pryce, Robert de Niro, Ian Holm, Bob Hoskins

Clockwork Orange

1971, GB
director   Stanley Kubrick
production   Polaris Productions/Warner Bros
screenplay   Stanley Kubrick
original novel   Anthony Burgess
cast   Malcolm McDowell, Patrick Magee, Warren Clarke,
                         Adrienne Corri

Close Encounters of the Third Kind

1977, USA
director   Steven Spielberg
production   Columbia/EMI
screenplay   Steven Spielberg
cast   Richard Dreyfuss, François Truffaut, Teri Garr

Dark City

1997, USA/Australia
director   Alex Proyas
production   New Line Productions
screenplay   Alex Proyas, Lem Dobbs, David S. Goyer
cast   Rufus Sewell, Kiefer Sutherland, Jennifer Connelly

Demolition Man

1993, USA
director   Marco Brambilla
production   Silver Pictures
screenplay   Peter M. Lenkov, Daniel Waters, Robert Reneau
cast   Sylvester Stallone, Wesley Snipes, Sandra Bullock, Nigel
                         Hawthorne

Event Horizon

1997, USA/GB
director   Paul Anderson
production   Paramount
screenplay   Philip Eisner
cast   Sam Neill, Kathleen Quinlan, Joely Richardson

Fahrenheit 451

1966, GB

director   François Truffaut
production   Anglo-Enterprise Film Productions/Vineyard Productions
screenplay   François Truffaut, Jean-Louis Richard
cast   Oskar Werner, Julie Christie, Cyril Cusack, Anton Diffring

Forbidden Planet

1956, USA
director   Fred M. Wilcox
production   Loew's Incorporated
screenplay   Cyril Hume
cast   Walter Pidgeon, Anne Francis, Leslie Nielsen

Futureworld

1976, USA
director   Richard T. Heffron
production   Aubrey Company
screenplay   Simon Mayo, George Schenk
cast   Peter Fonda, Blythe Danner, Yul Brynner, Arthur Hill

Gattaca

1997, USA
director   Andrew Wood
production   Columbia/Jersey Films
screenplay   Andrew Niccol
cast   Ethan Hawke, Uma Thurman, Alan Arkin, Jude Law

Incredible Shrinking Man

1957, USA
director   Jack Arnold
production   Universal-International
screenplay   Richard Matheson
original novel   Richard Matheson
cast   Grant Williams, Randy Stuart, April Kent

Independence Day

1996, USA
director   Roland Emmerich
production   Twentieth Century-Fox/Centropolis Entertainment
screenplay   Dean Devlin, Roland Emmerich
cast   Jeff Goldblum, Judd Hirsch, Randy Quaid

Invasion of the Body Snatchers

1956, USA
director   Don Siegel
production   Allied Artists
screenplay   Daniel Mainwaring
cast   Kevin McCarthy, Dana Wynter, Larry Gates

Invasion of the Body Snatchers

1978, USA
director   Philip Kaufman
production   Solofilm Company
screenplay   W.D. Richter
original novel   Jack Finney
cast   Donald Sutherland, Leonard Nimoy, Veronica Cartwright,
                  Jeff Goldblum

Invisible Ray

1936, USA
director   Lambert Hillyer
production   Universal
screenplay   John Colton
original story   Howard Higgin, Douglas Hodges
cast   Boris Karloff, Bela Lugosi, Frances Drake

Johnny Mnemonic

1995, Canada
director   Robert Longo
production   Alliance Communication Corporation
screenplay   William Gibson
original story   William Gibson
cast   Keanu Reeves, Dolph Lundgren, Ice-T

Just Imagine

1930, USA
director   David Butler
production   Fox-Movietone
cast   El Brendel, Maureen O'Sullivan, John Garrick

Looker

1981, USA
director   Michael Crichton
production   Ladd Company/Warner Bros
screenplay   Michael Crichton
cast   Albert Finney, James Coburn, Susan Dey

Max Headroom

1985–88, GB
pilot & 15 episodes
broadcast   Channel 4 Television/ABC
cast   Matt Frewer, Amanda Pays, George Coe

Metropolis

1926, Germany
director   Fritz Lang
production   Ufa
screenplay   Fritz Lang, Thea von Harbou
cast   Brigitte Helm, Alred Abel, Gustav Fröhlich

Silent Running

1971, USA
director   Douglas Trumbull
production   Universal
screenplay   Deric Washburn, Michael Cimino, Steve Bochco
cast   Bruce Dern, Cliff Potts, Ron Rifkin

Soylent Green

1973, USA
director   Richard Fleischer
production   MGM
screenplay   Stanley R. Greenberg
original novel Harry Harrison
cast   Charlton Heston, Edward G. Robinson, Joseph Cotten, Leigh
                Taylor-Young

Star Trek: The Motion Picture

1979, USA
director   Robert Wise
production   Paramount

screenplay	Harold Livingstone
original story	Alan Dean Foster
cast	William Shatner, Leonard Nimoy, DeForest Kelley, James Doohan

Star Trek: The Next Generation

1987–94, USA
176 episodes

| production | Paramount |
| cast | Patrick Stewart, Jonathan Frakes, Brent Spiner, LeVar Burton |

Star Wars

1977, USA

director	George Lucas
production	Lucasfilm/Twentieth Century-Fox
screenplay	George Lucas
cast	Mark Hamill, Harrison Ford, Carrie Fisher, Peter Cushing

Star Wars: The Empire Strikes Back

1980, USA

director	Irvin Kershner
production	Lucasfilm/Twentieth Century-Fox
screenplay	Leigh Brackett, Lawrence Kasdan
cast	Mark Hamill, Harrison Ford, Carrie Fisher, Billy Dee Williams

Star Wars: Return of the Jedi

1983, USA

director	Richard Marquand
production	Lucasfilm
screenplay	Lawrence Kasdan, George Lucas
cast	Mark Hamill, Harrison Ford, Carrie Fisher, Billy Dee Williams

Starship Troopers

1997, USA

director	Paul Verhoeven
production	TriStar Pictures/Touchstone Pictures
screenplay	Ed Neumeier
original novel	Robert A. Heinlein
cast	Casper van Dien, Dina Meyer, Denise Richards

Terminator

1984, USA
director   James Cameron
production   Cinema'84/Orion
screenplay   James Cameron, Gale Ann Hurd
cast   Arnold Schwarzenegger, Michael Biehn, Linda Hamilton

Terminator II: Judgment Day

1991, USA
director   James Cameron
production   Carolco Pictures
screenplay   James Cameron, William Wisher
cast   Arnold Schwarzenegger, Linda Hamilton, Edward Furlong

Things to Come

1936, GB
director   William Cameron Menzies
production   London Film Productions
screenplay   H.G. Wells
original novel H.G. Wells
cast   Raymond Massey, Ralph Richardson, Cedric Hardwicke,
                Margaretta Scott

THX-1138

1970, USA
director   George Lucas
production   American Zoetrope
screenplay   George Lucas, Walter Murch
original story George Lucas
cast   Robert Duvall, Donald Pleasance, Don Pedro Colley

Timecop

1994, USA
director   Peter Hyams
production   Largo Entertainment
screenplay   Mark Verheiden
cast   Jean-Claude van Damme, Ron Silver, Mia Sara

Total Recall

1990, USA

director	Paul Verhoeven
production	De Laurentiis Entertainment Group
screenplay	Steven Pressfield, Ronald Shusett, Dan O'Bannon, Gary Goldman
original novel	Philip K. Dick
cast	Arnold Schwarzenegger, Rachel Ticotin, Sharon Stone

2001: A Space Odyssey

1968, GB

director	Stanley Kubrick
production	MGM
screenplay	Stanley Kubrick, Arthur C. Clarke
original story	Arthur C. Clarke
cast	Keir Dullea, Gary Lockwood, William Sylvester

WAX, or The Discovery of Television Among the Bees

1991, USA

director	David Blair
production	Jasmone T Films
screenplay	David Blair
cast	David Blair, Meg Savlov, Florence Ormezzano

ZPG

1971, USA

director	Michael Campus
production	Sagittarius Productions
screenplay	Max Ehrlich, Frank de Felitta
cast	Oliver Reed, Geraldine Chaplin, Diane Cilento

BIBLIOGRAPHY

Abbott, Joe, 'They Came from Beyond the Center: Ideology and Political Textuality in the Radical Science Fiction Films of James Cameron', *Literature/Film Quarterly*, vol. 22, no. 1 (1994), pp. 21–8.

Ackerman, Forrest J. and A.W. Strickland (eds), *A Reference Guide to American Science Fiction Films*, vol. 1 (Bloomington: T.I.S. Publications, 1981).

Aleksander, Igor and Piers Burnett, *Reinventing Man: The Robot Becomes Reality* (London: Kogan Page, 1983).

Alliez, Eric and Michel Feher, 'Notes on the Sophisticated City', *Zone*, no. 1/2 (1986), pp. 41–55.

Amelio, Ralph J., *Hal in the Classroom: Science Fiction Films* (Dayton, OH: Pflaum Publishing, 1974).

Annas, Pamela, 'Science Fiction Film Criticism in the US', *Science-Fiction Studies*, vol. 7, no. 3 (1980), pp. 323–39.

Anobile, Richard J. (ed.), *Alien* (London: Futura Publications, 1979).

Appelbaum, Sam and Gerald Mead, '*Westworld*: Fantasy and Exploitation', *Jump Cut*, no. 7 (1975), pp. 12–13.

Ash, Brian (ed.), *The Visual Encyclopedia of Science Fiction* (New York: Harmony, 1977).

Balsamo, Anne, 'Reading Cyborgs, Writing Feminism', *Communications*, vol. 10, no. 3/4 (1988), pp. 331–41.

Balsamo, Anne, *Technologies of the Gendered Body: Reading Cyborg Women* (Durham, NC: Duke University Press, 1996).

Barns, Ian, 'Monstrous Nature or Technology? Cinematic Resolutions of the *Frankenstein* Problem', *Science as Culture*, no. 9 (1990), pp. 7–48.

Barringer, Robert, 'Skinjobs, Humans and Racial Coding', *Jump Cut*, no. 41 (1997), pp. 13–15, 118.

Baudrillard, Jean, 'Two Essays: Simulacra and Science Fiction; Ballard's *Crash*', *Science-Fiction Studies*, vol. 18, no. 3 (1991), pp. 309–29.

Baxter, John, *Science Fiction in the Cinema* (New York: Paperback Library, 1970).

Berenstein, Rhona, 'Mommie Dearest: *Aliens, Rosemary's Baby* and Mothering', *Journal of Popular Culture*, vol. 24, no. 2 (1990), pp. 55–74.

Berg, Charles Ramirez, 'Immigrants, Aliens and Extraterrestrials', *CineAction!*, no. 18 (1989), pp. 3–17.

Bergstrom, Janet, 'Androids and Androgyny', *Camera Obscura*, no. 15 (1986), pp. 37–64.

Bergstrom, Janet, Elizabeth Lyon, Constance Penley and Lynn Spigel (eds), *Close Encounters: Film, Feminism and Science Fiction* (Minneapolis: Minnesota University Press, 1991).

Best, Steve, 'In the Ditritus [*sic*] of Hi-technology', *Jump Cut*, no. 34 (1989), pp. 19–26.

Best, Steve, '*Robocop*: The Recuperation of the Subject', *Canadian Journal of Political and Social Theory*, vol. 13, no. 1/2 (1989), pp. 44–55.

Bick, Ilsa J., 'Boys in Space: *Star Trek*, Latency, and the Neverending Story', *Cinema Journal*, vol. 35, no. 2 (1996), pp. 43–61.

Bick, Ilsa J., 'The Look Back in *E.T.*', *Cinema Journal*, vol. 31, no. 4 (1992), pp. 25–41.

Bignell, Jonathan, 'Lost Messages: *The Handmaid's Tale*, Novel and Film', *British Journal of Canadian Studies*, vol. 8, no. 1 (1993), pp. 71–84.

Blair, Karin, 'The Garden in the Machine: The Why of *Star Trek*', *Journal of Popular Culture*, vol. 13, no. 2 (1979), pp. 310–20.

Blair, Karin, *Meaning in Star Trek* (New York: Warner Books, 1977).

Blair, Karin, 'Sex and *Star Trek*', *Science-Fiction Studies*, vol. 10, no. 3 (1983), pp. 292–7.

Brain, Bonnie, 'Saviors and Scientists: Extraterrestrials in Recent Science Fiction Films', *Et Cetera: A Review of General Semantics*, vol. 40, no. 2 (1983), pp. 218–29.

Bruno, Giuliana, 'Ramble City: Postmodernism and *Blade Runner*', *October*, no. 41 (1987), pp. 61–74.

Bukatman, Scott, 'The Artificial Infinite: On Special Effects and the Sublime', in Lynne Cooke and Peter Wollen (eds), *Visual Display: Culture Beyond Appearances* (Seattle, WA: Bay Press, 1995), pp. 255–89.

Bukatman, Scott, *Blade Runner*, BFI Modern Classics (London: British Film Institute, 1997).

Bukatman, Scott, 'The Cybernetic (City) State: Terminal Space becomes Phenomenal', *Journal of the Fantastic in the Arts*, vol. 2, no. 2 (1989), pp. 43–63.

Bukatman, Scott, 'Postcards from the Posthuman Solar System', *Science-Fiction Studies*, vol. 18, no. 3 (1991), pp. 343–57.

Bukatman, Scott, *Terminal Identity: The Virtual Subject in Postmodern Science Fiction* (Durham, NC: Duke University Press, 1993).

Bukatman, Scott, 'The Ultimate Trip: Special Effects and Kaleidoscopic Perception', *Iris*, no. 25 (1998), pp. 75–97.

Bundtzen, Lynda K., 'Monstrous Mothers: Medusa, Grendel and now *Alien*', *Film Quarterly*, vol. 40, no. 3 (1987), pp. 11–17.

Byers, Thomas B., 'Commodity Futures: Corporate State and Personal Style in Three Recent Science-fiction Movies', *Science-Fiction Studies*, vol. 14, no. 3 (1987), pp. 326–39.

Carter, Steven, 'Avatars of the Turtles', *Journal of Popular Film and Television*, vol. 18, no. 3 (1990), pp. 94–102.

Chevrier, Yves, '*Blade Runner*; or, the Sociology of Anticipation', *Science-Fiction Studies*, vol. 11, no. 1 (1984), pp. 50–60.

Chien, Joseph, 'Containing Horror: The *Alien* Trilogy and the Abject', *Focus Magazine*, no. 14 (1994), pp. 7–17.

Clough, Patricia Ticineto, 'The Final Girl in the Fictions of Science and Culture', *Stanford Humanities Review*, vol. 2, no. 2/3 (1992), pp. 57–69.

Coates, Paul, 'Chris Marker and the Cinema as Time Machine', *Science-Fiction Studies*, vol. 14, no. 3 (1987), pp. 307–15.

Cobbs, John L., '*Alien* as an Abortion Parable', *Literature/Film Quarterly*, vol. 18, no. 3 (1990), pp. 198–202.

Codell, Julie F., '*Murphy's Law, Robocop's* Body, and Capitalism's Work', *Jump Cut*, no. 34 (1989), pp. 12–19.

Cormier, Raymond, 'The Closed Society and its Friends: Plato's *Republic* and Lucas's *THX-1138*', *Literature/Film Quarterly*, vol. 18, no. 3 (1990), pp. 193–8.

Cranny-Francis, Anne, 'Sexuality and Sex-Role Stereotypy in *Star Trek*', *Science-Fiction Studies*, vol. 12, no. 3 (1985), pp. 274–84.

Creed, Barbara, 'From Here to Modernity: Feminism and Postmodernism', *Screen*, vol. 28, no. 2 (1987), pp. 47–67.

Creed, Barbara, 'Horror and the Monstrous-Feminine: An Imaginary Abjection', *Screen*, vol. 27, no. 1 (1986), pp. 44–70.

Critelli, Joseph W. and Jane Elizabeth Ellington, 'Analysis of a Modern Myth: The *Star Trek* Series', *Extrapolation*, vol. 24, no. 3 (1983), pp. 241–50.

Dadoun, Roger, '*Metropolis*: Mother City – "Mittler" – Hitler', *Camera Obscura*, no. 15 (1986), pp. 137–65.

Daso, Don and Peter Lehman, 'Special Effects in *Star Wars*', *Wide Angle*, vol. 1, no. 1 (1979), pp. 72–7.

Davis-Genelli, Lyn and Tom Davis-Genelli, '*Alien*: A Myth of Survival', *Film/Psychology Review*, vol. 4, no. 2 (1980), pp. 235–40.

Dean, Joan F., 'Between *2001* and *Star Wars*', *Journal of Popular Film and Television*, vol. 7, no. 1 (1978), pp. 32–41.

Dempsey, Michael, '*Blade Runner*', *Film Quarterly*, vol. 36, no. 2 (1982/3), pp. 33–8.

Dervin, Daniel, 'Primal Conditions and Conventions: The Genres of Comedy and Science

Fiction', *Film/Psychology Review*, vol. 4, no. 1 (1980), pp. 115–47.

Dery, Mark (ed.), *Flame Wars: the Discourse of Cyberculture* (Durham, NC: Duke University Press, 1994).

Design Quarterly, 'The City in Film', *Design Quarterly*, no. 136 (1987).

Desser, David, '*Blade Runner*: Science-Fiction and Transcendence', *Literature/Film Quarterly*, vol. 13, no. 3 (1985), pp. 172–9.

Desser, David, 'Race, Space and Class: The Politics of SF Film from *Metropolis* to *Blade Runner*', in Judith Kerman (ed.), *Retrofitting Blade Runner: Issues in Ridley Scott's Blade Runner and Philip K. Dick's Do Androids Dream of Electric Sheep* (Bowling Green, OH: Bowling Green State University Popular Press, 1991), pp. 110–23.

Doane, Mary Anne, 'Technophilia: Technology, Representation, and the Feminine', in Mary Jacobus (ed.), *Body/Politics: Women and the Discourses of Science* (London: Routledge, 1990), pp. 163–77.

Doll, Susan and Greg Faller, '*Blade Runner* and Genre: Film Noir and Science Fiction', *Literature/Film Quarterly*, vol. 14, no. 2 (1986), pp. 89–100.

Donnelly, Jerome, 'Humanizing Technology in *The Empire Strikes Back*: Theme and Values in Lucas and Tolkien', *Philosophy in Context*, no. 11 (1981), pp. 19–32.

Dumont, J.P. and J. Monod, 'Beyond the Infinite: A Structural Analysis of *2001: A Space Odyssey*', *Quarterly Review of Film Studies*, vol. 3, no. 3 (1978), pp. 297–316.

Elkins, Charles, 'Symposium on *Alien*', *Science-Fiction Studies*, vol. 7, no. 3 (1980), pp. 278–304.

Entman, Robert and Francie Seymour, '*Close Encounters* with the Third Reich', *Jump Cut*, no. 18 (1978), pp. 3–6.

Fisher, William, 'Of Living Machines and Living-Machines: *Blade Runner* and the Terminal Genre', *New Literary History*, vol. 20, no. 1 (1988), pp. 187–98.

Fitting, Peter, 'Count Me Out/In: Post-Apocalyptic Visions in Recent Science Fiction Film', *CineAction!*, no. 11 (1987/8), pp. 42–52.

Fitting, Peter, 'Futurecop: The Neutralisation of Revolution in *Blade Runner*', *Science-Fiction Studies*, vol. 14, no. 3 (1987), pp. 340–54.

Franklin, H. Bruce, 'Don't Look Where We're Going: Visions of the Future in Science Fiction Films', *Science-Fiction Studies*, vol. 10, no. 1 (1983), pp. 70–80.

Franklin, H. Bruce, 'Future Imperfect', *American Film*, vol. 8, no. 5 (1983), pp. 47–9, 75–6.

Franklin, H. Bruce, '*Star Trek* in the Vietnam Era', *Science-Fiction Studies*, vol. 21, no. 1 (1994), pp. 24–34.

Franklin, H. Bruce, 'The Vietnam War as American Science Fiction and Fantasy', *Science-Fiction Studies*, vol. 17, no. 4 (1990), pp. 341–59.

Frentz, Thomas S. and Janice Hocker Rushing, *Projecting the Shadow: The Cyborg Hero in American Film* (Chicago, IL: University of Chicago Press, 1995).

Friedman, Norman L., '*The Terminator*: Changes in Critical Evaluations of Cultural Productions', *Journal of Popular Culture*, vol. 28, no. 1 (1994), pp. 73–80.

Fuchs, Cynthia J., 'Death is Irrelevant: Cyborgs, Reproduction, and the Future of Male Hysteria', *Genders*, no. 18 (1993), pp. 113–33.

Gabbard, Krin, '*Aliens* and the New Family Romance', *Post Script: Essays in Film and the Humanities*, vol. 8, no. 1 (1988), pp. 29–42.

Geduld, Harry M. and Ronald Gottesman (eds), *Robots Robots* (Boston: New York Graphic Society, 1978).

Glass, Fred, 'The "New Bad Future": *Robocop* and 1980s Sci-Fi Films', *Science as Culture*, no. 5 (1989), pp. 7–49.

Glass, Fred, 'Totally Recalling Arnold: Sex and Violence in the New Bad Future', *Film Quarterly*, vol. 44, no. 1 (1990), pp. 2–13.

Goldberg, Jonathan, 'Recalling Totalities: The Mirrored Stages of Arnold Schwarzenegger', *Differences: A Journal of Feminist Cultural Studies*, vol. 4, no. 1 (1992), pp. 172–204.

Goodall, Jane R., '*Aliens*', *Southern Review*, vol. 23, no. 1 (1990), pp. 73–82.

Gordon, Andrew, '*Back to the Future*: Oedipus as Time Traveler', *Science-Fiction Studies*, vol. 14, no. 3 (1987), pp. 372–85.

Gordon, Andrew, '*Close Encounters*: The Gospel According to Steven Spielberg', *Literature/Film Quarterly*, vol. 8, no. 3 (1980), pp. 156–64.

Gordon, Andrew, '*Close Encounters*: Unidentified Flying Object Relations', *The Psychoanalytic Review*, vol. 82, no. 5 (1995), pp. 741–57.

Gordon, Andrew, '*E.T.* as Fairy Tale', *Science-Fiction Studies*, vol. 10, no. 3 (1983), pp. 298–305.

Gordon, Andrew, '*The Empire Strikes Back*: Monsters from the Id', *Science-Fiction Studies*, vol. 7, no. 3 (1980), pp. 313–18.

Gordon, Andrew, '*Return of the Jedi*: The End of Myth', *Film Criticism*, vol. 8, no. 2 (1984), pp. 45–54.

Gordon, Andrew, 'Science-Fiction Film Criticism: The Postmodern Always Rings Twice', *Science-Fiction Studies*, vol. 14, no. 3 (1987), pp. 386–91.

Gordon, Andrew, '*Star Wars*: A Myth for Our Time', *Literature/Film Quarterly*, vol. 6, no. 4 (1978), pp. 314–27.

Gordon, Andrew, 'You'll Never Get Out of Bedford Falls: The Inescapable Family in American Science Fiction and Fantasy Films', *Journal of Popular Film and Television*, vol. 20, no. 2 (1992), pp. 2–8.

Goscilo, Margaret, 'Deconstructing *The Terminator*', *Film Criticism*, vol. 12, no. 2 (1987/8), pp. 37–52.

Grant, Barry K., '*Invaders from Mars* and the Science Fiction Film in the Age of Reagan', *CineAction!*, no. 8 (1987), pp. 77–83.

Grant, Barry K., 'Looking Upwards: Reason and the Visible in Science Fiction Film', in Glenwood H. Irons (ed.), *Gender, Language and Myth: Essays in Popular Narrative* (Toronto: University of Toronto Press, 1992), pp. 185–207.

Gravett, Sharon L., 'The Sacred and the Profane: Examining the Religious Subtext of Ridley

Scott's *Blade Runner*', *Literature/Film Quarterly*, vol. 26, no. 1 (1998), pp. 38–45.

Greenberg, Harvey R., 'Fembo: *Aliens*' Intentions', *Journal of Popular Film and Television*, vol. 15, no. 4 (1988), pp. 164–71.

Greenberg, Harvey R., 'The Fractures of Desire: Psychoanalytic Notes on *Alien* and the Contemporary "Cruel" Horror Film', *The Psychoanalytic Review*, vol. 70, no. 2 (1983), pp. 241–67.

Greenberg, Harvey R., 'In Search of Spock: A Psychoanalytic Inquiry', *Journal of Popular Film and Television*, vol. 12, no. 2 (1984), pp. 52–65.

Greenberg, Harvey R., 'Reimagining the Gargoyle: Psychoanalytic Notes on *Alien*', *Camera Obscura*, no. 15 (1986), pp. 87–108.

Guerrero, Edward, 'AIDS as Monster in Science Fiction and Horror Cinema', *Journal of Popular Film and Television*, vol. 18, no. 3 (1990), pp. 86–93.

Hanson, Ellis, 'Technology, Paranoia and the Queer Voice', *Screen*, vol. 34, no. 2 (1993), pp. 137–61.

Haraway, Donna, 'The Actors are Cyborg, Nature is Coyote, and the Geography is Elsewhere', in Constance Penley and Andrew Ross (eds), *Technoculture* (Minneapolis: University of Minnesota Press, 1991), pp. 21–6.

Haraway, Donna, 'A Manifesto for Cyborgs: Science, Technology and Socialist Feminism in the 1980s', *Socialist Review*, no. 80 (1985), pp. 65–107.

Haraway, Donna, *Simians, Cyborgs and Women: The Reinvention of Nature* (New York: Routledge, 1991).

Hardcastle, Valerie Gray, 'Changing Perspectives of Motherhood: Images from the *Aliens* Trilogy', *Film and Philosophy*, vol. no. 3 (1996), pp. 167–75.

Hark, Ina Rae, '*Star Trek* and Television's Moral Universe', *Extrapolation*, vol. 20, no. 1 (1979), pp. 20–37.

Harmon, Gary L. and Louis A. Woods, 'Jung and *Star Trek*: The *Coincidentia Oppositorum* and Images of the Shadow', *Journal of Popular Culture*, vol. 28, no. 2 (1994), pp. 169–84.

Hawkins, Harriet, 'Paradigms Lost: Chaos, Milton and *Jurassic Park*', *Textual Practice*, vol. 8, no. 2 (1994), pp. 255–67.

Henning, C.M., '*Star Wars* and *Close Encounters*', *Theology Today*, vol. 35, no. 2 (1978), pp. 202–6.

Hermann, Chad, '"Some Horrible Dream about (S)mothering": Sexuality, Gender, and Family in the *Alien* Trilogy', *Post Script*, vol. 16, no. 3 (1997), pp. 36–50.

Heung, Marina, 'Why *E.T.* Must Go Home: The New Family in American Cinema', *Journal of Popular Film and Television*, vol. 11, no. 2 (1983), pp. 79–84.

Higashi, Sumiko, '*Invasion of the Body Snatchers*: Pods Then and Now', *Jump Cut*, no. 24/25 (1981), pp. 3–4.

Hoberman, J., 'Paranoia and the Pods', *Sight and Sound*, vol. 4, no. 5 (1994), pp. 28–31.

Huyssen, Andreas, 'The Vamp and the Machine: Technology and Sexuality in Fritz Lang's *Metropolis*', *New German Critique*, no. 24/25 (1981/2), pp. 221–37.

Instrell, Rick, '*Blade Runner*: The Economic Shaping of a Film', in *Cinema and Fiction: New Modes of Adapting, 1950–1990* (ed.), John Orr and Colin Nicholson (Edinburgh: Edinburgh University Press, 1992), pp. 160–70.

Jameson, Fredric, 'Progress versus Utopia; or, Can We Imagine the Future?', *Science-Fiction Studies*, vol. 9 (1982), pp. 147–58.

Jameson, Fredric, 'SF Novels/SF Film', *Science-Fiction Studies*, vol. 7, no. 3 (1980), pp. 319–22.

Jancovich, Mark, 'Modernity and Subjectivity in *The Terminator*: The Machine as Monster in Contemporary American Culture', *The Velvet Light Trap*, no. 30 (1992), pp. 3–17.

Jeffords, Susan, '"The Battle of the Big Mamas": Feminism and the Alienation of Women', *Journal of American Culture*, vol. 10, no. 3 (1987), pp. 73–84.

Jenkins, Henry and John Tulloch, *Science Fiction Audiences: Watching Star Trek and Doctor Who* (New York: Routledge, 1995).

Johnson, William (ed.), *Focus on the Science Fiction Film* (Englewood Cliffs, NJ: Prentice Hall, 1972).

Jordanova, L.J., 'Fritz Lang's *Metropolis*: Science, Machines and Gender', *Issues in Radical Science*, no. 17 (1985), pp. 5–21.

Joyrich, Lynne, 'Feminist Enterprise? *Star Trek: The Next Generation* and the Occupation of Femininity', *Cinema Journal*, vol. 35, no. 2 (1996), pp. 61–84.

Kaes, Anton, '*Metropolis*: City, Cinema, Modernity', in Timothy O. Benson (ed.), *Expressionist Utopias: Paradise, Metropolis, Architectural Fantasy* (Los Angeles: Los Angeles County Museum of Art, 1993), pp. 146–65.

Kavanaugh, James H., '"Son of a Bitch": Feminism, Humanism and Science in *Alien*', *October*, no. 13 (1980), pp. 91–100.

Kellner, Douglas, Flo Liebowitz, and Michael Ryan, '*Blade Runner*: A Diagnostic Critique', *Jump Cut*, no. 29 (1984), pp. 6–8.

Kerman, Judith B. (ed.), *Retrofitting Blade Runner: Issues in Ridley Scott's Blade Runner and Philip K. Dick's Do Androids Dream of Electric Sheep* (Bowling Green, OH: Bowling Green State University Popular Press, 1991).

Kinnard, Roy, 'The *Flash Gordon* Serials', *Film in Review*, vol. 39, no. 4 (1988), pp. 194–203.

Klein, Norman M., 'Building *Blade Runner*', *Social Text*, no. 28 (1991), pp. 147–52.

Knee, Adam, 'The Metamorphosis of the Fly', *Wide Angle*, vol. 14, no. 1 (1992), pp. 20–34.

Kolb, William M., '*Blade Runner*: An Annotated Bibliography', *Literature/Film Quarterly*, vol. 18, no. 1 (1990), pp. 19–64.

Kreitzer, Larry, 'The Cultural Veneer of *Star Trek*', *Journal of Popular Culture*, vol. 30, no. 2 (1996), pp. 1–28.

Kuhn, Annette (ed.), *Alien Zone: Cultural Theory and Contemporary Science Fiction Cinema* (London: Verso, 1990).

Lancashire, Anne, '*Return of the Jedi*: Once More with Feeling', *Film Criticism*, vol. 8, no. 2 (1984), pp. 55–66.

Landon, Brooks, *The Aesthetics of Ambivalence: Rethinking Science Fiction Film in the Age of Electronic (Re)production* (Westport, CT: Greenwood Press, 1992).

Landon, Brooks, 'Cyberpunk', *Cinefantastique*, vol. 18, no. 1 (1987), pp. 27–31.

Landon, Brooks (ed.), *Journal of the Fantastic in the Arts*, JFA Forum on Science Fiction Film, vol. 2, no. 2 (1989).

Landon, Brooks, 'Rethinking Science Fiction Film in the Age of Electronic (Re)production: On a Clear Day You Can See the Horizon of Invisibility', *Post Script: Essays in Film and the Humanities*, vol. 10, no. 1 (1990), pp. 60–71.

Landrum, Larry, 'Science Fiction Film Criticism in the Seventies', *Journal of Popular Film and Television*, vol. 6, no. 3 (1978), pp. 287–9.

Landy, Marcia and Stanley Shostak, 'Postmodernism as Folklore in Contemporary Science Fiction Cinema', *Rethinking Marxism*, vol. 6, no. 2 (1993), pp. 25–45.

Latham, Rob, 'Subterranean Suburbia: Underneath the Small Town Myth in the Two Versions of *Invaders from Mars*', *Science-Fiction Studies*, vol. 22, no. 2 (1995), pp. 198–208.

LaValley, Albert J., 'The Stage and Film Children of *Frankenstein*', in U.C. Knoepflmacher and George Levine (eds), *The Endurance of Frankenstein: Essays on Mary Shelley's Novel* (Berkeley: University of California Press, 1979), pp. 243–89.

LaValley, Albert J., 'Traditions of Trickery: The Role of Special Effects in the Science Fiction Film', in George E. Slusser and Eric S. Rabkin (eds), *Shadows of the Magic Lamp: Fantasy and Science Fiction Film* (Carbondale: Southern Illinois University Press, 1985), pp. 141–58.

Leach, James, '*The Man Who Fell to Earth*: Adaptation by Omission', *Literature/Film Quarterly*, vol. 6, no. 4 (1978), pp. 371–6.

LeGacy, Arthur, '*The Invasion of the Body Snatchers*: A Metaphor for the Fifties', *Literature/Film Quarterly*, vol. 6, no. 3 (1978), pp. 285–92.

Lem, Stanislaw, 'On the Strucutral Analysis of Science Fiction', *Science-Fiction Studies*, vol. 1 (1973), pp. 26–33.

Lem, Stanislaw, 'The Time Travel Story and Related Matters of Science Fiction Structuring', *Science-Fiction Studies*, vol. 1, no. 3 (1974), pp. 143–54.

Lev, Peter, 'Whose Future? *Star Wars*, *Alien* and *Blade Runner*', *Literature/Film Quarterly*, vol. 26, no. 1 (1998), pp. 30–37.

Liddel, Elizabeth and Michael, '*Dune*: A Tale of Two Texts', in John Orr and Colin Nicholson (eds), *Cinema and Fiction: New Modes of Adapting, 1950–1990* (Edinburgh: Edinburgh University Press, 1992), pp. 122–39.

Lightman, Herb A. and Richard Patterson, '*Blade Runner*: Production Design and Photography', *American Cinematographer*, no. 63 (1982), pp. 684–91, 715–25.

Literature/Film Quarterly, '*Blade Runner* Issue', *Literature/Film Quarterly*, vol. 18, no. 1 (1990).

Liu, Albert, 'The Last Days of Arnold Schwarzenegger', *Genders*, no. 18 (1993), pp. 102–12.

Lowentrout, Peter M., 'The Meta-Aesthetic of Popular Science Fiction Film', *Extrapolation*, vol. 29, no. 4 (1988), pp. 349–64.

Luciano, Patrick, *Them or Us: Archetypal Interpretations of Fifties Alien Invasion Films* (Bloomington: Indiana University Press, 1987).

Malmgren, Carl D., *Worlds Apart: Narratology of Science Fiction* (Bloomington: Indiana University Press, 1991).

Mann, Karen B., 'Narrative Entanglements: *The Terminator*', *Film Quarterly*, vol. 43, no. 4 (1989/90), pp. 17–27.

Marder, Elissa, '*Blade Runner*'s Moving Still', *Camera Obscura*, no. 27 (1991), pp. 88–107.

Markey, Constance, 'Birth and Rebirth in Current Fantasy Films', *Film Criticism*, vol. 7, no. 1 (1982), pp. 14–25.

Matheson, T.J., 'Marcuse, Ellul and the Science-Fiction Film: Negative Responses to Technology', *Science-Fiction Studies*, vol. 19, no. 3 (1992), pp. 326–39.

McMahon, David F., 'The Psychological Significance of Science Fiction', *Psychoanalytic Review*, vol. 76, no. 2 (1989), pp. 281–95.

McNamara, Kevin R., '*Blade Runner*'s Post-individual Worldspace', *Contemporary Literature*, vol. 38, no. 3 (1997), pp. 422–46.

Metz, Christian, 'Trucage and the Film', *Critical Inquiry*, vol. 3, no. 4 (Summer, 1977), pp. 657–75.

Michelson, Annette, 'Bodies in Space: Film as "Carnal Knowledge"', *ArtForum*, vol. 7, no. 6 (1969), pp. 54–63.

Miklitsch, Robert, '*Total Recall*: Production, Revolution, Simulation-Alienation Effect', *Camera Obscura*, no. 32 (1993), pp. 5–39.

Miles, Geoff and Carol Moore, 'Explorations, Prosthetics and Sacrifice: Phantasies of the Maternal Body in the *Alien* Trilogy', *CineAction!*, no. 30 (1992), pp. 54–62.

Miller, Martin and Robert Sprich, 'The Appeal of *Star Wars*: An Archetypal-Psychoanalytic View', *American Imago*, vol. 38, no. 2 (1981), pp. 203–20.

Miller, Mark Crispin, '*2001*: A Cold Descent', *Sight and Sound*, vol. 4, no. 1 (1994), pp. 18–25.

Mizejewski, Linda, 'Total Recoil: The Schwarzenegger Body on Postmodern Mars', *Post Script: Essays in Film and the Humanities*, vol. 12, no. 3 (1993), pp. 25–34.

Morrison, Rachael, '*Casablanca* Meets *Star Wars*: The Blakean Dialectics of *Blade Runner*', *Literature/Film Quarterly*, vol. 18, no. 1 (1990), pp. 2–10.

Nagl, Manfred, 'The Science Fiction Film in Historical Perspective', *Science-Fiction Studies*, vol. 10, no. 3 (1983), pp. 262–77.

Naureckas, Jim, '*Aliens*: Mother and the Teeming Hordes', *Jump Cut*, no. 32 (1987), pp. 1, 4.

Neale, Stephen, 'Issues of Difference: *Alien* and *Blade Runner*', in James Donald (ed.), *Fantasy and the Cinema* (London: British Film Institute, 1989), pp. 213–23.

Necakov, Lillian, '*The Terminator*: Beyond Classical Hollywood Narrative', *CineAction!*, no. 8 (1987), pp. 84–6.

Nestriek, William, 'Coming to Life: *Frankenstein* and the Nature of Film Narrative', in U.C. Knoepflmacher and George Levine (eds), *The Endurance of Frankenstein: Essays on Mary*

Shelley's Novel (Berkeley: University of California Press, 1979), pp. 3–30.

Neumann, Dietrich, 'Before and After *Metropolis*: Film and Architecture in Search of the Modern City', in Dietrich Neumann (ed.), *Film Architecture: Set Designs from Metropolis to Blade Runner* (Munich and New York: Prestel-Verlag, 1996), pp. 33–8.

Neustadter, Roger, 'Phone Home: From Childhood Amnesia to the Catcher in Sci-Fi – The Transformation of Childhood in Contemporary American Science Fiction Films', *Youth and Society*, vol. 20, no. 2 (1989), pp. 227–40.

Ohlin, Peter, 'Science-Fiction Film Criticism and the Debris of Postmodernism', *Science-Fiction Studies*, vol. 18, no. 3 (1991), pp. 411–19.

Owens, Nancy, 'Image and Object: Hegel, Madonna, *Metropolis*', *Spectator: The University of Southern California Journal of Film and Television Criticism*, vol. 12, no. 2 (1992), pp. 58–63.

Parish, James Robert (ed.), *The Great Science Fiction Pictures II* (Metuchen, NJ: Scarecrow Press, 1990).

Patalas, Enno, '*Metropolis*, Scene 103', *Camera Obscura*, no. 15 (1986), pp. 165–74.

Peary, Danny (ed.), *Omni's Screen Flights/Screen Fantasies: The Future According to Science Fiction Cinema* (New York: Doubleday, 1984).

Penley, Constance, 'Time Travel, Primal Scene and the Critical Dystopia', *Camera Obscura*, no. 15 (1986), pp. 67–84.

Pielke, Robert G., '*Star Wars* vs. *2001*: A Question of Identity', *Extrapolation*, vol. 24, no. 2 (1983), pp. 143–55.

Rabkin, Eric S. and George E. Slusser (eds), *Aliens: The Anthropology of Science Fiction* (Carbondale: Southern Illinois University Press, 1987).

Rabkin, Eric S. and George E. Slusser (eds), *Shadows of the Magic Lamp: Fantasy and Science Fiction Film* (Carbondale: Southern Illinois University Press, 1985).

Robertson, Robbie, 'The Narrative Sources of Ridley Scott's *Alien*', in John Orr and Colin Nicholson (eds), *Cinema and Fiction: New Modes of Adapting, 1950–1990* (Edinburgh: Edinburgh University Press, 1992), pp. 171–9.

Roth, Lane, 'Death and Rebirth in *Star Trek II: The Wrath of Khan*', *Extrapolation*, vol. 28, no. 2 (1987), pp. 155–66.

Roth, Lane, '*Metropolis*, The Lights Fantastic: Semiotic Analysis of Lighting Codes in Relation to Character and Theme', *Literature/Film Quarterly*, vol. 6, no. 4 (1978), pp. 342–47.

Roth, Lane, 'The Rejection of Rationalism in Recent Science Fiction Films', *Philosophy in Context*, no. 11 (1981), pp. 42–55.

Roth, Lane, 'Vraisemblance and the Western Setting in Contemporary Science Fiction Film', *Literature/Film Quarterly*, vol. 13, no. 3 (1985), pp. 180–86.

Rubey, Dan, 'Not So Long Ago, Not So Far Away', *Jump Cut*, no. 41 (1997), pp. 2–12, 130.

Rubinstein, Diane, 'The Anxiety of Affluence: Baudrillard and the Sci-Fi Movies of the Reagan Era', in William Stearns and William Chaloupka (eds), *Jean Baudrillard: The Disappearance of Art and Politics* (London: Macmillan, 1992), pp. 65–81.

Ruddick, Nicholas (ed.), *State of the Fantastic: Studies in the Theory and Practice of Fantastic Literature and Film* (Westport, CN: Greenwood Press, 1992).

Ruppersburg, Hugh, 'The Alien Messiah in Recent Science Fiction Films', *Journal of Popular Film and Television*, vol. 14, no. 4 (1987), pp. 159–66.

Ruppert, Peter, '*Blade Runner*: The Utopian Dialectics of Science Fiction Films', *Cineaste*, vol. 17, no. 2 (1989), pp. 8–13.

Rusher, Janice Hocker and Thomas S. Frentz, *Projecting the Shadow: The Cyborg Hero in American Film* (Chicago, IL: University of Chicago Press, 1995).

Rushing, Janice Hocker, '*E.T.* as Rhetorical Transcendence', *Quarterly Journal of Speech*, no. 71 (1985), pp. 188–203.

Rushing, Janice Hocker, 'Evolution of "The New Frontier" in *Alien* and *Aliens*: Patriarchal Co-optation of the Feminine Archetype', *Quarterly Journal of Speech*, vol. 75, no. 1 (1989), pp. 1–24.

Rutsky, R.L., 'The Mediation of Technology and Gender: *Metropolis*, Nazism, Modernism', *New German Critique*, no. 60 (1993), pp. 3–32.

Sammon, Paul M., *Future Noir: The Making of Blade Runner* (New York: HarperCollins, 1996).

Sammons, Todd H., '*Return of the Jedi*: Epic Graffiti', *Science-Fiction Studies*, vol. 14, no. 3 (1987), pp. 355–71.

Saunders, Ian, 'Richard Rorty and *Star Wars*: On the Nature of Pragmatism's Narrative', *Textual Practice*, vol. 8, no. 3 (1994), pp. 435–48.

Schelde, Per, *Androids, Humanoids and Other Science Fiction Monsters* (New York: New York University Press, 1993).

Schmertz, Johanna, 'On Reading the Politics of *Total Recall*', *Post Script: Essays in Film and the Humanities*, vol. 12, no. 3 (1993), pp. 35–43.

Schwab, Gabriele, 'Cyborgs: Postmodern Phantasms of Body and Mind', *Discourse: Journal for Theoretical Studies in Media and Culture*, no. 9 (1987), pp. 64–84.

Schwartz, Nancy, '*THX 1138* vs. *Metropolis*', *The Velvet Light Trap*, no. 4 (1972), pp. 18–23.

Scigaj, Leonard M., 'Bettelheim, Castaneda and Zen: The Powers Behind the Force in *Star Wars*', *Extrapolation*, vol. 22, no. 3 (1981), pp. 213–36.

Scobie, Stephen, 'What's the Story, Mother? The Mourning of the Alien', *Science-Fiction Studies*, vol. 20, no. 1 (1993), pp. 80–93.

Sconce, Jeffrey, 'Brains from Space: Mapping the Mind in 1950s Science and Cinema', *Science as Culture*, vol. 23 (1995), pp. 277–302.

Selley, April, 'Transcendentalism in *Star Trek: The Next Generation*', *Journal of American Culture*, vol. 13, no. 1 (1990), pp. 31–34.

Senior, W.A., '*Blade Runner* and Cyberpunk Visions of Humanity', *Film Criticism*, vol. 21, no. 1 (1996), pp. 1–12.

Shapiro, Benjamin, 'Universal Truths: Cultural Myths and Generic Adaptation in 1950s Science Fiction Films', *Journal of Popular Film and Television*, vol. 18, no. 3 (1990), pp. 103–12.

Sharrett, Christopher, 'Myth, Male Fantasy and Simulacra in *Mad Max* and *The Road Warrior*', *Journal of Popular Film and Television*, vol. 13, no. 2 (1985), pp. 80–92.

Shelton, Robert, 'Rendezvous with HAL: *2001/2010*', *Extrapolation*, vol. 28, no. 3 (1987), pp. 255–68.

Shumaker, Conrad, 'More Human than Humans: Society, Salvation and the Outsider in Some Popular Films of the 1980s', *Journal of American Culture*, vol. 13, no. 4 (1990), pp. 77–84.

Silverman, Kaja, 'Back to the Future', *Camera Obscura*, no. 27 (1991), pp. 109–32.

Slade, Joseph W., 'Romanticizing Cybernetics in Ridley Scott's *Blade Runner*', *Literature/Film Quarterly*, vol. 18, no. 1 (1990), pp. 11–19.

Slattery, Dennis Patrick, 'Demeter-Persephone and the *Alien*(s) Cultural Body', *New Orleans Review*, vol. 19, no. 1 (1992), pp. 30–35.

Sobchack, Vivian, 'Child/Alien/Father: Patriarchal Crisis and Genetic Exchange', *Camera Obscura*, no. 15 (1986), pp. 7–34.

Sobchack, Vivian, 'Cities on the Edge of Time: The Urban Science Fiction Film', *East/West Film Journal*, vol. 3, no. 1 (1988), pp. 3–19.

Sobchack, Vivian, *The Limits of Infinity: The American Science Fiction Film* (New York: A.S. Barnes and Co., 1980).

Sobchack, Vivian, 'Science Fiction', in Wes D. Gehring (ed.), *Handbook of American Film Genres* (Westport, CN: Greenwood Press, 1988), pp. 229–47.

Sobchack, Vivian, *Screening Space: The American Science Fiction Film* (New York: Ungar, 1987).

Sobchack, Vivian, 'The Virginity of Astronauts: Sex and the Science Fiction Film', in Eric S. Rabkin and George E. Slusser (eds), *Shadows of the Magic Lamp: Fantasy and Science Fiction Film* (Carbondale: Southern Illinois University Press, 1985), pp. 41–57.

Sofia, Zoë, 'Exterminating Fetuses: Abortion, Disarmament and the Sexo-Semiotics of Extraterrestrialism', *Diacritics*, vol. 14, no. 2 (1984), pp. 47–59.

Sontag, Susan, 'The Imagination of Disaster', in *Against Interpretation* (London: Eyre & Spottiswoode, 1966), pp. 208–25.

Springer, Claudia, *Electronic Eros* (London: Athlone Press, 1996).

Springer, Claudia, 'Muscular Circuitry: The Invincible Armored Cyborg in Cinema', *Genders*, no. 18 (1993), pp. 87–101.

Springer, Claudia, 'The Pleasure of the Interface', *Screen*, vol. 32, no. 3 (1991), pp. 303–23.

Staiger, Janet, 'Future Noir: Contemporary Representations of Visionary Cities', *East–West Film Journal*, vol. 3, no. 1 (1988), pp. 20–44.

Stern, Michael, 'Making Culture into Nature: or, Who Put the "Special" into Special Effects', *Science-Fiction Studies*, vol. 7, no. 3 (1980), pp. 262–9.

Stewart, Garret, '*Close Encounters* of the Fourth Kind', *Sight and Sound*, vol. 47, no. 3 (1978), pp. 167–74.

Stewart, Garrett, 'The Photographic Ontology of Science Fiction Film', *Iris*, no. 25 (1998), pp. 99–132.

Strick, Philip, 'The Age of the Replicant', *Sight and Sound*, vol. 51, no. 3 (1982), pp. 168–72.

Strick, Philip, 'Future States', *Monthly Film Bulletin*, no. 661 (1989), pp. 37–41.

Tarratt, Margaret, 'Monsters from the Id', in Barry K. Grant (ed.), *Film Genre: Theory and Criticism* (Metuchen, NJ: Scarecrow Press, 1977), pp. 161–81.

Telotte, J.P., 'The Dark Side of the Force: *Star Wars* and the Science Fiction Tradition', *Extrapolation*, vol. 24, no. 3 (1983), pp. 216–26.

Telotte, J.P., 'The Doubles of Fantasy and the Space of Desire', *Film Criticism*, vol. 7, no. 1 (1982), pp. 56–68.

Telotte, J.P., 'Enframing the Self: The Hardware and Software of *Hardware*', *Science-Fiction Studies*, vol. 22, no. 3 (1995), pp. 323–32.

Telotte, J.P., 'The Ghost in the Machine: Consciousness and the Science Fiction Film', *Western Humanities Review*, vol. 42, no. 3 (1983), pp. 249–58.

Telotte, J.P., 'Human Artifice and the Science Fiction Film', *Film Quarterly*, vol. 36, no. 3 (1983), pp. 44–51.

Telotte, J.P., '*Just Imagine*-ing the *Metropolis* of Modern America', *Science-Fiction Studies*, vol. 23, no. 2 (1996), pp. 161–70.

Telotte, J.P., *Replications: A Robotic History of the Science Fiction Film* (Urbana: University of Illinois, 1995).

Telotte, J.P., 'Science Fiction in Double Focus: *Forbidden Planet*', *Film Criticism*, vol. 13, no. 3 (1989), pp. 25–36.

Telotte, J.P., '*The Terminator, Terminator II* and the Exposed Body', *Journal of Popular Film and Television*, vol. 20, no. 2 (1992), pp. 26–34.

Telotte, J.P., 'The Tremulous Public Body: Robots, Change and the Science Fiction Film', *Journal of Popular Film and Television*, vol. 19, no. 1 (1991), pp. 14–23.

Telotte, J.P., '*Westworld, Futureworld* and the World's Obscenity', in Nicholas Ruddick (ed.), *State of the Fantastic: Studies in the Theory and Practice of Fantastic Literature and Film* (Westport, CN: Greenwood Press, 1992), pp. 179–88.

Telotte, J.P., '*The World of Tomorrow* and the "Secret Goal" of Science Fiction', *Journal of Film and Video*, vol. 45, no. 1 (1993), pp. 27–39.

Testa, Bart, 'Technology's Body: Cronenberg, Genre and the Canadian Ethos', *Post Script: Essays in Film and the Humanities*, vol. 15, no. 1 (1995), pp. 39–57.

Torry, Robert, 'Politics and Parousia in *Close Encounters of the Third Kind*', *Literature/Film Quarterly*, vol. 19, no. 3 (1991), pp. 188–97.

Tulloch, John, 'Genetic Structuralism and the Cinema: A Look at Fritz Lang's *Metropolis*', *Australian Journal of Screen Theory*, no. 1 (1976), pp. 3–50.

Tyrell, William Blake, '*Star Trek* as Myth and Television as Mythmaker', *Journal of Popular Culture*, vol. 10, no. 4 (1977), pp. 711–19.

Vaughn, Thomas, 'Voices of Sexual Distortion: Rape, Birth, and Self-Annihilation Metaphors in the *Alien* Trilogy', *Quarterly Journal of Speech*, vol. 81, no. 4 (1995), pp. 423–35.

Warrick, Patricia S., *The Cybernetic Imagination in Science Fiction* (Cambridge, MA: MIT Press, 1980).

Westfahl, Gary, 'Where No Market Has Gone Before: "The Science-Fiction Industry" and the *Star Trek* Industry', *Extrapolation*, vol. 37, no. 4 (1996), pp. 291–301.

Wilcox, Clyde, 'To Boldly Return Where Others Have Gone Before: Cultural Change and the Old and New *Star Trek*s', *Extrapolation*, vol. 33, no. 1 (1992), pp. 88–100.

Williams, Alan, 'Structures of Narrativity in Fritz Lang's *Metropolis*', *Film Quarterly*, vol. 27, no. 4 (1974), pp. 17–24.

Williams, Tony, 'Close Encounters of the Authoritarian Kind', *Wide Angle*, vol. 5, no. 4 (1983), pp. 22–9.

Wood, Denis, 'Growing Up Among the Stars', *Literature/Film Quarterly*, vol. 6, no. 4 (1978), pp. 327–42.

Wood, Denis, 'The Stars in Our Hearts: A Critical Commentary on George Lucas' *Star Wars*', *Journal of Popular Film and Television*, vol. 6, no. 3 (1978), pp. 262–79.

Wood, Robert E., 'Cross Talk: The Implication of Generic Hybridization in the *Alien* Films', *Studies in the Humanities*, vol. 15, no. 1 (1988), pp. 1–12.

NOTES ON CONTRIBUTORS

Will Brooker researches and teaches at the Tom Hopkinson Centre for Media Research at the University of Cardiff. He is the author of several articles on popular media texts and their audiences, and co-editor (with Peter Brooker) of *Postmodern AfterImages*.

Scott Bukatman is Assistant Professor of Film Studies at Stanford University, and author of *Terminal Identity: The Virtual Subject of Postmodern Science Fiction*, and of *Blade Runner* in the BFI Modern Classics series.

Catherine Constable is a Lecturer in Film Studies at Sheffield Hallam University, and holds a PhD in Philosophy from the University of Warwick. Her doctoral thesis explores psychoanalytic and philosophical constructions of Woman as pure appearance, and links these to the films of the Dietrich/von Sternberg cycle.

David Desser is Professor of Cinema Studies at the University of Illinois, Urbana–Champaign. He has authored and edited several books on Japanese and Chinese cinema, as well as a number of essays on science-fiction cinema.

Barry Keith Grant is Professor of Film Studies in the Department of Communications, Popular Culture and Film at Brook University, Ontario. He is the author or editor of eight books, including *Voyages of Discovery: The Cinema of Frederick Wiseman, Film Genre Reader*, and *The Dread of Difference: Gender and the Horror Film*. His writings on film and popular culture have appeared in the journals *Post Script*,

Film Quarterly, Journal of Popular Film, Jump Cut, Film/Literature Quarterly, Wide Angle, Journal of Film and Video, CineAction and *Persistence of Vision.*

Annette Kuhn is Reader in Cultural Research at Lancaster University, and an editor of *Screen.* She is the editor of *Alien Zone: Cultural Theory and Contemporary Science-Fiction Cinema,* and her recent books include *Family Secrets: Acts of Memory and Imagination* and *Screen Histories: A Screen Reader* (co-edited with Jackie Stacey).

Brooks Landon is Professor of English at the University of Iowa. He has written numerous articles about science fiction and science-fiction film, and is the author of *Science Fiction after 1900: From the Steam Man to the Stars* and *The Aesthetics of Ambivalence: Rethinking Science Fiction Film in the Age of Electronic (Re)production.*

Linda Mizejewski is an Associate Professor of English at Ohio State University, and author of *Divine Decadence: Fascism, Female Spectacle, and the Makings of Sally Bowles* and *Ziegfeld Girl: Image and Icon in Culture and Cinema.*

Vivian Sobchack is an Associate Dean and Professor of Film and Television Studies at the UCLA School of Theater, Film and Television. The first woman to be elected president of the Society for Cinema Studies, she is now on the Board of Trustees of the American Film Institute. Her books include *Screening Space: The American Science Fiction Film, The Address of the Eye: A Phenomenology of Film Experience;* two edited anthologies, *The Persistence of History: Cinema, Television and the Modern Event* and *Meta-Morphing: Visual Transformation in the Culture of Quick Change;* and a forthcoming collection of her own essays, *Carnal Thoughts: Bodies, Texts, Scenes and Screens.*

Claudia Springer is a Professor in the English Department and Film Studies Program at Rhode Island College. She is the author of *Electronic Eros: Bodies and Desire in the Postindustrial Age.*

Janet Staiger is Professor of Radio–TV–Film at the University of Texas at Austin. Her most recent book is *Bad Women: Regulating Sexuality in Early American Cinema.*

Garrett Stewart is the author of four books of literary criticism and theory: *Dickens and the Trials of the Imagination, Death Sentences, Reading Voices,* and *Dear Reader;* and of the forthcoming *Between Film and Screen: Modernism's Photo Synthesis.* He is James O. Freedman Professor of Letters at the University of Iowa.

INDEX